CORPORATE COMMUNICATION AND PROMOTION MANAGEMENT

CORPORATE COMMUNICATION AND PROMOTION MANAGEMENT

Edited by

M.K. Singh
&
A. Bhattacharya

DISCOVERY PUBLISHING HOUSE PVT. LTD.
NEW DELHI-110 002

Edition-2011

ISBN 978-81-8356-909-5

Published by

DISCOVERY PUBLISHING HOUSE PVT. LTD.
4831/24, Ansari Road, Prahlad Street,
Darya Ganj, New Delhi-110002 (India)
Phone: 23279245, 43764432 • Fax: 91-11-23253475
E-mail: discoverypublishinghouse@gmail.com
dphbooks@rediffmail.com

Printed at:
Mehra Offset Press
Delhi

Preface

The phenomenal growth of commercial enterprises in the past decade or so has been the outcome of an equally remarkable spurt in surplus purchasing power, wage increase, liquidity of holdings and the advent of consumerism impelled by the remarkable technological development during the period. Enterprises and industrial conglomerates, trading services and hire-purchase firms alike have had to move fast to be equal to the opportunities provided by a growing national as well as international market. Industry and enterprises have had to change gears in a big way.

The purpose of this representative cross-section is to bring to both students and scholars of management the basic methodologies of conceiving, creating and implementing communication strategies that seek to project and promote the corporate objective of increasing profitability with due recognition of social and national responsibility. The forms and varieties of corporate communication are numerous. From the everyday routine letter of the middle-level executive to the decision-making communiques of the Board of Director, from the instruction manual for the enterprises' workshops and factories to the Annual Reports and Chairman's speech delivered at the Annual General Meeting—the content and quality of each of these is of extreme importance. All together the various forms and varieties of corporate communication form a distinct and vital component of the corporate entity.

In our efforts we have been assisted in generous measure by our many colleagues and friends, professional managers and experts consultants. They would be too numerous to list—suffice it to say that without their guidance these papers and articles would not have been brought together into a cohesive whole. Nonetheless, we feel it our bounden duty to acknowledge the fruitful discussions we have had with Prof. P. Sarveshwar and Dr. Arun Nimbalkar of the Institute of Corporate and Industrial Management, Bombay; Dr. S. Ganesan of the Textile Managers Association, Aurangabad; Shri K. R. Wadhawan of the Centre for Research in Management Sciences, Manila, and Smt. Urvashi Palekar, Documentation Officer, Institute of Corporate Management, Faculty of Economics, University of Lagos, Nigeria.

Excellent computer and secretarial support services were provided by S/Shri Sameer Kak, Arvind Goswami and Raghuraj T. We are grateful to them.

We have attempted to minimise all printing errors, but hasten to add that we alone are responsible for those that still remain.

M. K. SINGH
A. BHATTACHARYA

Introduction

Management may be defined as the process of efficient functioning based on correct choices and actions. However, in the modern world which is increasingly dependant on large organisations, the most significant situations are those which require organisational management. This implies decision and action in a context which is characterised by organised group or collective activity and the goals or objectives towards which the group effort is directed.

These objectives are pursued by managers, who make decisions pertaining to the desired objectives and concerning relationships among resources—the people, money and machines, materials and methods which can be effectively deployed to attain those objectives. Managers then see that their decisions are carried out and that they have the desired effect. When necessary, they use *control actions* to redirect their resources toward the desired objectives. Since managers of large organisations cannot literally to each and every thing that is required as a result of the decisions that are made, organisational management is a process of *working through others* to achieve broad organisational objectives, such as profit or social welfare, or specific objectives such as the development of a new product with success potential of the efficient and time-bound construction of a power plant.

Management may thus be thought of as involving two major elements, *planning* and *control.* These two aspects of management apply to all areas of organised activity, such as the modern large firm represents. Planning involves decisions and actions concerning the future of the organisation. What type of business should be taken up? What kinds of manpower mix will be needed for effective functioning in the 1990s? What impact will increased leisure time have on the utilisation of the contemplated products?

Control involves decisions and actions related to the present organisations. How should production be scheduled to optimise machine-utilisation time? What should be the efficient allocation of workload among various levels of manpower? What mix of newspaper-radio-TV advertising would be best suited to the products?

Every manager is involved to some degree in both planning and control, but the jobs of many managers emphasise the control component. This is, in fact, true of many jobs which have the word 'planning' in their designation. The job of a production planning manager, for instance, is largely control oriented as it stresses the present and the immediate future rather than the long-term future—which is an intrinsic aspect of correct planning.

In similar and parallel terms a communications manager, as distinct from a systems analyst or management information system expert, would seek to control and collate all information relating to the corporate entity he serves. The two obvious levels of functioning are: internal communications for the benefit of increased efficiency within the enterprise and external communications designed with the objective of promoting the corporate image and its material interests. The latter is generally entrusted to someone who in more conventional parlance is known as 'public relations' or 'publicity' officer. The former, on the other hand, handles a task which though contained within the perimeters of the corporate enterprise is of far-reaching significance. While the external communications manager links the corporate entity to the outside world, the internal communications officer networks or ties together all the workers within the organisation into an effective whole.

The internal communications person welds, while the external communications expert builds bridges.

Understanding of the various aspects of management is closely related with understanding of the psychology of communication, both interpersonal and intrapersonal. Communication managers, if trained and experienced, usually have little understanding of what managers do and how they do it. The key factor therefore is that in all communications designs the principal requirement in view should be the actual day-to-day needs of the section heads at all levels. Organisation and methods experts, and also communications personnel, unlike information system or computer/EDP analysts, do know something about the nature of the managerial beast. For instance, it is worth quoting the six prime characteristics of managerial work, as derived from a vast amount of empirical work in this area by Mintzberg (1975):

(i) Managers prefer issues that are current, specific and *ad hoc*.

(ii) Managerial activity is characterised by variety, fragmentation and brevity.

(iii) The manager performs a great quantity of work at an unrelenting pace.

(iv) Despite the preponderance of obligations, the manager appears to be in control of his affairs.

(v) The manager sits between his organisation and a network of contacts.

(vi) The manager demonstrates a strong preference for the verbal media.

While these six characteristics do not claim to represent a definitive understanding of the nature of managerial functions in their totality, they are of obvious value to the communications manager in feeding the correct and appropriate does of information to the managers he networks.

The nature of communications internal to an enterprise would of necessity be very different from that applicable to say an academic research institution (seminars, symposia, conferences with sister institutions) or a government undertaking with specific social and parametric objectives. The commercial enterprise or firm would have an in-house communications system in terms of desk-to-desk networking, intra-departmental and interdivisional or inter-plant meetings, instruction manuals for the shop-floor, rules and regulations for all categories of employees, information sheets for factory and plant workers related to the prevention of accidents, for instance, or the meeting hours and conduct of union meetings. On the external front, there would be sales, publicity and promotional brochures and leaflets, product instruction booklets, liaison with advertising agencies for publicity through newspapers, journals and other print media and a special cell for audio-visual preparation, promotion and monitoring. The role of television in India is now one of the predominant considerations.

In recent years corporate communications in India has taken a giant leap forward. This is due to the high degree of sophistication which has been brought into the dynamics of publicity and promotion of the corporate image as well as the corporate product. Beginning with the new well-known success story of a famous brand of fast-food noodles, Indian advertising has come of age. Equally laudable has been the effort of several Indian corporate entities to participate in the public good (*e.g.*, the welcome and most useful insertions by the Loss Prevention Association of India and the Petroleum Conservation Research Institute). All this is great, but the composite picture of Indian advertising are the corporate image and product is rather confusing. The high degree of sophistication that it has injected into the media has sidelined the hundreds of millions of our fellow-citizens who can only be bewildered at the vast array of luxury electronic goods, cosmetics, gadgetry and similar trivia that seem to be the very blood and breath of the urban fellow-citizens. Advertising shorts have become the agency's work of art instead of carrying a message as simply as possible. The imagery of the commercial on Indian TV is a confusing mix of fantasy and vague futurism; tyres plagiarise mystical moments of Spielberg's "Close Encounters" and TV sets reach out to us from galactic distances. The possibilities of the visual media and the small screen are endless but endless sophistication too is boring. The admen who manage the corporate image and the corporate product would seem to be in dire need of the pause that refreshes.

It needs to be recognised that corporate communications should be based primarily on utility and effectiveness, on the one hand, and a reaffirmation of the identity of interests of the corporate entity and the society it belongs to. There is no need for a committed corporate entity, or a totally subservient corporate image projected to hundreds of millions of fellow-citizens—The prime need is for a high degree of corporate responsibility and an impeccable sense of integrity. All corporate communications, it need not be reiterated, should be based on the larger consumer and public good. Junk food and coloured condoms do not belong to a nation where over one-third of the population worries about the next meal.

The purpose of these papers is to present as representative a cross-section as possible of the nature and form of corporate communications for both internal and external use. The intended readership would comprise both students and scholars of management as well as publicity and public relations executives and communications managers of all corporate enterprises and organisations.

Contents

PREFACE v

INTRODUCTION vii

1. Publicity Programme for Business Organisation 1
JOHN PARRY

2. Criteria for Selecting Trade Representation Offices Abroad 68
JOHN R. HEALY

3. Trade Information: State Trading Organizations 84
H K. RAINA

4. Arranging Transport and Customs Formalities for Trade Shows 94
BRUCE BENDOW

5. Trade Fair Participation 122
BRUCE BENDOW

6. Developing Your Own Case Materia's 201
CLAUDE CELLICH

7. Complexity of Corporate Communications 211

8. Communication: A Tool for Motivation 232
DR. NIRAJ KUMAR

9. Organisational Effectiveness through Management Information Systems 254
B.B. SAKSENA

10. Writing Effective Business Letters 264
ANN RAINE THOMSON

11. Commercial Reporting: Obtaining and Relaying Market Information Effectively 281
J.M. KNOWLES

12. Radio as a Trade Promotion Tool 298
BILL MCCABE

13. A Management Overview of Public Relations 311
R. P. BILLIMORIA

14. Audit of Information and Reporting Systems 318
P. CHATTOPADHYAY

1

Publicity Programme for Business Organisations

JOHN PARRY*

I

Chambers of commerce and other business organizations should carefully plan their publicity activities to support their trade promotion work. Chambers of commerce and other business associations need an effective publicity programme to carry out their trade promotion work successfully. In their supporting role in trade promotion to the national export promotion agency (which has overall responsibility for coordinating trade promotion on the national level), chambers need to publicize their foreign trade services to local business community so that these firms receive full benefit from the chamber's activities.

*John Parry is a specialist in publicity who has served as a consultant for several ITC technical cooperation projects in developing countries. This article is based on publication that he recently wrote, *The Preparation of Publications and Publicity Material. A Guide for Chambers of Commerce*, which is one of a series of guides being produced under ITC's technical cooperation programme with national chambers of commerce.

They also often need to make their trade promotion activities better known in government circles so that they can get adequate recognition and back-up for their work. Furthermore chambers must provide their members with information on overseas marketing opportunities and business conditions so that foreign business transactions can expand. They should likewise alert businessmen abroad to trading opportunities that exist in the chamber's country, such as products available for export, import goods sought by local firms and investment possibilities.

To carry out these publicity and information tasks effectively, a chamber should draw up a comprehensive publicity programme that takes into account the over all aims of the organization's publicity work, the means at its disposal to undertake publicity activities and the best available techniques to achieve these aims. One person in the chamber should be responsible for overseeing the planning and implementation of this publicity programme.

THE TARGET AUDIENCES

Every publicity activity should be aimed at a specific audience, and a publicity campaign for a chamber of commerce is no exception. When drawing up a publicity programme, and before embarking on any kind campaign, the management of the chamber should consider carefully which audience—or audiences—it is trying to reach, and with which techniques. In the case of a chamber these audiences are many—the government and administration of the country in question; the members of the chamber itself: others in the country who are interested in business but are not members of the chamber; foreign governments and companies considering doing business with the country in question; the media at home and abroad; and eventually the general public.

The overseas targets of this publicity campaign are perhaps especially important. In many cases they include potential buyers or suppliers, or persons working in services concerned with trade such as the organizers of overseas shows and exhibitions.

TYPES OF INFORMATION

Before attempting to address these various target audiences, a chamber of commerce should clearly set down its publicity objectives. In drawing up these objectives, which are part of its overall publicity programme, a chambers' management and its publicity specialist should ask:

Who is the chamber trying to reach and why?

Is the particular information technique selected the best means for getting the message across to the target audience?

Is the cost justified in terms of the publicity that the chamber is trying to get for itself and its members, and are there sufficient financial resources to cover the expense?

Because a chamber's trade promotion activities should be considered part of the country's overall export promotion effort, an additional question should be answered:

Is the chamber's publicity effort completely integrated with that of the export promotion board, and are the chamber's efforts complementary to, and not repetitive of, the publicity activities of the board and other trade promotion bodies?

Once these question have been asked and satisfactorily answered within the context of the chamber's overall aims and the government's trade policy, a question of a more technical nature arises:

What types of information need to be disseminated?

The list of information subjects is somewhat long and is discussed in more detail later in the article. A comprehensive programme should be drawn up describing the publicity aims, means and techniques. However, some of the types of information that a chamber should collect and disseminate are:

Information for the home govefnment on business developments within the country and abroad.

Explanation of government decisions to the business community and in particular clarification of the many international regulations being formulated by bodies such such as European Community, UNCTAD and GATT; also, an explanation of the impact on the business community of actions taken by other governments and international bodies.

What the chamber itself is doing.

"How to" information, that is, practical material that chamber members can use in their export efforts. The Singapore International Chamber of Commerce for example, has produced a fact-filled handbook, *How to Export*, which covers in detail all the facets of exporting. Other information of this kind could cover such practical aspects as how to participate in a trade fair abroad and how a company can produce publicity material to promote its exports. Some of the purely commercial information that a chamber should collect for dissemination to its various target audiences is described in the checklist on page 8-9

Information on products that can be supplied to foreign buyers and on items that local firms are seeking to import from foreign suppliers, for dissemination to foreign businessmen and their official commercial representatives abroad.

SELECTING TECHNIQUES

Every publicity activity that a chamber undertakes should be aimed at a specific audience. When drawing up its publicity programme in addition to determining its target audiences, setting down the aims of its programme, and deciding on the types of information to provide, a chamber should carefully consider the techniques to applly to achieve its publicity goals.

In choosing a particular information technique, whether it be a newsletter, press release, handbook, audiovisual presentation or other, the chamber officials responsible for publicity should have a clear aim from the outset: whether to inform the reader on the affairs of the chamber per se or whether to disseminate a wider range of information on trade and industry at home and abroad. In some techniques a combination of these two aims is possible. This is particularly so in the case of a newsletter, which provides an opportunity to tell interested parties at home or abroad exactly what the chamber is doing. A newsletter also easily tends itself to widespread diffusion. Press releases and media relation achieve maximum publicity at minimal cost.

Audiovisual presentations, besides being relatively costly, are seldom used by chambers of commerce in their publicity programmes abroad. Press releases and media relations, on the other hand, achieve maximum publicity at minimal cost and in many instances provide the chamber the exposure it needs to the media in its own country. Chambers usually do not issue press releases outside their own country except on such occasions as trade fair participation abroad.

In creating lts information policy, a chamber should also consider other means of communication such as issuing directories of members, producing literature to assist members in foreign marketting techniques (either individually or ns a group), participating in foreign trade fairs and exhibitions, preparing leaflets on individual subjects such as products available from member companies, and organizing seminars and courses.

In opting for publicity programme containing one or several of these elements, a chamber must take the basic decision to carry through the programme and the various activities within it until the goals set at the beginning have been achieved. This is particularly important in the case of a publication to be issued. The world is littered with the remains of would be publications started by trade organizations in various countries with no clear idea of their target audicnce, the cost involved or the effort required to bring the idea to fruition. Many of these publications have never appeared after the first issue.

To be a success a publication should he carefully developed and produced to meet the needs of its readers. The material needs to be written and presented in such a way as to make its readers, however few or numerous they may be, look forward to receiving it and use the information it contains. Moreover the publication should be seen as part of an integrated publicity programme covering the entire spectrum of communications methods available.

AN INFORMATION OFFICER

To be effectively carried out, a chamber's publicity programme should be administered by a professional information officer who works under the direct supervision of a senior officer of the chamber. This officer should be responsible for collecting information on the chamber, its work and related subjects, and for disseminating it to the target audiences described above. He should thus be accountable for coordinating all publicity inputs and for producing publications and generating publicity. For this he needs a background in public relation journalism and/or advertising as well as a "nose" for news.

However, budgetary restrictions may make the employment of such a person impossible. In this case a chamber could use the services of a publicity consultant, who could work in liaison with a staff member designated to supervise the publicity work. This is particularly advisable in advertising and magazine production, but such profeesional assistance is also required in any other areas.

A full-time information officer can usually be found in the ranks of trained journalists in the country concerned. Business journalists are particularly useful because of their grasp of the subject matter of the chamber's information programme.

If the chamber decides not to employ a full-time information officer, it is desirable to give the staff member responsible for the information programme some kind of journalistic and communications training. Administering a programme of this type, covering as it does all facets of communications requires many complex skills. If the staff member does not already have at least a basic knowledge of these skills, it will probably be useful for him to spend some time in short apprenticeships with outside consultants.

Such short training periods are generally easy to arrange. For example, the staff member could spend several weeks working with a local advertising agency to learn the basic techniques of producing publications that contain advertising. He could work for a short time either with a local business magazine or, if this does not exist, with the business editor of a local newspaper to study the techniques of gathering and presenting news.

International news agencies such as Reuters and Agence France Presse also make available training facilities of this kind. However their news-gathering techniques are perhaps not as specialized as those required by an information officer in a chamber of commerce.

The International Public Relations Association, whose headquarters are in Switzerland (20, quai Gusitive Ador, 1207 Geneva), can arrange training courses in public relations (PR), usually with a PR agency in the country concerned or, if required, in other countries where the PR function is more developed.

The checklist on pages 8-9 gives the basic decisions to be made in setting up a chamber of commerce's publicity programme.

PRESS RELEASES AND MEDIA CONTACTS

One of the essential elements of a chamber's publicity programme will probably be to produce press material and cultivate

CHART 1-A

Checklist of Main Ifems of Commercial Information that a Chamber should Collect Regularly

1. Foreign news, by product

   Supply and demand trends abroad.

   Foreign market development and overseas business opportunities.
   International commodity market news'

   National and international trade statistics.

   Foreign sales leads of use of members; overseas buyers interested in specific products; public tenders abroad.

2. Foreign market news, by country and area

   Import and export statistics of overseas markets.

   Economic trends abroad.

   Demand trends in foreign markets.

   New about competing suppliers in other countries.

   Other trends and developments that could affect demand for the home country's products in the particular export market, such as shifts in consumer tastes and technological developments.

   Tariff and quota changas, government regulations, and other commercial policy and political developments in the market abroad.
   Trade channels overseas; lists of importers in other countries and their methods of doing business.

3. Foreign exchange developments

4. Intemational political developments (if relevant to local businessmen).

5. Trade agreements involving foreign firms and govemments

6. Shipping news

   Arrivals and departures of freight carriers (if necessary or possible), freight rates, port regulations, shipping conference agreements, new shipping services.

7. Foreign trade incentives.

Available trade promotion services; fiscal incentives for export business.

8. Regulations affecting trade

New trade restrictions or procedures, both at home and abroad.

9. Overseas promoiions

Forthcoming trade fairs and exhibitions abroad, store promotions in foreign markets; outgoing trade missions.

10. Arrival of visiting buyers (if of interest to the chamber's target audiences)

11. New information sources on foreign trade

News of new studies, book reviews etc.

12. Problems facing the export sector.

---

media relations, Dealing with the press and other media calls for a professional, well planned approach. "Let's get it published in the newspaper" is a phrase uttered casually every day by thousands of people seeking to publicize an idea, a message or an event. The statements presupposes that newspaper and magazine editors sit patiently in their offices waiting for people to bring them "news" to fill their columns. Newspapers and magazines do not operate in this fashion and, far from having empty columns waiting for news to fill them, their space is extremely restricted. Moreover, editors have their own ideas about what to print, and these may not coincide with those of would be contributors.

Press publicity. Nevertheless, press publicity is one of the most efficient ways of getting a chamber's message across to a wide public, provided that the person responsible for the chamber's information programme can identify the news needs of the various media and tailor his information accordingly. For despite the fact that newspapers and magazines have much news competting for their space, editors—and particularly business editors of specialized business magazines—are usually

CHART 1-B

Points to Consider in Planning a Chamber's Publicity Programme

To whom is the programme addressed ?

What sort of information is to be collected to send to the various target audiences ?

Where can this information be collected and how will it be sifted to extract the maximum value?

What techniques will be used to disseminate this information?
Will a professional information officer be hired to handle the administration of this programme?

If not, is the person who is handling it sufficiently trained in communications techniques? If he is not, will outside consultants be employed to assist this person in his work?

interested in printing news from their local chamber of commerce, particularly if it is genuinely newsworthy, concisely written and well presented. Verbosity is counter productive, as editors are busy persons and have no time for long dissertations.

The most effective vehicle for carrying chamber's message to the media is the press release. It is also one of the most inexpensive to use. Anyone with a typewriter and a duplicating machine (or preferably access to an offset printing shop) can issue press releases at minimal cost.

Care should be taken in using press releases as a communications technique, however, to assure that the releases are of sufficient interest to the reader in many countries editors are deluged with releases. The edittor of the London *Daily Mail*, for example, has estimated that as many as 500 releases come into his paper's editorial room every day.

Moreover, press releases must be seen as part of a wider ranging media relations programme involving not only the press but also television and radio. The press release is an essential tool of communication with the press, but it should not be seen as a means to itself.

Nevertheless press releases are extremely important, because they are probably the best way for a chamber to present its news to the public. From time to time it is possible to place material on the radio or on television, but such occasions are rare, as radio and TV time is limited. Moreover, news heard on the radio tends to become blurred in the listener's memory two or three days later.

Thus most of the press relations work conducted by a chamber will be with the written media, very often mostly the business press. The aim of a chamber's press release programme should be to encourage and assist the media to publish news and other material that will advance the chamber's objectives.

To do this, it is essential to know the media and the types of audiences the chamber is seeking to reach. This task is simplified for a chamber since it is assumed that its press relations programme will concentrate on the media at home and will not extend to other countries.

One way for the chamber's information officer to identify the media with whom he should be dealing is to ask members which publications they read. This will show which newspapers and periodicals are considered by the business community as the most valuable. The next step is to find out what news and other information these publications need and ensure that this is made available to them. At this stage a certain amount of personal contact between the person in charge of the chamber's information policy and journalists is necessary.

The mechanics of producing press releases: The most effective way to carry a chamber's message to the media is the press release. Press releases can cover all aspects of a chamber's work: seminars, conferences, appointments, dealings with other countries and so on. They should be issued whenever there is a genuine item of news to be disseminated, but the technique should not be over used Too many releases containing too little news will tend to make journalists throw away future releases—which might contain real news-unread.

CHART 1-C

Questions to be Answered in Planning a Media Campaign

What is the message the chamber is trying to get across?

Which media are most receptive to receiving it?

Has an informal poll of members been carried out to ascertain which media they find the most valuable in their work?

Have business journalists been sounded out about the information they want from the chamber?

Has a crisp, easy-on-the-eye layout been established for the press release paper?

Are all those who should be receiving the press releases on the list? Is this list constantly updated?

Is the writing style of the press releases crisp enough to attract the attention of professional journalists?

Before scheduling a press conference has it been determined that the conference is really needed? Would a release be better?

A press release should normally be typewritten, double spaced and printed (or photocopied) on A 4 size paper. If possible, in order to attract the attention of the reader, it should be reproduced on a striking letterhead, designed especially for the chamber. Recto-verso printing (*i.e.*, on both sides of the sheet of paper) is acceptable, but there should be plenty of white space left around the text.

The news in a press release should be kept as simple as possible, with the salient facts concisely conveyed. No press release should run longer than two typewritten pages, double spaced, a name and telephone number for further information should be prominently featured for readers wanting more details.

Press conferences: The press conference is another frequently employed media-relations technique that—again if used with care—can provide valuable exposure for a chamber's ideas. But as with press releases, it cannot be stressed too often that this technique must be used with care. In sehedulling a press conference the chamber's information officer must ask himself whether the event really merits a conference, or whether a release would not do just as well. Furthermore he must ask this question not from the viewpoint of the chamber but from that of journalists who will be invited to come. Journalists are busy and often have to choose between several competing events. Thus, if a chamber calls a press conference on a subject important to it but not to the media, it runs the risk of holding a conference with no journalists. Publicity fiascos can easily be avoided by maintaining close contact with journalists, by informally exchanging views and by soliciting their advice from time to time.

The checklist on pages 12 lists some of the questions an information officer should ask himself in embarking on a press and media relations campaign.

(See next issue of FORUM for a continuation of the discussion on different publicity techniques that a chamber can use.)

II

When planning a publicity programme, a chamber of commerce should look into the different types of activities that could be included. Chambers of commerce and other business organizations have an important publicity function to carry out in ths trade promotion work that they undertake in liaison with the national export promotion agency. Using appropriate publicity techniques to support this work is vital if a chamber wishes to succeed in its trade promotion activities. A number of different techniques can be used to achieve a chamber's publicity aims. Some of these are press releases and media contacts, a glossy magazine, newsletters and other periodicals, ad hoc publications, a handbook on how to export and an official chamber directory. The techniques selected should be incorporated into the chamber's overall publicity programme and carried out in coordination with other activities under that programme.

Some of the factors to consider when selecting individual publicity techniques are discussed below. (The first article in this series, in the previous issue of FORUM, dealt with a chamber's overall publicity plan and the use of press relations as a publicity tool.)

A GLOSSY MAGAZINE

Producing a glossy magazine may be one of the elements to include in a chamber's publicity programme. Nothing looks more attractive in the offices of a chamber than a well produced, brightly coloured and copiously illustrated magazine. Often printed in four colours on glossy paper, it can serve as effective advertising for the chamber.

Alas too often a chamber magazine remains unread. Businessmen are busy, and however well produced the magazine, they are hard-pressed for time to read it, particularly if, as is frequently the case, its text is heavily interspersed with photographs not relevant to the text and with advertising. Moreover a multitude of glossy magazines are put out by commercial companies, throughout the world, many of them containing much of the same information being disseminated by chambers of commerce. The average businessman's desk usually contains half a dozen professional periodicals, international magazines (such as L'Express or Asian Business) and daily newspapers.

A businessman, whose day is taken up with the effort of running his company, does not have time to read all this material. Thus he tends to be highly selective in his reading, and in many cases the glossy magazine put out by his local chamber of commerce goes to the bottom of his pile of reading matter—and is quite often thrown away without ever having been read at all!

Research carried out by ITC over a number of years has shown that very few chambers of commerce, particularly in developing countries. are capable of putting out a glossy magazine that contains sufficient information to make the reader pick it up ahead of, say *Jeune Afrique*. The reasons for this are many:

The cost of four colour printing is often too high for the chamber's budget.

The task of collecting interesting and topical news and feature material is too much for the modest production staff, particularly if a professional information officer is not available.

The magazine cannot be circulated efficiently to those who would like to make the most of it.

Readers, or would-be readers, are unwilling to pay the relatively high price required to cover the production costs a magazine of this kind.

Producing a magazine: Thus, the idea of publishing a magazine should be thought through very carefully. If a decision to publish is taken, care should be exercised that the product is of the highest quality, capable of competing on equal terms with other publications available to the projected readership. This means giving close attention to the editorial content, consultation with a graphic designer to make sure the design is as eye-catching as possible and strict control of the budget.

A glossy magazine does offer several advantages over other types of publications. If it is well produced, it serves as a prestige outlet for the chamber's news. For this purpose its graphics, particularly on the front page need to be attractive.

A magazine also offers greater scope for longer articles, a larger number of photographs and more statistics than, for example, a newsletter. Its formal allows the editor more space to pesent the news he has collected and more freedom of choice in what he prints. A magazine format, for example, allows the editor to present detailed statistics on import opportunities in other countries. It gives him the space to reproduce the full texts of important international or governmental decrees affecting business community. It offers him the possibility to print long articles from abroad about trade opportunities, or articles by chamber members describing aspects of their work that are of use to fellow members.

The format also gives the opportunity to use photographs, both black-and-white and colour, and to sell advertising to members of the chamber to help finance the publication. Most chambers of commerce accept advertising for their magazines and indeed many depend on it as their major source of revenue from publications. Some even earn a profit from it. Thus while a case could be made for not having advertising in other publications. It would seem essential to carry as much as possible in a glossy magazine.

Printing: The printing of a magazine is of utmost importance, for however valuable the information it contains, the magazine is sold as much on its content. Wherever feasible, it is recommended that a chamber engage a graphic designer to plan the most eyecatching layout possible. For a one-time fee, this professional can design the proposed magazine, suggest (with a printer) the type of paper to be used, and generally make the format as appealing to the reader as possible within the chamber's budget.

Sales: The sales strategy for the publication should aim at bringing in revenue, but care should be taken not to charge too high a price. The publication will compete with other commercial publications above, as described, and it must therefore be reasonably priced in comparison.

A case can well be made for selling the publication at a lower price to chamber members than to outsiders, or for including the cost of the magazine in membership fees. In budgeting for a magazine, however, an effort must be made to balance production and distribution costs with subscription and advertising revenue. This is often difficult to do, at least in the initial stages, but it is the goal towards which any editor of a chamber's magazine—or indeed, the editor of any magazine—should strive.

The checklist on page 20 shows some of the points a chamber of commerce should consider in deciding whether it should produce a glossy magazine.

NEWSLETTERS AND OTHER PERIODICALS

A good mix of types of information should be developed for a magazine or a newsletter. A newsletter can be an effective publicity technique for a chamber if the information it contains is relevant and current, if distribution is rapid and if a mailing list has been suitably, developed to cover key persons in the target audience.

What is news?: The *Oxford English Dictionary* defines news as "report of recent happenings, fresh information; tidings; intelligence," All these definitions apply to a chamber's newsletter.

To "sell" a newsletter to the reader, the editor must produce an interesting and readable selection of news. Given the wealth of information available, this would seem to be a simple task, for a large amount of material flows into a chamber every day, in the form of communications from members, communications from governments and international organizations, domestic and foreign publications, and reports on the chamber's meetings and the activities of its members. Yet compiling a digest of what the readers of the newsletter really want to read is extremely difficult. The checklist on page 25 list some of the basic questions that the editor should ask himself in planning the newsletter. When these basic questions have been answered, he can begin his task of assembling news for a trial issue.

It is essential to produce a trial issue or issues for internal use—and criticism—before the publication is actually launched. The proceedure of assembling news and presenting it in interesting and informative way is highly complex, and it will be necessary to experiment with various combinations of news before the right mix is achieved for the first edition of the newsletter.

Sources of information: An advisable news mix for a four or eight-page newsletter is in general one page of news on the chamber's activities and three (or seven) pages of more general information of interest to members and others.

Developing sources of information is an important part of an editor's task. He should know where to acquire information on a wide variety of subjects, either at home or abroad. Published reference books are useful, and all chambers should have a basic library containing such major works. But personal cantact is even more valuable, and as his work proceeds an editor may find it' useful to compile a card index of persons who can help him, either by providing facts or writing short news items for inclusion in the newsletter. These persons can be the government, in private in business and members of the press, either in the chamber's home country or abroad.

A second source of information is the chamber itself. The editor, as has been seen above, will presumably be an official of the chamber and thus have access to details on its inner workings. In corperation with the managing director or director general, he should inform himself of the news that needs to be disseminated publicly and ensure that it is presented concisely and factually. He must be careful about selecting items for publication. While calendars of meetings and reports of the chamber's initiatives on behalf of members are usually of interest, the managing director or other officials may not want to see some such activities publicized. The editor must bear in mind that no confidential information should appear in the newsletter unless the chamber's management specifically authorizes it.

The third major source of information is published material. It will obviously not be possible for the editor to read the thousands of publications available from around the world. Furthermore the chamber's budget is usually not large enough to cover the cost of subscriptions to more than a small fraction of them. Selectivity is therefore the key, and the editor must ensure that he has access to the main newspapers and periodicals that deal with the subjects on which the chamber is seeking to inform its readers.

What news to publish: The major objective of a newsletter, as discussed above, is to give the chamber wider exposure. This in turn will attract new members and thus increase the influence of the chamber. A second objective is to provide members and other readers with information they may not have seen elsewhere, using the sources of information described above.

The International Chamber of Commerce (headquartered in Paris), in describing its own activities, has drawn up a valuable checklist of the subjects with which a chamber could concern itself. This list can be used as a subject guide by an editor of a newsletter. It covers the following; arbitration; banking; international activities of chambers of commerce throughout the world; competition law; international business conferences and congress; East-West trade, North-South trade and South-South trade; energy; the environment; industrial property; investments; marketing; telecommunications; trade facilitation; trade and commodity policy; trade fairs; and transport. Although far from exhaustive, the list pinpoints the basic subjects on which a chamber's publication should seek to inform its readers.

Production: As with a magazine, the way a newsletter looks is as important as what it says. Most people are scanners, that is, they will skim through a publication before reading it in earnest. Thus in planning a newsletter, a chambers's management should engage a professional design consultant to design a layout that will catch the eye, particularly the front page.

CHART 1-D

Checklist for Deciding Whether to Publish a Glossy Magazine

What other magazines is the business community reading?

Can the chamber produce an editorially and graphically attractive product that will compete with them?

Does the chamber's budget allow it to do so?

What will the editorial content be? Where will it come from?

How much advertising will be accepted, given that the more advertising the magazine carries the better the balance between income and expenditure?

What is the pricing policy *vis-a-vis* (a) members and (b) other readers?

A well designed publication is usually easier to produce on an issue-to-issue basis than one that does not follow any particular style and format, because once the decision on design has been made, the editor simply follows it for each issue. The design should include a distinctive logotype the establishes the identity of the publication (and of the organization). In most cases, this will be the logotype of the chamber itself. The masthead should carry the name of the newsletter, the name of the chamber of commerce, the volume number and issue date.

Circulation: The major question arises of whether readers should pay for the newsletter or instead get free. The budgetary restrictions to which most chambers of commerce are subject are a natural argument in favour of requiring readers to pay. However, the chamber's members may initially resist paying for something that they consider—rightly or wrongly—part of the services that they are entitled to receive when they join the chamber and pay their membership fees.

One way around this problem may be to include a subscription to the newsletter in the regular member ship dues. Another is to offer the newsletter at a reduced rate to members and at a higher rate to nonmembers. Local considerations play an important role in determining the choice between these alternatives.

OTHER PUBLICATIONS

In addition to the newsletter, the information programme of a chamber should include other publications aimed at achieving specific objectives. These would cover, for example, trade opportunities, market studies, educational materials and new publications in the chamber's library.

These publications can be issued whenever there is a need. A bulletin on trade opportunities, for example, can be in a newsletter format and be quite simply produced. The key to a successful trade opportunities bulletin is speed. The publication must appear frequently—weekly if possible—and transmission time form the editor's desk to the hands of the reader must be kept to an absolute minimum.

It is important that all other publications closely resemble the newsletter in style, in order to preserve the corporate identity of the chamber. It should be clear from a glance at their mastheads that are issued by the chamber and that they complement each other. A selection should be made from the large amount of material that flows into a chamber.

AD HOC PUBLICATIONS

In addition to the regular newsletter or magazine and the semi-regular publications described above, a chamber should publish ad hoc bulletins and other materials as the need arises. Even if the chamber does produce a regular journal of some kind, there should be a regular flow of ad hoc publications, because the frequency and format of a journal are not suitable for all types of information. Even the subject of trade opportunities sometimes lends itself to such an approach.

In developing countries where the flow of information on trade opportunities is considerable, a more regular bulletin of the type described in the last section is the best solution. But in other countries with fewer trade opportunities to be brought to the attention of a smaller number of interested parties, an ad hoc approach is sometimes better. This would simply consist of the quick production of a leaflet nothing the opportunities, and its distribution by the chamber to the persons most interested in them.

Market studies are another type of ad hoc publication of value to chambers of commerce. In many cases these can simply be typed in the chamber's offices and photocopied for members. The information they contain can be obtained from the general flow of information into the chamber, from embassies and consulates abroad, and from foreign trade representatives stationed locally. If this method of distribution is too expensive, the chamber might consider producing and distributing from time to time a list of the country and market studies available. Its members can then ask for copies of those that interest them.

Ad hoc leaflets can also be issued to describe new legislation at home and abroad, report on education material, discuss the chamber's services and, in particular, announce courses, seminars and other events run by the chamber. Changes in the management of the chamber. In addition to being publicized in the newsletter or journal, can also be announced in this way.

Other ad hoc leaflets might carry international trade statistics; lists of international trade fairs and exhibitions of interest to members; lists of supplisrs, manufacturers, importers and exporters; price data on various products; and information on customs tariffs abroad.

A HANDBOOK ON HOW TO EXPORT

While a newsletler is invaluable for keeping members up to date on current events and news of the chamber itself, some members need a more specialized information tool to help them in their work. For instance, many members in developing countries would like to increase their exports but are unsure of how to go about it.

In many developing countries small and medium-size industries have only a limited knowledge of the export business. While they would like to export thhir products, they are uncertain about how to identify their major markets, are unfamiliar with export pricing and overseas import regulations, are uninformed about which documents are needed and where and, in many cases, are not equipped with the necessary expertise to obtain export financing.

All of these problems tend to inhibit small businessmen in developing countries. A small exporter needs help in mastering the intricacies of the overseas market and, as a member of the local chamber of commerce, he is entitled to look to it for this help.

Sometimes a newsletter or magazine will provide, some basic information on all or part of the subjects mentioned above. But a newsletter. through its very design, aims at providing short and concious information about wide-range subjects in limited space. This is not enough for a would-be exporter. Moreover, the very specialized nature of the information he requires is not of interest to everyone.

A newsletter is meant to be a publication of general interest. The inclusion of too much information on a highly complicated and specialized subject would irritate its readers and perhaps cause them to withdraw their support from the newsletter as a whole. A strong case can be made, than, for a chamber to publish a handbook or brochure on how to export, aimed at telling the small and medium-size businessman all he needs to know about entering export trade.

A chamber should approach the publication of such a handbook with care, however, for it can raise a number of problems.

The export promotion agency: The first thing a chamber should consider in discussing whether to produce a handbook on how to export is: "What is our national export promotion agency doing in this regard? Mady export promotion bodies, often in cooperation with ITC, produce such documents, and it is important for the chamber to find out at the very beginning what the agency itself has been doing. Duplication of effort is a waste not only of time but also of money for all concerned, ITC also produces publications of this type for developing countries.

What information to include: What does a would-be exporter in the chamber's own country need to know? Just as the structure of chambers varies from country to country, so does the information needed by companies seeking to enter export trade.

In countries with a considerable export tradition, small and medium-size companies already have access to certain sources of information on foreign markets. In others. it is necessary for the handbook's compilers to start from scratch, beginning with the initial stages of an export operation. The editor of a handbook should therefore conduct an informal opinion survey among exporters or would be exporters to find out what sort of information they are looking for. After all, they will be buying the publication when it is completed, and it must therefore satisfy their needs.

In compiling a handbook of this type, it is essential that the presentation be simple and clear. The tendency to address the subject in complicated economic and social terms or to explain everything in too simple a language must be raised. What readers want from a handbook of this kind is facts, not opinions or rhetoric.

CHART 1-E

Editorial Questions to be Answered in Planning the First Issue of a Chamber's Newsletter

What is the basic concept of the publication? What are its aims and its function within the chambers?

What is the editorial plan for, or message to, the readers (*i.e.* how are the goals of the publication to be explained to them)?

Who are the target readers or subscribes?

How will the publication help them? What concrete benefits will they realize from reading it?

What is the competition (*i.e.* what other publications do readers read)? What can the newsletter offer readers that is exclusive?

Does the publication need a question-and-answer feature on a major topic of concern?

Should tables or graphs be used to illustrate some of the news?

Should specific points be emphasized so that readers can, if necessary, take action on these points for themselves?

What are the sources of information? How can they be developed and new ones be created?

What topics should be covered: Every exporter should ask ten basic questions before entering the export market. These questions, treated in more detail, should form the basis of any plan for exporters, and the basis for any book on how to export. They are:

1. Is there a demand for the firm's products in a particular foreign market, taking into account that marketing conditions there differ from those at home?

2. Who are the competitors, and how strongly are they established in this market?
3. What is the most effective method of designing and packaging products for this market? (In some countries, political, national and religious susceptibilities play an important role in these marketing factors).
4. In what language should the sales material, packaging, brochures and correspondence with potential buyers be prepared?
5. Is it desirable to advertise in the target country, and if so how should this be done and how much will it cost?
6. What are the means and cost of distribution?
7. Are the firm's products competitivey priced in relation to those of its competitors and local market conditions?
8. What are the firm's relations with potential buyers and credit agents in the country in question? Are they trustworthy?
9. What is the degree of stability in the foreing country, and what is the state of its national economy?
10. What is the extent of import restrictions, tariffs and exchange controls?

To answer these questions the following basic subjects should be covered:

How to find markets abroad.

How to sell abroad.

Foreign import regulations.

Export pricing.

Export contracts.

Documents.

Export financing.

Export incentives.

Export licensing.

Foreign exchange controls.

Insurance.

Transport and freight forwarding.

Export packaging.

Export quality control.

Where to find the information: In many cases the sources of information for a "how to export" handbook are identical with, or similar to, those for a newsletter or magazine. In other cases the library of the export promotion agency or the information facilities of the ministry of commerce or trade will have the information required.

The handbook should not deal with market information on specific countries, as this would make it unwieldy and too prone to go out of date. Rather it should concentrate on synthesizing the Information available and identifying sources of information that readers can use to answer more specific queries.

Physical production of the handbook: A handbook can be published to help small and medium-size businessmen in their exporting. In many ways, production of a handbook on how to export resembles, albeit on a somewhat more elaborate scale, the production of a newsletter. For both, the following simple rules apply:

The writing should be clear.

The graphic design should make optimum use of the space available without filling every centimeter with text.

The circulation policy should be clearly set out and aim at achieving maximum sales.

The last point is particularly important, for while a chamber could, in certain cases, justify giving away its newsletter as a goodwill gesture provided the budget so allows, no such justification can be made for the brochure. Its physical production costs preclude such generosity on the part of the chamber. It must be sold, and preferably at a profit.

As with the newsletter, the editor should consult a graphic designer for the handbook's initial layout. It might well be the same person as the designer used for the newsletter since a continuity could thus be established from a graphics point of view between the newsletter (presumbly already established) and the booklet.

Circulation: Since the handbook is a commercial venture, it must be sold energetically to avoid substantial financial loss. Issuing the book in association with a publishing house can lessen this financial risk. Such a firm would absorb part of the assumption that it, too would profit from sales. But if no such publishing house exists, the chamber itself must undertake a campaign to market its handbook among members and non-members.

Advertising: There are arguments both for and against the inclusion of advertising in a handbook of this type. Carrying advertising from chamber members, perhaps grouping the ads in two blocks at each end of the text, could be a useful source of revenue to help defray the cost of publication.

Unless a chamber has an advertising expert on its staff, it should ask a professional advertising and space sales agency to advise on rates to be charged and eventually to sell space against a commission. Inexperienced executives often set their advertising rates too low in publications of this type and fail to realize the profit they had been expecting. Or, rates may be set so high that no one will pay them and no advertising is sold for the handbook. A chamber would therefore be advised to enlist the help of a professional in setting advertising policy.

A CHAMBER'S OFFICIAL DIRECTORY

Every major publishing house has what is calls its "flagship" publication. In essence, this is what the owners of the publishing house consider its most important publication. It is not necessarily the publication that sells the most copies, is the most graphically eye-catching, has the most pages. contains the most advertising, or carries the most sensational or comprehensive news. It is simply the publ:cation that has the greatest influence on its national or regional readers and that the management considers its most important representative to the outside world. For a chamber of commerce such a publication is inevitably the official directory of its members. Without a directory of this type, the chamber and its members would go unknown, not ɔnly in the domestic market but also overseas.

Without an official directory of its members, a chamber goes unknown at home and abroad. A chamber directory is more than a simple list of members. It presents to various outside audiences the official face of the chamber. It is one of the yardsticks by which the chamber is judged. It is therefore essential that it is even more of a prestige publication then the magazine, the newsletter and the other publications. This does not necessarity mean that the directory needs to cost a great deal of money. But it does mean that it should be planned with great care and that every effort should be made to make it look as attractive and professional as possible, given the financial resources available.

What it should contain: A chamber's directory should contain as a minimum a listing of members, their speciality, address, telephone and telex numbers, and chief executives. But a good directory contains much more than this. Without impinging on the other publications of the chamber, it should provide a broad overview of the business climate of the country concerned so that a foreign company seeking to do business there will know at once which persons to contact.

The optimum solution would seem to be to limit the directory to a listing of members, classified by product and market, while at same time including a broad overview of what the chamber is trying to achieve and what its structure and constitution are. This means that first section of the directory, where the overview is given, must be "tightly" written, that is, it must befactual and not verbose. It thus requires a well disciplined writtining style of its editor.

Production: Every world that has been said about the production of magazines, newsletters, handbooks and other publications in this and the preceding article can be repeated here, with emphasis, for a directory. A directory must look attractive in addition to containining the basic information described above. It is, after all, the showpiece or "flagship" among the chamber's publications.

Advertising: As with other chamber publications, the question of whether the directory should carry advertising is of primary importance. Once again, the budget plays a role. If the budget is tight, advertising revenue from chamber members will be a welcome addition to the cash flow.

Care should be taken, however, to ensure that the directory is not swamped by advertising. The directory should not appear to the uninitiated reader as a series of advertisements interspersed with occasional pages of text. Balance must be achieved, and if it seems to the editor that the advertising is taking over from the editorial content, it may be preferable for him to regroup the advertising in two blocks at the beginning and end of the text, as was suggested for the handbook on how to export. There is no rule of thumb on this: One must simply attempt to gauge the ratio between advertising and editorial content and make sure that neither heavily outweights the other;

Directories without advertising are, of course, equally possible. However financial constraints frequently lead to graphic design and printing of poor quality. Advertising revenue can therefore often be used to improve the overall quality of the publication itself.

CONCLUSIONS

Too often the mere issuance of a publication appears to be as important to commercial companies or organizations as its use-a case of the means justifying the end. However the publications deseribed in this and tbe preceding article are designed to be used as working tools with which chambers can achieve two objectives:

Publicize the chamber and its activities, and disseminate to members and other interested parties commercial and official information that will help them in their work.

Improve the efficiency of members in export trade.

The key point to remember in producing publications of the types described above is that they should be derigned to serve their readers. The readers ultimately make or break a publication, for it cannot exist as a viable commercial entity if nobody buys or reads it.

III

Staffing for Foreign Trade Activities*

Chambers of commerce and similar organizations should have a basic number of staff to carry out their trade promotion functions effectively until recently, most chambers of commerce and industry tended to give priority to their traditional role as the business sector's forum for reviewing problems and its

*By Charles Aubert, formerly the Director of the Geneval Chamber of Commerce. This article is based on a study that he recently prepared. Organization and Structure of Chambers of Commerce. which is one of a series of guides produced under ITC's technical cooperation programme with chambers of commerce.

representative vis-a-vis the government; Because trade expansion has taken on greater importance for national economic growth in recent years, however, particularly in developing countries, trade promotion functions have become a major preoccupation of many national chambers. As chambers move into this domain of activity, in partnership with the government's national trade promotion agency, the question often arises of the number and type of personnel required to carry out this expanded role. Although funds for administering chambers are often limited, especially in developing countries, a certain minimum staff is needed if chambers are to undertake trade promotion functions effectively

REORGANIZING FOR TRADE PROMOTION

Although some chambers try to operate with only one official, the secretary general, such a staffing arrangement is usually not viable, particularly as a chamber takes on responsibilities in export promotion. Various routine tasks will take up much of the official's time, so he will not be able to devote sufficient attention to more important business matters. Therefore, if finances permit, a chamber in a developing country that is reorganizing its set-up and work programme to include trade promotion activities should be administered by several persons if it is to carry out these new functions successfully during its early years of operation. An ideal number of stall for a restuctured chamber would be eight, which would consist of the following:

The secretary general. The secretary general is the chamber's permanent executive officer. He implements the chamber's decisions and, above all proposes means to achieve its aims. (The term "secretary-general" is used by chambers establis-hed under public law in-most of continental Europe and "director-general" or "director" by chambers established under private law in English-speaking and Scandinavian countries, among others). He should have a university education and practical experience in business or administration and, preferably, know several languages commonly used in international's business.

In dischagring the chamber's administrative tasks, the secretary general works closely with the president and other officers of the chamber's board of directors. He reports to the board on matters within its jurisdiction. He establishes and maintains contact with members, public authorities, the national organization to which his chamber belongs, and local economic and professional groups. In chambers run under private law, he is also responsible for recruiting members.

Aside from his managerial tasks, he takes charge, with the assistant secretary-general, of conducting economic and legal studies. It is through these studies that the chamber shapes the views it expresses in policy statement to the authorities and the public.

He and his assistant also play an active role in the chamber's trade promotion activities. For instance, they organize trade missions for businessmen, receive foreign delegations, organize participation in trade fairs abroad, set-up contacts and arrange conferences. They likewsse represent the business community vis-a-vis public authorities concerning the expansion of international trade.

Assistant secretary-general. If the secretary-general is an economist, it would be advisable if his assistant is a lawyer. He should know at least one language commonly used in international trade. He can be put in charge of certain administrative responsibilities, such as central bookkeeping and staff management, in addition to the other duties he carries out with the secretary-general.

An executive in charge of the department of foreign trade. He should know at least two foreign languages used in international business. He oversees the following priority tasks during the first years of the chamber's operation:

—Provide information on export and import formalities.

—Issue the certificates and attestions required for international trade, if the chamber is empowered to issue them.

—Provide information on customs matters, indirect taxation on imports and exports, and rules governing international payments.

—Provide information on trade fairs to assist local firms to penetrate foreign markets.

—Provide information on facilities and assistance available to exporters.

His responsibilities will expand as the chamber grows in size and scope of operations.

An assistant to the head of the foreign trade department. He helps the department head and replaces him in his absence. He is responsible for keeping the records and files of the documents on which the issure of various types of commercial certificates and attestations is based. He should be familiar with the regulations covering their issue and the collection of the relevant fees.

An executive in charge of information. Every chamber must collect information that will enable it to answer inquiries of all types from members, the authorities, the public and correspondents abroad. This official oversees the expansion of the chamber's collection of documentation in order to provide such information.

An executive secretary and shorthandtypist, conversant with at least one language commonly used in international trade.

A shorthand-typist for the information service'

An employee in charge of such tasks as running errands, setting up meeting rooms, addressing mall, shipping and document reproduction.

AS CHAMBERS GROW

Experience shows that the number of staff required to administer a chamber, particularly when it has taken on trade promotion functions, is likely to rise fairly quickly.

As a chamber's membership increases, the volum of its work expands. A staff of eight is therefore not able to cope with all the requests for services from businessmen as its responsibilities grow.

If financial means are available, chamber should hire several additional staff members during this period of expansion, such as the following:

For the secretary-general's office, two or three university graduates could be hired to take over the secertary-general's responsibility for undertaking studies and to increase the range and depth of these studies, thus enabling the chamber to make more authoritative policy statements. One of these should be a legal expert to deal with taxation and legislation.

In the foreign trade department, two or three persons could be added to the staff, depending on demands on the chamber for advice on international and domestic trade regulations. for services related to conventions on temporary admission to goods (such as the ATA carnet system) and for its trade promotion activities. [The ATA ("admission temporaire/temporary admission") carnet system provides for the duty-free import of goods, such as products to be exhibited at trade fairs, that are to be re-exported within a specified time period under a system of controls.] An additional two or three officers will be required if the chamber acts as the secretariat of the national guarantor for the ATA system.

Two more persons may also be needed to collect and disseminate up-to-date business information and to maintain a trade information library, working under the officer in charge of information.

Additional personnel involved in administration will also probably be necessary by this stage. These include a switchboard operator, possibly a telex operator; an assistand bookkeeper; and two shorthand-typists.

This would bring the number of staff to about 20.

For example the chamber of commerce in Geneva, Switzerland, which has a private law status, has a staff of 19. Sixteen work for the chamber itself. These include the director (a university graduate) and four executives, who handle legal, economic and commercial matters. Three other staff members, including a university graduate, work with the guaranteeing association for the ATA carnet system, which is a legally separate entity. The Geneva chamber is not equipped for data processing and relies, as far as commercial information is concerned, on the Office Suissee d'Expansion Commerciale (Swiss, Office for the Development of Trade). When workloads peak, it hires additional personnel.

The Zurich chamb r, which is also one of the largest in Switzerland, has a staff of roughly the same size.

ADVANCED STAGE OF DEVELOPMENT

As a chamber develops, its staffing requirements also evolve. In what could be termed an advanced stage of development, a chamber of commerce could, for example set-up training institutes, provide technical assistance in export management for small and medium-size enterprises, and introduce computerized data processing.

At this stage the type and number of additional staff hired depend on the specialized directions in which the chamber moves Staff of some of the larger chambers in industrialized and also developing countries sometimes run up to several hundred.

For instance, not counting the staff of its educational institutions (who number 3,100), the Paris Chamber of Commerce and Industry has 600 employees, 90 who work on tasks related to international trade. Total staff in the London chamber is 168, with 62 involved in foreign trade matters; of the Stockholm chamber, 50, with 9 in foreign trade; Stuttgart, 200, with 15 foreign trade specialists; and Zurich, a total of 16, with 10 in trade matters.

In Colombia, the Camara de Comercio de Bogota has 170 staff members, 13 of whom deal with international trade (including one director, three department heads, four analysts, four secretaries.) The staff of Costa Rica's chamber is 18, 13 in trade; Kuwait, 60, with 4 trade specialists; Dhaka (the Metropolitan Chamber of Commerce and Industry), 50, 5 in trade matters.

A 1979 survey by the Kuwait Chamber of Commerce and Industry showed that the average number of staff of private-law chambers in the Middle East stood at 30, with the largest at 95 and the smallest 10.

PROFESSIONAL REQUIREMENTS OF STAFF

The secretary general of a chamber and his assistant, as well as certain officers in larger chambers, such as department heads and staff in the legal and tax department, should be university graduates in economics, business administration, law or related fields. The other categories of staff need not have university degrees, particularly if they have acquired practical experience in such sectors as international trade, banking, business journalism or transport, or have worked in government offices such as the customs department or the ministry of foreign trade.

Anyone wishing to occupy a high position in the chamber must know one or more foreign languages that are used in international business. It is advisable, therefore, for chambers to encourage their staff to take language courses. Chambers in France, for instance, organize such courses in their own training institutes; other chambers simply administer language tests and issue certificates to those who qualify (for instance in the United Kingdom and Switzerland).

A chamber should provide continuous training to the staff of its foreign trade department to enable it to adapt its procedures to changes in international and domestic trade regulations. On its own or together with other chambers, should hold discussions on new regulations for the benefit of its staff with senior officials from such government offices as the ministry of foreign trade and the customs department. It should also invite heads of export departments of private firms for discussions on the same subjects. Some chambers offer regular courses to their staff through their educational institutes, for instance the Institut Consulaire de Perfectionnement in Le Havre, France.

Institutes of higher education run by chambers of commerce in industrialized countries are frequently open to candidates from developing countries who wish to establish a carree in chambers of commerce. The German (Federal Republic), Austrian, Spanish and especially the French chambers provide such training.

On the international level, ITC and the International Chamber of Commerce (ICC), the latter through its International Bureau of Chambers of Commerce (IBCC) in Paris, assist in training executives of chambers of commerce in developing countries. They organize training seminars either at their headquarters or in the countries themselves. Information on such courses can be obtained by writing to the secretariats of these organizations.

IV

How Chambers of Commerce can Increase their Resources to Offer Expanded Services*

To finance an expanded range of services, including trade promotion functions, chambers can undertake income-generating activities Chambers of commerce have been established to promote and protect the interests of trade and industry. They vary widely in size and range of activities but hold in common their role of representing the interests of the business community vis-a-vis national and local authorities, and of providing services to their members, including services dealing with trade promotion.

Their trade promotion activities are often carried out in cooperation with national trade promotion organizations.

To carry out these functions effectively, chambers of commerce must have adequate resources. To supplement their main source of financing, which is membership fees, chambers can carry out different types of activities that generate income. They can thereby strengthen their operations in general and their role in promoting trade in particular.

Some of the services that a chamber can organize that can be wholly or partly financed by special fees are discussed in this article. Such income-generating activities have been carried out by chambers of commerce in Sweden and many other countries. The following examples illustrate the variety of services that a chamber can offer to its members against a fee.

*By Seven Swarting, Managing Director of the Stockholm Chamber of Commerce and Secretary General of the Association of Swedish Chambers of Commerce and Industry. This article is based on a study that he recently prepared for ITC and the International Chamber of Commerce entitled *income-generating Activities of Chambers of Commerce*, which is one of a series of guides being produced under ITC's technical cooperation programme with national chambers of commerce.

ORGANIZING TRADE MISSIONS

One way in which chambers can generate supplemental income is by organizing trade missions. Chambers of commerce are in a good position to organize trade missions abroad to promote both exports and imports, because they can work through their counterparts in foreign countries. For example, the itinerary and other arrangements can be made in cooperation with the chamber of commerce in the host country. Working through the foreign chamber is less expensive for the organizing chamber than undertaking all the planning itself, but is, of course, based on an arrangement of mutual assistance.

If the government provides financial support for such joint trade promotion activities, the chamber of commerce can act as a channel for reimbursements and other assistance. The chamber's administrative and other expenses can be financed by government subsidies, by fees charged to participants or by a combination of both.

HOSTING INCOMING TRADE MISSIONS

A good way of promoting exports is to extend invitations to foreign businessmen who are able to influence their country's export trade. This can be organized by the host chamber of commerce in cooperation with the chamber in the guests' home country.

The organizing chamber of commerce should have the support of a number of local companies, which should be ready to shoulder most of the costs of the project. The chamber could handle the administrative aspects of the visit, for example, extending the invitation and arranging receptions, dinners and visits to the sponsoring companies.

For instance, when the chamber has obtained a binding promise in writing from 25 companies for financial support, it could invite about 15 prominent businessmen from abroad to visit the host country. The invitees could be selected by the local sponsoring companies and by their commercial representative at the local embassy. The sponsors could pay for the visitors' hotel and meal costs and compensate the chamber for its administrative expenses. The guests could defray the costs of their travel.

PROVIDING EXHIBITION SERVICES

A chamber of commerce can assist a group of companies wishing to take part in an exhibition or trade fair abroad by booking space; booking group travel to obtain lower rates; running a common information desk at the fair; and providing secretarial, translation and interpretation services.

It the government provides financial support for such joint trade promotion projects, the chamber of commerce can also act as a channel for reimbursements or contributions from it.

The chamber's administrative costs for such services should be defrayed either by fees charged to the participating companies, or where possible, by government trade promotion funds.

MANAGEMENT OF EXHIBITIONS

Some chambers of commerce actively engage in the management of fairs and exhibitions. These are chambers that have their own premises for temporary exhibitions by foreign trade missions. Several chambers of commerce in the Middle East offer these services for a fee.

Other chambers of commerce are part-owners of international exhibition complexes. Those are usually managed by a separate company on whose board of directors the chamber of commerce is represented. The Stockholm Chamber of Commerce and the Birmingham Chamber of Industry and Commerce, for instance, each own part of their respective international exhibition centres. These centres are financed by rental of exhibition space and by entrance fees for visitors.

JOINT EXPORT MARKETING GROUPS

A chamber of commerce active in export promotion may find that a number of companies have common or interrelated problems, markets or ranges of products. In order to assist them and to realize economies of scale, the chamber can initiate the formation of joint export marketing groups. The chamber of commerce can handle the group's administration, advise it on collective marketing, and arrange contacts with chambers of commerce abroad, and can change a fee for these services.

EXPORT SALESMEN FOR HIRE

Some companies find it difficult for various reasons, including costs, to employ their own export salesmen. Others may need extra salesmen for a temporary export drive or to test a new market or a new product for export.

One method of assisting such companies is for a chamber of commerce to make available export salesmen for hire. Two or more companies can share the costs of the foreign travel of a common salesman. The latter may be an export manager, an experienced export salesman or a retired senior executive. This technique is practiced in Sweden.

ISSUING EXPORT DOCUMENTS

One of the most common services offered by chambers of commerce is the issuing of certificates of origin and the certification of other export documents. For many chambers of commerce, this activity is the most important source of income after membership dues.

Chambers of commerce in most countries are entrusted with issuing general certificates of origin, and in some countries they are also entrusted with issuing certificates for preferential treatment.

The export of some goods may be restricted by bilateral government agreements, mostly on export quotas. Certain export documents are required, and the duty of monitoring the quotas and issuing the documents may also be entrusted to the chamber of commerce. The fees collected from exporters applying for export documents can finance the activity.

In some countries, certain technical or quality standards are required for the import or the export of goods, and certificates of inspection must be issued. In most cases, inspection to ascertain conformity with standards is carried out by governmental authorities or authorized inspection companies. However, it may be possible for a chamber of commerce to manage an inspection system on a commercial basis and to hire experts to carry out the inspection.

Chambers of commerce often certify the authenticity of documents used in international trade, such as invoices and insurance policies. This activity can also be financed by fees paid by the exporter.

ATA CARNETS

The issue of ATA carnets is an income-generating activity for many chambers of commerce and is a service very much in line with their aim of facilitating trade. Three major groups of goods—samples of value, goods for presentation or use at exhibitions or fairs, and professional equipment—can be temporarily admitted duty free if covered by an ATA carnet.

The ATA system is currently used in 39 countries, in all of which tbe carnet is issued by chambers of commerce that are members of an international chain set up for the purpose by the International Bureau of Chambers of Commerce (IBCC) Members of the chain guarantee payment of the import duties or taxes due on goods that are not re-exported. When that happens, these charges an first paid by the member of the chain in the country of temporary importation, which then recovers the sum from the chain's affiliate in the goods' country of origin. The latter in turn claims payment from the firm to which the carnet was delivered.

COLLECTION OF COMMERCIAL DEBTS

A system of assistance in the collection of commercial debts, based on cooperation among chambers of commerce, has been set up under the auspices of IBCC. The system facilitates the collection of commercial debts by informing creditor enterprises about the procedures available to them and by transmitting their claims to debtor enterprises through the network of chambers of commerce. It does not apply any legal sanctions nor do chambers take a position on the dispute.

The system is enforced in countries whose national organization of chambers of commerce, or of chambers performing their functions, has agreed to participate. At the international level, interventions between chambers of commerce are free of charge. At the national level, however, the creditor's chamber is free to charge the creditor a fee to cover its costs.

ARBITRATION

The status and the impartially of a chamber of commerce make it especially suited to take part in the arbitration of commercial disputes between companies. Thus, several chambers of commerce have established arbitration institutes.

The primary duty of an arbitration institute is to appoint arbitrators in business disputes, normally from among exports not employed by the chamber. It is important that the disputing parties have access to offices and services of different types, such as telex,. telephone and secretarial assistance in legal and general matters. Some services should be provided by the institute; secretarial assistance is often provided by staff employed by the chamber.

Such an institute is financed by the parties in dispute, who pay a general administration fee for its maintenance and a fee for the services utilized. The latter fee is, in principle, based on costs.

PROMOTING BUSINESS CONTACTS

Chambers of commerce frequently receive inquiries from abroad, for information on marketing opportunities for their products.

The more serious inquirers are often willing to pay a fee for a service more extensive than a lisling in a bulletin or a list of companies. In response to more demanding inquiries, a chamber of commerce may offer a marketing service, consisting of a brief market analysis for the product in question. statistics, analysis of competition and some hints on possible distribution channels.

The Stockholm Chamber of Commerce offers such marketing services in addition to the traditional service of publishing inquiries in bulletins and supplying inquirers with lists of companies. Its marketing service is undertaken by a group of four independent marketing agencies. Under the terms of an agreement with the chamber, these agencies charge their usual fee plus a commission to the chamber.

INVESTMENT SERVICES

For companies intending to invest or participate in a joint venture abroad, the chamber of commerce in the host country is a natural source of information. A potential investor needs to know the regulations on establishing a company, taxation and so on. Chambers of commerce can thus play an active role in the promotion of investment from abroad. Where a special investment organization already exists, the chamber can play a complementary role. A foreign investor may feel more at ease discussing his plants with a chamber of commerce than with a governmental agency.

Capital investment from abroad, whether in a manufacturing plant or in a trading subsidiary, is generally regarded as beneficial to the community. Services in connection with such investment are therefore usually provided free of charge to the foreign firm. But the chamber of commerce may be able to obtain compensation from government funds for its expenses in promoting foreign investment.

CONSULTANCY AND ADVISORY SERVICES

As part of their normal services to members, chambers of commerce provide information and advice on a wide range of business matters. However, sometimes they may receive demands for time consuming and highly specialized counselling requiring extensive research or considerable expertise. Such services would, in many cases, exceed a member's ordinary claim to services and, if offered free of change, would impair the chamber's ability to service its members in general. Some chambers of commerce therefore provide the services for a fee.

Possible services of this type include the compilation of special statistics or other data; assistance in drawing up special contracts; assistance in wording appeals against administrative decisions; consultation regarding the internal administration of a company; and research concerning a special line of business.

The Stockholm Chamber of Commerce offers a wide range of legal services. Its legal department has a number of experienced lawyers specializing in different areas of business law. It assists companies in drawing up contracts and gives legal advice and counsel, in and out of courts. These services are carried out in the name of the Law Office of the Chamber of Commerce, a subsidiary of the chamber.

ADMINISTRATION OF SERVICES FOR GROUPS OF COMPANIES

A chamber of commerce may sometimes offer the advantage of scale to small and medium-size companies within the limits posed by legislation and the business environment. Examples of possible areas for the administration of collective services are pension schemes, insurance schemes and the collective purchase of services for neighbouring companies, such as industrial security, cleaning, catering, transport and maintenance. These services reduce costs for participating companies while generating income for the chamber.

Some Swiss chambers of commerce have formed special bodies to act as guarantors for loans given by banks to small and medium-size companies. They charge a fee for the service.

ADMINISTRATION OF ASSOCIATIONS

Smaller trade associations, foundations or economic organizations may lack the resources to set up an efficient secretarial and accounting administration of their own. Such an association may find it suitable to use the resources of a chamber of commerce, under an agreement specifying the services and fees.

The chamber of commerce may use its own staff for such activities as preparation and distribution of notes for the association, collection of membership dues and bookkeeping. The chamber's premises and facilities may be used for meetings and as a telex service and a mailbox. As the chamber normally does not take on additional personnel or office space for these services, they result in a more efficient use of its existing resources.

AUTHORIZATION OF FIRMS

Chambers of commerce also aim at developing and maintaining good business practices for instance, by granting authorizations to professionals or companies that meet certain standards. A chamber's right to grant authorizations may arise from governmental decree, tradition or demand from the business community.

For example, the Stockholm Chamber of Commerce authorizes real estate agents. The activity is financed by a fee paid at the application for or renewal of; authorization. As the system is authorized by governmental decree, the fee is fixed by the Government; it covers all costs, including that of compensation to the secretariat of the chamber.

Other professionals may be authorized in the same way. In Finland, for instance, the Central Chamber of Commerce authorizes auditors, translators and forwarding agencies. The regional chambers of commerce authorize auditors and goods inspectors. Auditors and translators pay a fee for authorization and for renewal once a years other authorized experts pay no renewal fee. The Central Chamber also recommends fairs and exhibitions on the basis of their quality. The fair organizers pay a fee each time they are included on the recommended lists. All fees are determined by the Chamber.

COURSES AND SEMINARS

Business training in schools and universities can often be complemented by practical courses arranged by chambers of commerce for all levels of office employees. They may range from complete professional courses, such as secretarial courses, to short seminars on special subjects such as management techniques, accounting procedures and taxation. Chambert often run courses on foreign trade, for example, expors documentation, transport planning and contract clauses.

Courses and seminars can be financed by participants' fees, and those that are deemed beneficial for the promotion of exports may be subsidized by the government. Seminar documentation can also be sold to persons unable to participate.

The Central Chamber of Commerce of Finland, for instance, arranges week long export seminars abroad for groups of Finnish managers to enable them to learn from local experts how to market their exports, in, or to improve their imports from, the countries visited.

DIRECTORY OF MEMBERS

A common source of income for a chamber of commerce is its directory of members, which is much used by companies and government authorities. These directories also carry advertising on companies, for example, that sell goods and services to the business community (banks, insurance companies and airlines). Members may also like to advertise their names and products in such directories, and in some directories members are offered the possibility of using their own logotype, against a fee.

Directories of members are thus mainly financed from advertising income, and in many cases earn the chamber a profit.

NEWSLETTERS AND FACT SHEETS

Many businessmen find it difficult to folllow economic and commercial developments in foreign countries. The international contacts of chambers of commerce render them especially qualified to be information centres. Information that is available at the chamber or that can readily be obtained can be made available to the members through the sale of fact sheets, newsletters or other publications. If necessary, they can be tailor-made to the requirements of certain companies for information about specific countries, markets or products.

TEMPORARY OFFICE PERSONNEL

One of the major income generating activities of the Stockholm Chamber is its bureau for the temporary employment of secretaries. It provides companies with temporary secretarial help in case of sick leave, maternity leave and peaks in workload.

The Stockholm chamber has a register of persons who have declared that they are willing to take on temporary office employment, and it acts as an inntermediary when a company requests temporary secretarial assistance. The chamber pays the temporary secretaries and invoices the companies for an amount including the secretary's compensation and a commission to cover administrative costs. It arranges about 3,000 periods of temporary employment annually, and has a list of about 1,000 persons on its register.

OFFICE SPACE

Chambers of commerce often have centrally located offices and can temporarily rent out spare space for board and other business meetings. Companies with cramped offices outside the city, for instance, can rent a room at the chamber of commerce, which can serve as a prestigious and convenient place to meet foreign businessmen. Similarly, foreign businessmen wishing to meet local entrepreneurs can use the chamber as a base.

The chamber may also rent out space for conferences and for small temporary exhibitions by foreign companies or trade missions. For the latter, it may provide related services, such as issuing invitations to interested companies.

GROUP TELEX SERVICES

The telex is an important means of rapid communication in international business. As the coal of installing and operating it may be too high for small firms, a chamber of commerce may, if it is so permitted by the telex authority, operate a group telex service for these firms. This service would make the chamber's own telex installation less costly.

For example, each subscriber can pay an annual fee and an additional fee each time it utilizes the service to send messages.

The chamber of commerce can undertake to receive telex messages and to post them to the subscriber immediately (or to communicate them by telephone). A copy of outward messages can be posted to the subscriber.

TAX-FREE SYSTEMS

Governments in many countries allow tourists to buy goods without paying local taxes. Sometimes this privilege is granted only at airports and similar areas, but in other instances goods are tax exempt if they are delivered to the buyer at the point of departure, for instance the port or airport.

When the regulations stipulate that the goods must be delivered to a special area, a chamber of commerce can manage the tax-free systems. It can set up a service at the airport, for instance, where tourists can pick up their goods. It should be able to finance the service with fees paid by the stores utilizing it. For example, the Barbados Chamber of Commerce runs a tax-free service at the international airport and at the harbour.

PROFESSIONAL CLUBS

The councils and committees of chambers are normally composed of company chief executives and chairmen. To attract middle management, chambers can form professional clubs.

The Stockholm Chamber of Commerce has established The Swedish Traders Club, which consists of persons actively engaged in foreign trade. The club aims to promote the exchange of ideas, to provide professional training, to arrange conferences and to represent the interests of members vis-a-vis the authorities, airlines and so on. The club is financed by annual membership fees covering the chamber's administrative costs. Each gathering is financed by an entrance fee.

CONCLUSION

The types of income-generating activities that chambers of commerce can undertake are numerous and quite varied. Those described in this article are only examples. Other services could also be added to the list, depending on the demand for specific services, a chamber's particular areas of interest and its means to offer such services.

V

Finnish Chambers of Commerce: Their Foreign Trade Services*

Finland's chambers of commerce offer a range of services to their business members of promote their foreign trade operations. The Finnish chambers of commerce, like chambers in many other countries, are in a good position to provide foreign trade services to their members in conjunction with the national trade promotion agency, for several key reasons. First, the international network that the Finnish chambers belong to, consisting of over 6,000 chambers in 145 countries, offers extensive possibilities for foreign business contacts. Because chambers in this network all have basically the same functions —to provide services to member companies and to influence the government in business matters—such contacts are easy to establish, even among chambers as yet unknown to each other and located far apart. Second as chamber membership in Finland covers the broad spectrum of the business sector, including all types of firms involved in foreign trade (importers, exporters, agents, carriers, forwarding agents and so on), the chambers by nature have an integrated outlook on business and can offer comprehensive trade promotion services of interest to all parties concerned. Finally, the way in which the Finnish

*Sakari Yrjonen is General Manager of the Central Chamber of Commerce in Finland.

chamber of commerce organization is set up, with regional chambers working under a central national chamber, allows them to assist export companies on the spot throughout the country.

The foreign trade services that the Finnish chambers offer are focused on taking advantage of these organizationai features—the international network, the broad-based business membership and the branch set-up throughout the country. These servires are concentrated on providing information and expertise on foreign markets and on export marketing techniques, promoting contracts, with businessmen abroad, assisting with foreign trade documents and procedures, and presenting the views of business to the Government. These trade promotion services complement those of the Finnish Foreign Trade Association, which is the official export promotion agency in the country, and the Finnish Institute of Export, the central organization for export training.

PROVIDING INFORMATION AND EXPERTISE

The most important service that the Finnish chambers offer to their members is keeping them up to date on such matters as new business laws and regulations, economic and commercial trends, new marketing methods and events of interest to the business community. Providing information on foreign trade matters is a part of this function. The principal means of conveying this information are circular letters, the chamber's periodical *Kauppakamari*, seminars, visiting lecturers, expert advice and other expert services.

Publications: By far the most popular service and the number-one incentive for a company to join the chamber is the chamber's publication of circulars and bulletins containing brief, concrete and easily digestible information on current topics of interest to the business community. All 22 regional chambers in Finland now have regular bulletins (issued at least once a month) in which information on new foreign trade regulations plays an important part.

The chamber's magazine *Kauppakamari* is included in the membership subscription fee and is delivered monthly to each of the 13,000 members in the country directly from the Central Chamber of Commerce (located in Helsinki). The periodical contains articles and practical information on foreign trade. A regular feature in the magazine is requests received from abroad for business contacts in Finland.

Seminars: In 1970 the Central Chamber and the Helsinki chamber launched a series of one-day information seminars on topics of current interest to the business community, which were quite successful. The first of these dealt with foreign trade. Since than an average of one seminar per month has been held on some narrowly defined subject of potential interest to chamber members. Attendance averages from 150 to 170 participants for each session. About one-fourth of the 150 seminars held in this series so far have entirely concerned foreign trade, and most of them have included a foreign trade aspect. A few examples of the topics covered:

"Taxation on business operations abroad".

"Barter and compensation deals".

"Customs clearance practice today".

"New rules on markings origin".

"Collecting debts".

"Cutting travelling expenses".

"Profit or loss on foreign currency transactions".

The other 21 regional chambers in Finland also arrange information seminars on a regular basis. In 1984 they organized a total of 229 events of this type, an average of more than ten per chamber.

The seminars are a self-financing activity. The current charges for the one-day events held in Helsinki are US $ 80.

for a representative of a member company and US $ 120, for others.

Expert visits: Because of their worldwide contacts, combined with their thorough knowledge of local conditions. Finnish chambers are able to bring international market and marketing expertise directly to the companies needing the information, through the local chamber network. This saves the butinessmen the time and expense of travelling out of the region to get the information elsewhere.

For instance the regional chambers regularly invite Finland's official commercial representatives and industrial attaches stationed in the country's diplomatic and commercial posts abroad to visit the chambers and meet with their members. Finland's network of commercial attaches, employed by the Ministry of Foreign Affairs, covers about 60 countries. The task of these officials is to promote Finland's exports to their post countries or areas. When a commerical attache visits a chamber, he usually gives a lecture on marketing conditions in the country where he is posted and afterwards consults individually with representatives of the host chamber's member companies. The same procedure is used for visits of industrial attaches stationed abroad, employed by the Technical Research Centre of Finland, whose duty is to keep up to date with technical developments in their respective post countries.

In addition to commercial and industrial attaches a wide variety of other experts on foreign trade is made available to chamber members, through various advisory services.

Advisory activities: Some of Finland's chambers have export advisers on their staff who are paid either by the Finnish Foreign Trade Association, another export organization, the chamber itself, local business firms or a combination of these. The use of these advisers is one way that the chamber strengthens its resources as a regional service centre in the country in cooperation with other bodies.

Other experts who work for the chamber but are in some cases partly on the payroll of another organization include industrial experts, legal and tax advisers, specialists in data-processing and information technologies, and, in at least one case, on expert on materials management. These persons usually advise the chamber on part-time basis only, for instance one afternoon a week. Businessmen can come to the chamber during the specialist's office hours and discuss specific export problems with him. For example, in one of the orgional chambers, a local bank official spends one afternoon a week in the chamber for consultations with firms. The specialist's salary during this afternoon is paid by the bank that regularly employs him. In another chamber, a legal adviser is paid by the chamber for his consultation hours. The largest chambers employ full-time legal and tax advisers themselves.

A considerable part of these various advisory activities in foreign trade matters deals with the legal aspects of doing business abroad. Subjects that are frequently covered in such counselling include foreign trade contracts, agency agreements, conditions of delivery and payment, taxation, patents, trade-marks, arbitration, establishing a business, rules of competition and marketing law. Advice is usually given free of charge to members, but for practical reasons it must be limited to fairly short consultations for each member company.

Library: A library in the Central Chamber's Foreign Trade Department provides basic information on exprt markets. The information files in the library are kept up to date through informal contacts that the chamber maintains with other chambers worldwide and through reports of the country's official commercial representatives abroad. The extensive information in the library on foreign markets is provided free of charge to businessmen as background for their foreign marketing trips.

PROMOTING BUSINESS CONTACTS

The Finnish chambers promote contacts between local businessmen and those in foreign countries in several ways. These include handling trade inquiries from abroad, organizing trade missions to foreign markets and providing administrative services for binational chambers operating in Finland.

Trade inquiries: The Finnish chambers receive about 3,000 requests a year from foreign companies seeking buyers, sellers or agents in Finland. These requests are regularly published in the chamber's periodical and in circulars of the Helsinki chamber. If the number of potential contacts is small, the requests are disseminated directly to the companies concerned.

There are far fewer requests from Finnish companies for foreign trade contacts. Recently the chamber has been trying to encourage outgoing requests by introducting a standard application from from for this purpose.

Incoming trade inquiries are handled free of charge by the Finnish chambers. For outgoing requests the chamber charges the business firm a nominal fee.

Trade missions: One of the best ways of promoting contacts between chamber members and foreign businessmen is to arrange and host trade missions to and from foreign countries. A trade mission carried out under the auspices of a chamber is likely to have many doors opened to it that would perhaps not be open to exporters and importers travelling individually. It is an unwritten law of cooperation between chambers of commerce that the host chamber arranges a few joint meetings and visits for the foregin chamber-sponsored delegation and in addition provides each members with an individual programme according to his wishes.

Trade missions from Finland to foreign countries are arranged primarily by the Central Chamber, but some delegations, particularly to neighbouring countries, are organized by regional chambers in the country. The participants pay their own travel and accommodation expenses for such missions.

Administrative support for bi-national chambers: Another way in which the Finnish chambers promote contacts with business-men abroad is by .providing secretarial assistance for nine binational chambers set up in Finland. This secretarial help is handled at the Central Chamber's offices. Examples of these associations are the Finnish-Hungarian, Finnish-Indian and Finnish-Belgian chambers. These associations have been founded to promote trade between the two countries in question by exchanging trade delegations, information, countacts and other trade promotion services. The member companies of the associations pay a separate membership fee of approximately US $ 50. a year.

FOREIGN TRADE DOCUMENTS AND PROCEDURES

Because of their semi-official status, the Finnish chambers have been entrusted with certain tasks to facilitate businessmen's export operations. These concern the issuing of foreign trade documents and the certification of various types of foreign trade specialists and enterprises.

Forign trade documents: The chambers are responsible for issuing most of the foreign trade documents required by importing countries. These consist mainly of certificates of origin and "full confidence" certificates, and the certification of export documents. The chambers also issue ATA-carnets for the simplification of temporary importation and exportation of commercial samples, exhibition goods and professional equipment. The guarnteeing association in Finland of this international inter-chamcer chain is the Central Chamber. A fee is changed for all certificates. Chamber members get a considerable reduction in charges for such services.

Authorization: The chambers also have the task of recommending or authorizing certain expects or institutions used by the business community. The Central Chamber authorizes translators specialized in foreign trade and forwarding agencies, while the regional chambers authorize goods inspectors. The goods inspectors are neutral experts who check mainly imported goods for compliance with quality and quantity requirements. In recent years, however, some of them have also carried out pre-shipment inspection of export goods. The chambers likewise authorize auditors, timber measurers and other experts, and recommend certain fairs to the business community. Authorization is strictly limited to people or organizations fully competent to serve the business community in their respective fields. In addition to formal competence, much importance is attached to practical experience when authorization is being considered,

A fee is charged for authorization and, in the case of auditors, for the preceding examination.

INFLUENCING GOVERNMENT DECISIONS

The Finnish chambers strive to promote free competition and a free flow of goods in domestic as well as international trade. This involves working to abolish trade barriers in the form of unnecessary regulations, simplify documents and trade procedures, and provide other means for successful and competitive foreign trade operations. These activities entail preparing policy statements, initiating proposals and working in committees that are responsible for preparing, for instance, new legislation affecting foreign trade.

The majority of the regional chambers of commerce in Finland have established foreign trade committees as a part of a very comprehensive network of committees of experts in various fields. These foreign trade experts are of great help in preparing statements and proposals, as well as in providing services to members in foreign trade matters.

The chambers in the country have very good relations with the government authorities dealing with the different aspects of foreign trade. For instance, the chambers hold frequent negotiations with the customs authorities. The customs officials also cooperate with the chambers in providing certain services to chamber members, such as seminars on customs clearance procedures and changes in regulations.

Recent chamber initiatives on foreign trade matters have concerned proposals to improve the system of tax-free sales to tourists, improve and diversify the teaching of foreign languages in schools, and set up a value-added tax system to improve export competitiveness.

COOPERATION WITH OTHER CHAMBERS

In addition to their informal working relationship with chambers of commerce throughout the world, the Finnish chambers have somewhat more formal cooperation agreements with the chambers of the Nordic countries (Denmark, Iceland, Norway and Sweden) and the Baltic Sea countries (the Scandinavian countries, the Federal Republic of Germany, the German Democratic Republic, Poland and the USSR). Representatives of these chambers meet regularly to discuss business contact services, transportation, trade barriers, tourism, symposia and so on.

Finland is also an active member of the International Bureau of Chambers of Commerce (IBCC). It participates in the IBCC chain for ATA-carnets and the inter-chamber system for the collection of commercial debts, as well as in the IBCC's development programme. Finland is also strongly in favour of the new IBCC system under which chambers will systematically extend the same practical services to members of foreign chambers as they do to their own. The Finnish chamber likewise works closely with the International Chamber of Commerce (ICC), the Finnish section of which operates in connection with the Central Chamber. Services to businessmen in cooperation with the ICC include, for instance, dissemination of the ICC's rules and guidebooks.

There are also joint efforts between regional chambers of commerce across Finland's borders. Because the chambers of the middle regions of Norway, Sweden and Finland were

CHART 1-F

Finnish Chamber of Commerce Plan for 1985

1. Finances and Members

1.1 Budget for 1985:

Membership fees	Other Income	Total Income
————————	———————	———————

1.2 Number of members:

Estimate by the end of 1984:——————————

of which corprate members:——————————

Target by the end of 1985:——————————

of which corporate members:——————————

1.3 Possible tragets for membership drives (types of business, names of towns, size range of companies ete.) and major methods of expanding membership:——————————————

——————————————————————

——————————————————————

1.4 Basis of membership fees:	1984	1985 (target)
— company membership fees: minimum/maximum fees	————	————
— community membership fees: minimum/maximum fees	————	————
— other organization membership fees	————	————
— professionals' membership fees	————	————
— individual membership fees	————	————

2. Organization

2.1 Number of office personnel (*e.g.*, 1+1, 1+1½, 2½+2) 1984 ——— 1985 ———

Remarks——————————————

2.2 Any changes in office set-up foreseen for 1985:

——————————————————————

2.3 District and expert committees and commissions—possible changes in 1985:——————————————————

——————————————————————

Existing district and expert organizations whose activity will receive particular attention during 1985, and how this will be achieved:——

——————————————————————

Community liaison officers in 1985 in——communities out of a total of——in the district.

2.4 Information and training (internal)—During 1985 internal information and training will be provided as follows:

For office personnel:——————————————————

——————————————————————

For board and commission members:——————————

——————————————————————

For others (*e.g.*, community liaison officers, community officers on business matters, chamber's representatives in district authorities' organizations):——————————————————

3. Influencing Government in 1985

3.1 Possible major emphasis theme:——————————————

3.2 Influence on the national level—targets, issues and methods of work:——————————————————————

3.3 Influence and cooperation on the provincial level—initiatives and methods:

Provincial government:——————————————————

—provincial department of education:——————————

Others:——————————————————————

——————————————————————————

Chamber's representation in district authorily organization in 1985 (list various organizations):——————————————

——————————————————————————

The chamber's contracts with these representatives as well as the representation itself will be developed as follows:——————

——————————————————————————

3.4 Influence and cooperation on the community level—initiatives and methods; contacts for creating an atmosphere favourable to business:——————————————————————

——————————————————————————

Local activities and community discussions:——————————

——————————————————————————

Local traffic and transportation issues:——————————

Educational questions—cooperation with local schools and colleges:——————————————————————

3.5 Cooperation with neighbouring chambers:——————————

——————————————————————————

3.6 Activities will be supported by external information and public relations as follows:

Major channels:——————————————————

Major methods:——————————————————

The chamber will be in news media approx.——times a month.

4. Membership Services in 1985

4.1 Possible particular emphasis:——————————————

——————————————————————————

4.2 Membership information—methods and frequency:

____

____

4.3 Informative seminars – number, subject, time: ____________

____

____

4.4 Export visits, lectures discussions—number, subjects, time: ______

____

4.5 How expert services will be developed and increased: ________

____

How the chamber will provide the following services:

Advice on foreign trade: ________________________

Advice on legal matters: ________________________

Advice on taxation: ____________________________

Others services: ______________________________

____

4.6 Advisory clinics (based on individual confidential advice that will be arranged):

"Seting up a business" clinic: ____________________

"Developing competitveness" clinic (for existing companies): ____

____

Tax clinic: ____________________________________

4.7 Other services and developments planned during the next few years: ______________________________

____

____

Budget to be made on the basis of the above plan. Please return copy of plan to the Central Chamber of Commerce by 15 November 1984.

dissatisfied that most of the trade tended to go in a north-south direction in each country separately, they began to work several years ago towards achieving more direct contacts. This so-called mid-Nordic cooperation has resulted in a considerable increase in direct trade between the three middle sections, as well as new transportation routes, a general increase in direct business, and reinforced educational and tourist ties across the three national borders in that area.

ANNUAL PLANNING

To carry out those various activities the Finnish chambers at the national and regional levels undertake an annual planning exercise. The purpose of the plan is to set targets for quantifiable aspects of chamber development (an increase in membership, subscriptions and personnel) and to achieve more cohesion and systematic approach to such activities as the provision of services.

As the Central Chamber assists in and oversees the operations of the regional chambers, it coordinates the work of drawing up the individual chambers plans. In September each year it sends out a form to each regional chamber asking for details on the chamber's services and operations for the coming year, including activities in foreign trade (*see example of form on pages 61-64*) Suggestions for completing the from are provided in writing as well as in person, if necessary.

The forms must be filled in and returned to the Central Chamber by 15 November each year. The Central Chamber reviews these and sometimes discusses suggested changes with the chamber concerned. At the same time the annual plan of the Central Chamber is compiled as a synthesis of suggestions from the regional chambers and from the various departments of the Central Chamber. Copies of the plan of the Central Chamber are sent to each of the 22 regional chambers after approval by the Board.

Throughout the coming year the individual plans are monitored by each regional chamber, as well as by the Central Chamber. The chambers are expected to follow through with their programmed activities to the extent possible. At the end of the year a final evaluation is made of the success in achieving the quantified targets set.

In their plans the regional chambers usually give considerable emphasis to foreign trade matters. Examples of recent chamber services planned in this area are the employment of additional foreign trade experts; seminars and theme days on certain foreign markets; customs seminars, particularly on the new harmonized tariff; lobbying for new airline connections; and, in general, helping member companies "internationalive" (*i.e.*, extend their business operations abroad).

The planning activity has helped the chambers over the years to focus their activities on the subjects of most interest to their business members and to assure that services are coordinated among the regional chambers and the Central Chamber when possible.

FINANCING

Although the Finnish chambers have a semi-official status, they are not subsidized by the state. Instead they finance their operations almost entirely from membership fees. As membership in the chambers is voluntary in Finland, efforts are continually being made to attract new members and thereby increase the financial resources of the chambers. The membership fees charged to companies are usually based on the firm's taxable income.

In addition to membership fees, the Finland earn revenue through some of the services they provide to firms (for instance the seminars and export documents discussed above). Chamber members are charged lower fees for such services than outside companies. (However some of the chamber's services are free of charge, for example most expert advisory activities).

In 1984 the Finnish chambers had a total of 13,000 members. Revenue from membership fees came to US $ 1.9. million. Each regional chamber levies and keeps its own fees. Income of the regional chambers from other sources in 1984 amounted to $850,000 from charges for services, seminars, documents and so forth. The income of the Central Chamber in 1984 came to about $1 million, financed entirely through similar income-generating activities.

RELEVANCE FOR OTHER COUNTRIES

Finland's economy is greatly dependent on foreign trade, which currently accounts for one-third of the country's gross national product (GNP). Continued expansion into foreign markets by Finland's companies, even small and medium-size firms, is of primary importance for sustained economic growth. The role of the chambers of commerce in promoting this process is of increasing significance.

Trade may plan an equally important role in the economic growth of many developing countries. The chambers in those countries should therefore carry out the trade promotion activities required by there business communities to support this export growth, in conjunction with the national trade promotion organization. Some of the specific foreign trade services provided by the Finnish chambers could possibly be adapted by chambers in developing countries for their own programmes. For example, the use of part-time trade experts from outside organizations can be an inexpensive yet highly effectixe chamber service for businessmen, and, on the management side, annual planning can help chambers to organize their activities more effectively. Any such activities adopted, however, should be carefully geared to the requirements of the developing country's foreign trade sector.

2

Criteria for Selecting Trade Representation offices Abroad

JOHN R. HEALY*

When setting up or enlarging its overseas office network, a commercial representation service should systematically evaluate potential locations. Developing countries that are setting up or enlarging their of the commercial representation services abroad often face difficulties in determining where to extend their network of posts. Obviously, it is impossible to try to cover all foreign markets with resident trade officials. Few, if any, developing countries—or developed countries—have the fesources to develop such an all-encompassing network, and, rurthermore, most would not need commercial representation in such a wide spread of markets. What is required instead is a select number of overseas posts that yield high benefits in terms of increased business with the markets concerned. The exercise

*John R. Healy is Assistant Chief Executive for Exporter Services of Coras Trachtala/Irish Export Board. This article is based on papers that he recently presented at an ITC workshop in Beijing on institutional aspects of a national trade commissioner service, attended by officials of the Chinese Ministry for Foreign Economic Relations and Trade.

of choosing these locations and deciding on the staffing required should be carried out systematically if positive results are to be achieved.

The most important determinant of the number, size and location of a country's official trade posts abroad is the objectives that these posts are expected to achieve. Once these objectives have been clearly defined, decisions can be taken on where the posts are to be set up, staffing required and other operational features. Such decisions should be based on a systematic evaluation of potential posts against a standard set of criteria. The procedures outlined below illustrate how a national trade representation service can under take such an appraisal in order to develop a network that will help promote the country's trade interests abroad.

DETERMINING OBJECTIVES

A national commercial representation service may set up overas posts to fulfill one or more goals. When it is establishing or expanding its network abroad it must decide which objectives are to receive priority. These could include to:

1. Establish and maintain a government-to-government trading relationship. A trade representation post with such an objective will be concerned largely with implementing the government's foreign trade policy, negotiating inter-governmental trade agreements and managing state-to-state trade dealings.
2. Promote exports of raw materials or primary commodities.
3. Promote trade in manufactured goods. Trade representation services are generally concerned with promoting the exports of their country. However, some services also facilitate imports from the host country.
4. Promote investment or tourism. In some countries the seeking of investment funds for industrial developmen

is an important function of the national trade representation service.

5. Gather economic and commercial information on the host country for transmission to headquarters. (This should not, however, be the prime function of the service. Some services devote too large a part of their resources to merely gathering information).

Coras Trachtala/Irish Export Board (CTT), for example, has clearly defined the objectives of its trade representation offices abroad as being to promote exports of Irish manufactured goods.

CRITERIA FOR LOCATION

Having identified the objective(s) of these offices, those responsible for the trade representation service must next decide on the number and location of the posts. A preliminary list of possible locations should be drawn up and should include both countries that are already important trading partners of the exporting country and countries in which there is believed to be potential for increased trade. These possible locations should then be examined according to a set of "macro," or broad criteria and also of narrower "micro" factors. This analysis will provide an opportunity to assess the market potential of the posts under examination in both the short and medium term. (It is important to evaluate the medium-term prospects as well as expected immediate gains, because the investment that a trade representation service makes in establishing an office abroad cannot be expected to bring returns such as increased exports immediately). The evaluation process will help identify business opportunities in the potential host country and will assist in defining the role that a new office could play in establishing closer trade relations between the two countries.

MACRO CRITERIA

The broad criteria against which potential locations for trade representation offices should be measured are:

Economic conditions: A review of the trends in the economy of a prospective host country should be carried out in some depth. Factors to be studied include population size and growth, gross national product (GNP) and rate of increase, main economic sectors and growth trends, and the foreign trade situation and trends. For example, a country whose economy has shown little growth in recent years may not merit a new trade representation office, in contrast with a country whose economy is rapidly expanding and whose imports are swiftly increasing.

Political relationships: The political relationship between the exporting country and the potential host country should be reviwed. Political differences can obviously hinder the development of close economic links. The exporting country must therefore decide if the current political relationship with the other country, and the likely development of these ties in the future, will provide a suitable framework for closer trade links. For example, whether the country has already opened an embassy in the potential post would be one factor to consider.

Existing trade links: Existing trade ties between the exporting country and the potential host country should be reveiewed. This includes examining the volume and value of trade between the two in recent years, the structuse and components of that trade, and any special trade treaties concluded between them. Rapid growth in trade between two countries in recent years may not, of itself, provide a reason for establishing a new post. Examination of that trade might show, for example, that it is concentrated on a limited number of products that might not be assisted by a new trade representation office. On the other hand, a careful examination of trade statistics might identify in a potential host country growth trends that could be greatly stimulated by a new post.

Sales opportunities: Sales opportunities for the home country's exporters should be identified in the potential market. A survey should be made of the prospects for supplying goods to the different market sectors in that country. For example, the analysis might show that good opportunities existed for sales of canned foods and leisure goods, while openings for industrial machinery and components were limited. Depending on the home country's exports, this survey would either favour or provide arguments against establishing a trade office there.

Presence of competitors: An evaluation of the potential of the host country should include an examination see pages (79-13), of the presence in that market of competing trade representation services or industry groups from other exporting countries, particulariy in the sectors that offer the most promising opportunities for sales. It is particularly useful to monitor the overseas representation policies of countries that compete internationally with the exporting country. The establishment of new posts by such countries should cause the exporting country to carry out a preliminary examination of the potential of the countries in which the new posts are located.

"*Extra market*" *activities*: It is useful to assess the potential of the proposed host market for carrying out what might be described as "extra market" promotional activities, *i.e.*, promotion to other countries through special facilities or opportunities provided by that market. A good example of such potential is the market of the Federal Republic of Germany. In itself, the Federal Republic presents favourable sales opportunities in a number of product lines because of the size and openness of its market. In addition, many of the major international trade exhibitions are held there including the Anuga food fair, the Heimtextil exhibition of home textiles and the Hanover fair for industrial products. These exhibitions, plus many others held in the country, are visited by business people from a number of other countries. Resources spent to set up a trade representation office in such a market would therefore have an impact on sales to other markets as well.

Investment potential: If one of the objectives of the trade representation service is to seek foreign investment funds for industrial development at home, an assessment should be made of the potential of the host country as a source for such funds. Factors to consider include the strength of its economy, current levels of industrial investment and the existence of industry sectors that both have a propensity to invest overseas and are compatible with the economy of the exporting country.

Import system: The potential of an overseas market can be greatly reduced by the existence of strict import controls. It is thus necessary to study the degree to which exports from the home country have free access to that market. An analysis should be made of the level of customs duties, quantitative import restrictions, the import licensing system, the price control system (if one exists), the scale of internal taxes and the incidence of nontariff barriers. If controls are too stiff, it may not be worth-while to establish a post in the market.

MICRO CRITERIA

The points mentioned above are broad criteria against which the trade representation service can measure the opportunities for its country's products and services in a foreign market. In addition to these, a number of micro factors should be examined. These concern the experience of individual firms in that market, their future strategies there and the ways in which a new post could assist them. The final selection of the countries in which posts should be located is then based on the conclusions of the evaluation of these two sets of criteria.

CTT, for instance, starts its examination of the micro criteria by identifying the Irish export enterprises that are active in the market being reviewed, CTT staff meet with these exporters to assess the potential of the market in question, learn about the specific problems they have encountered in setting there, obtain information about their future business plans in that market and identify ways in which a trade representation office could help them. Such an analysis enables CTT to quantify the number of export firms that require the sort of services there that a trade office could offer. Such services could include assisstance in contacting buyers, identifying agents, doing market research and providing information on import regulations.

For example, several years ago when CTT was studying the possibility of setting up a trade representation office in Tokyo, it consulted Irish exporters on such points. Based on these discussions, CTT realized that although Japan was a large market, the opportunities there for the average Irish exporter were limited because of the costs and complexity of establishing a foothold there. CTT was also aware however, that, given the geographical distance between Ireland and Japan, as well as the difference in language and business customs between the two countries, an intermediary between an Irish seller and a Japanese buyer was often found to be necessary, both to maintain existing sales and to develop new business. For these reasons, CTT decided to set up a new post there. The Irish office now operating in Tokyo has increasingly assumed this role of intermediary, which in itself justified the expense of setting up the office.

SELECTING A COMMERCIAL CENTRE

Once a trade representation service has decided to establish an office in a particular country, it must choose an appropriate location. The fundamental rule is to select a city that is a major trading centre.

For trade representation offices that are part of a country's diplomatic service, difficulties arise when the host country's capital is not also its commercial centre. For example, in the United States the capital is Washington, D.C., but the commercial hub of the country is New York. Choosing the location can also be difficult in a country that has several equally important commercial cities. An obvious example is the Federal

Republic of Germany. Bonn, the capital, does not rank commercially with such cities as Dusseldorf, Frankfurt, Hamburg and Munich, all of which could merit a irade office.

Some countries whose trade commissioners are part of their diplomatic services have, however, overcome these difficulties and have, succeeded in locating their trade representation offices in commercial centres rather than diplomatic capitals, for example the services of Australia and the United Kingdom.

In the case of Ireland this problem does not occur, as CTT's trade officers abroad do not have diplomatic status and are not part of the country's embassy network, except in special circumstances. (They are employees of CTT.) CTT thus has the freedom to set up its foreign offices in the most appropriate commercial locations.

EXAMPLE OF IRELAND

CTT's overseas office network has been developed as a result of the type of exercise outlined above, *i.e.*, an analysis of the composition of the country's trade and of the exporting needs of its industry. The location, concentration and size of overseas offices in particular markets reflects the relative or potential importance of those markets to the Irish export community. The United Kingdom, for example, Ireland's largest export market, has five offices, while posts are also located in markets of growing commercial significance for Irish exporters, such as Nigeria and the Middle East.

The overseas office network is subdivided into four section: Europe (excluding Great Britain); North America; Great Britain; and the Middle East, Africa and Asia. The offices in Europe are located in Brussels, Amsterdam, Copenhagen, Dusseldorf, Paris, Milan, Stockholm, Zurich, Madrid, Vienna and Moscow. Those in the British market are located in London, Manchester, Birmingham, Bristol and Glasgow. In North America the locations are New York, Chicago and Toronto. The remaining posts are in Sydney, Tokyo, Bahrain, Lagos, Beijing and Singapore.

COSTS VS. BENEFITS

The analytical process outlined above is aimed at establishing the home country's likely return on the investment it makes in setting up a trade office in a new location. The scale of that return must be considered in relation to the amount of investment required.

When deciding to invest in a new overseas office, a trade representation service is making a long-term commitment from which it will be difficult to extract itself. Ideally, the service should operate in a flexible and pragmatic manner, deploying resources as market conditions dictate. The reality, however, is somewhat different. Once an overseas office has been established, it is difficult to close it.

Four types of investment that must be made in a new trade representation office should be taken into consideration in this cost-benefit analysis:

Establishment costs.

Recurring costs.

Consequential costs.

Human resources.

Establishment costs: The costs of setting up an office abroad include obtaining office space and living accommodation, which in some countries can be expensive, and furnishing and equipping those premises. The costs of transferring staff from headquarters to the new location must also be taken into account.

Recurring costs: Recurring costs are those that arise, throughout the operation of the office and must therefore be budgeted for. They include rent, salaries, travel and entertainment, purchase of information, communication and local promotion.

Consequential costs: In addition to the costs of setting up and running an overseas office, a trade representation service also needs to budget for the costs of a variety of activities that naturally follow from the establishment of a new post. These include such expenditures as participating in trade fairs, organizing selling missions, arranging retail promotions and handling other special promotional activities In other words, these are activities that help to take advantage of the market opportunities that the trade officers have identified. In most trade representation services these costs are met out of the headquarters budget.

Human resources: A trade representation office abroad can function only if it has adequate human resources. This includes not only hiring a sufficient number of staff at appropriate professional levels, but also training them as needed.

The practice in CTT, for example, in to appoint as Irish national as the manager of each of its overseas posts, because it is considered easier for an Irish official to become familiar with the particular features of an overseas market than it is for a foreign national to get a throough understanding of CTT operations and of the Irish manufacturing sector. However, CTT employs locally recruited staff as secretaries and, in some cases, as support officers.

The number of staff in each CTT office is related to the importance of that particular market for Irish exporters and the level of the trade office's activity in that market. In the larger offices the manager is usually assisted by several marketing advisers and/or locally employed marketing officers. In smaller offices the manager often works with the assistance of a local secretary only.

In an effort to expand its trade representation service rapidly toward the end of the last decade, CTT established a number of small trade offices abroad that were staffed by only an Irish manager and a locally recruited secretary. Of the 25 overseas offices that CTT is currently operating, 13 are manned by only two such staff. If finances permitted, however, CTT would increase the strength of most of these offices, because a post that is run by just a manager and a secretary spends too much of its time on administrative and representational matters and too little on marketing assistance, which is the core of its work overseas.

In 1982 the cost to CTT of maintaining its 118 overseas based staff amounted to US $ 45,000 per staff member. This figures did not include any of the establishment costs or the consequential costs of promotional events, which were part of the headquarters budget.

The staff in CTT's five offices in the United Kingdom cost, on average, $35,000 each to maintain, whereas the comparable average in Western Europe and North America was $43,000 per person. There is a significant difference between staff costs in these and other locations. In case of its 11 officers serving in five posts in Africa, Asia and the Middle East, the cost to CTT per staff member in 1892 was $ 81,000.

Training is an additional staff cost. The posting of officers abroad can entail a substantial amount of training. In CCT this training falls into three areas:

1. Language training: This is a necessity in most locations and can be a considerable expense.
2. Consultancy and appraisal skills: CTT invents a large sum of money in training its marketing advisory staff, both at home and abroad, in these important areas.
3. Marketing skills: CTT believes that it is important for its trade officers to be fully conversant with current marketing theory and techniques and, accordingly, it organizes both internal and external training programmes for them in these subjects.

The four costs areas must be taken into consideration when trying to calculate the real cost of establishing a new trade representation office. The costs thus calculated must be compared with the potential of the host market and the likelihood of a trade representation office contributing towards the realization of the potential.

APPENDIX A

How Ireland's Trade Representation System Operates

Ireland's trade representation service operates under the aspices of the Irish Export Board/Coras Trachtala (CTT), which is the Government's focal point for promoting and developing Irish exports. CTT oversees the trade representation service along with its other export promotion activities, which include marketing advisory services and facilities, group promotions, incentive grants, market, research, trade information, transport information services, design and publicity. One of CTT's four major divisions is responsible for its network of trade representation offices abroad.

STAFF POSTED ABROAD

Each of CTT's 25 overseas offices (*see list on page 75*) in run by an Irish manager, who is responsible to the area director based in the region.

The trade representation service's marketing advisers, who work in the larger overseas posts under the direction of the office manager, usually spend three years at CTT's head office before being posted abroad. The normal period of service in an overseas office is from three to five years. Upon return to the head office they are usually assigned to a product section. Further overseas postings depend on the number of vacancies arising and the performance of the individual concerned.

The marketing advisers are usually recruited from private industry, the state sector or from within CTT. These staff, who carry out the core of CTT's export promotion work, generally hold a degree of professional qualifications related to marketing and have at least three years' commercial experience. It is unusual to recruit persons as marketing advisers who have just graduated from the university.

At the end of 1982, total CTT staff numbered 319, of whom 118 were serving abroad in the trade representation service.

MAIN RESPONSIBILITIES

The basic functions of the Irish trade representation service are to carry out market research for Irish export companies, advise exporters on correct marketing strategies, identify opportunities in the host markets for Irish industry and provide an information service to buyers in the post locations. They also give exporters assistance in such areas as promotion and publicity.

Market research: Market research accounts for the work of an overseas CTT office. This varies from basic scouting for retail price information to in-depth market studies. As exporters want practial information that enables them to make marketing decisions, an overseas tradc office usually concentrates its efforts on gathering and disseminating specific trade information related to the products of a company or group of companies. This includes details on distribution patterns; pricing structures, including discount practices; business terms; and background on specific buying enterprises and their operations.

Exporter servicing: Expansion of a country's exports depends to a great extent on an intensive marketing effort by individual export companies. The existence of an overseas office encourges exporters to visit that martket. It also increases the likelihood that such visits will be successful, because the office can arrange appointments with buyers in advance. Irish trade representatives are encouraged to accompany visiting exporters to meetings to improve their own knoweledge of home firms' products and also to develop and maintain contact with trade buyers in their host countries.

Opportunity identification: Actively seeking out export opportunities in the host country is also an essential part of an overseas office's work. It usually involves briefing buyers on the range of products available from Ireland in order to generate interest in that country for Irish products.

Group promotions: Group promotions entail the organization of national and group stands at trade fairs and store promotions. The work of the overseas office includes liaison between the fair and store authorities and the head office in Dublin to ensure that the total project is effectively coordinated. In addition, some offices help coordinate the arrangements for trade missions undertaken to their particular markets.

Publicity: Publicity generation and press liaison are essential functions of an overseas office. Providing information request to the media; disseminating press releases orignating at the head office; and actively seeking media coverage for Irish exporting activities are some of the broader aspects of an Irish trade representative's publicity role.

COORDINATION WITH FIELD OFFICES

The management and control of a distant overseas office can sometimes be difficult. CTT operates a number of written and unwritten controls to make the management link between representatives and headquarters more effective.

The written controls include "management-by-objectives" procedures and monthly financial statements. "Management by objectives" is a system whereby each executive identifies the most vital tasks to be undertaken during a six-month period and undertakes to carry out these tasks to agreed standards.

In addition, each field office sends a precise statement of its expenditure to the head office accunts department of its expenditure to the head office accounts department once a month. Each overseas office is given an annual budget at the beginning of the year, which is subdivided into categories such as salaries, rent, buyer entertainment, telephones, travel and telex. The overseas office is responsible for controlling total expenditure and also the expenditure within each of these categories.

The unwritten controls include periodic visits by CTT's Assistant Chief Executive for overseas operations tot he regional directors of the overseas office network and, it turn, visits by the directores to the managers of the overseas offices. Regular visits to the Dublin office by overseas personnel are also necessary in order them to keep up to date with headquarters priorities.

EVALUATION SYSTEM

The systems that CTT uses to evaluate the work of the overseas offices are monthly reports and an annual assessment.

Once a month each field office has to submit a report on the activities that it has carried out during the previous month. This report is divided into the following categories; market research, trade fairs and exhibitions, exporter servicing, buyer servicing, press and public relations, administration and visitors to the office.

The annual assessment is a process whereby the strengths and weaknessess of the overseas representative are identified jointly by each representative and his or her manager, and action is agreed upon to help eliminate or reduce these weaknesses.

STAFF DEVELOPMENT

CTT's management-by-objectives (MBO) system seeks to integrate the organization's need to identify, agree upon and achieve its objectives with the individual's need to develop himself. or herself. It does this by establishing overall organizational objectives that are broken down by division, department and section, with each individual's job priorities identified and agreed upon with his manager. This system is applied to overseas staff as well as headquarters personnel.

The continuing review of an individual's training and development needs to enable him to achieve the objectives of his job is one of the aims of the MBO system. Weaknesses that can be overcome by training are highlighted, and arrangements are made for staff to attend external courses or "in-house" training programmes.

Marketing advisers, for example, need to have a knowledge of finance, communications, business principles and, in many cases, foreign languages. A weakness in any of these areas can be identified and rectified through special training courses suited to the officer's particular needs.

Financial assistance is also available to staff who wish to attend parttime courses of study; outsidc of working hours.

3

Trade Information: State Trading Organizations

H.K. RAINA*

State trading organizations cannot carry out their trading operations effectively without having access to relevant market information. State trading organizations (STOs) in developing countries have a wide spectrum of differing objectives, roles, organizational patterns, financial structures and corporate forms. Likewise they enjoy varying degrees of monopoly rights or trading privileges for import, export and/or domestic trade. Some STOs have a complete monopoly for the import or export of a commodity or a group of commodities. Others enjoy no such privilege: They are required to compete with private traders. Again, some STOs have partial monopoly rights either for one commodity or one market or both.

*H.K. Raina is Senior General Manager of the Minerals and Metals Trading Corporarion of India, Ltd. This article is extracted from a paper that he presented at the International Symposium of State Trading Organizations of Developing Countries, organized recently in Ljubljana, Yugoslovia, under the auspices of UNCTAD, ITC and the International Centre for Public Enterprises (ICPE).

Given STOs' pronounced diversities, it is obvious that no single market information set-up can be prescribed for all STOs. Each STO will have to determine its own specific information needs and the most appropriate information system, subject to the overall resources available to it.

ROLE OF TRADE INFORMATION

The basic role of market intelligence for STOs, as commercial enterprises, is the same as for any business. Without information, a business simply cannot survive. The decision-making process in any business involves the identification of a problem, recognition of an opportunity, determination and evaluation of an alternative course of action, and selection of the most desirable and feasible method of implementation. Information is needed by an STO in each one of the above areas for its commercial decisions.

STOs in most developing countries have, however, been created to achieve various socio-economic objectives and have often been assigned special roles and responsibilities. Governments have also bestowed upon some STOs special privileges or facilities. For these reasons, an STO cannot evaluate and select alternative courses of action solely on the commercial profitability criterion relevant in a competitive business environment. Information needs thus have a special role for an STO and will have to be related to the tasks assigned to it.

DETERMINING MARKETING STRATEGIES

Information has an important role for an STO in evolving an optimal marketing strategy both for exports and imports.

An STO may find it useful to pursue a strategy of long-term contracting in certain areas. With proper information, an STO will know which new customers are likely to seek long-term arrangements and on what terms and conditions.

Similarly, STOs that procure essential consumer goods, such as foodstuffs and raw materials critical for maintaining production in an industry may find it useful to enter into long-term contracts if analysis of past data shows that supplies in the international market are prone to cyclical variations. Information on existing market conditions will also help an STO to decide whether or not it would be necessary to the up supplies through such an arrangement.

For assured future supplies, longer term trends in the international market may indicate the need for an STO to offier to collaborate with another STO (for a prospective producer) in another developing country through equity participation and agreed production sharing. Similarly, the strategy of inducing a prospective buyer to invest along with an STO in the development of a new source of supply may be warranted on the basis of information on market conditions likely to prevail in the future.

Diversifying Marketing Operations

An STO will also need information if it is seeking to diversify its export or import operation. Identification of new export marketing opportunities is possible only on the basis of information on growth in demand in existing and emerging markets. Information on specifications of the product in demand will help in assessing whether the product an STO has to offer will be accepted as it is, or will need to be adapted or modified. Information on prices, commercial policy, taxes, distribution margins, freight rates, and tariff and nontariff barriers will be necessary in assessing whether the product will be competitive or not. Similarly, information on competitives' product characterties, marketing channels and the like help in assessing the possibility for market penetration in new areas.

For diversification of sources of supplies for import items, information will help in discovering where the potential exists or is developing. Information on total exportable surplus will be required to assess how much surplus may be available from any one source. Information on commitments made and firm contracts which may have already been signed by the potential supplier or which other sellers and buyers may have concluded for the same commodity is equally relevant.

STOS' SPECIPIC INFORMATION REQUIREMENTS

Imports: An STO's specific information needs are fairly extensive for imports. These will, however, vary with the commodity and the size of the import operations. In general the following are some of the essential areas where information on imports will be necessary:

(a) Current prices and recent past trends. For commodities traded on the institutional markets, the futures price gives a broad indication of the expected supply and demand conditions in the short-term.

(b) Changes in factors likely to affect supply and demand conditions, for instance, weather conditions in important producing or consuming countries, crop forecasts, strikes and lockouts, manufacturing and trading activities of major producers and consumers, national policy decisions such as stockpile operations and multilateral agreements on commodities.

(c) Freight market situation.

(d) Foreign exchange rates: persent and future outlook.

(e) General world economic outlook—more particularly, growth in output and employment in industrially advanced countries, changes in interest rates and so on.

Prices: One of the key elements in a purchasing decision and strategy for a commodity is its price. Prices of commodities rarely remain static. Some fluctuate violently from day to day and even during the course of the same day. Information on prices, therefore, is one of the most important elements in the decision-making process. When to buy, how much to buy and where to buy from, to a large extent, are decisions which are strongly influenced by current and future prices. Thus, price information has to be a specific input of decisions involving imports.

Specification; STOs in developing countries are generally entrusted with the task of importing essential items. Usually, these items are available according to various specifications conforming to diverse quality standards. To ensure that an STO procures the goods that users prefer, it is necessary to collect information on the precise specifications preferred by them. At the same time the STO will also have to locate supplies that conform to these specifications. (Usually, trade directories listing various suppliers of a country give an indication of the specifications offered by different producers. Product lists and price lists published by large companies also give descriptions of the available specifications.)

Sources of supply: Diversification of sources of supply is an important strategic planning tool to ensure steady supplies, at competitive prices, of items which the STO needs to import in large quantities and for a long period. Information is, therefore, required to identify new sources of supply. Specifically, it will be necessary to know whether the output is or is not already committed and what is likely to be available for export. To assess its competitive position, an STO requires information on production costs, infrastructural facilities available for shipment and any export subsidies on the commodity. Some of this information will be patricularly useful for commodities and products not traded on any institutional market.

Export regulations: Export regulations of different countries differ for various reasons. Information on export controls and regulations in a potential supplying country will be required for assessing effective supply capability. Information on the regulations on minimum prices, export taxes, quality control standards and regulations by way of quotas or outright ban due to local shortages and the like will be useful in this regard.

Contracting practices: Apart from the above, for most commodities, it is important to know the standard terms and conditions governing sales. Some commodities are sold with reference to prices at a commodity exchange. Others are sold mosty at "producers" prices." There are likewise differences in pricing periods and other terms. Contracting terms also depend on the bargaining strength of the parties. The relative bargaining strengths keep changing, on account of changing demand and supply conditions as well as other reasons. An STO must remain abreast of changing contracting practices.

Transport costs: Information on sandling, forwarding and freight rates will enable STO to arrange for these services at competitive rates. This knowledge can help STOs to assess the relative merits of supply offers that may be quoted on FOB or CIF terms.

Exports: Export market development involves promotional costs. It is therefore important to the STO to assess the target market's political and economic viability and the potential demand that the market will offer, not only in the immediate future but also over a longer period. From this point of view, it is useful to look for some of the macro-economic attributes that affect overall demand and supply for a commodity. Macro-economic information required will cover:

(a) Population and its growth rate.

(b) National come and per capita income.

(c) Share of agriculture and industry in the gross national product.

(d) Consumption patterns.

(e) Structure of foreign trade.

(f) General level and composition of imports.

(g) Tariff and nontariff barriers.

(h) Preferential treatment.

(i) State of the balance of payments and foreign exchange resources.

(j) Future development plans and strategies.

(k) Exchange control.

While items on the above list are a necessary part of market information. their importance varies from product to product, and in particular, exporter to exporter, depending on the volume of exports being contemplated. For STOs that have to dispose of an occasional marketable suplus, all that may be relevant would be information on latest prices and recent trends in consumption and growth of demand.

Apart from the macro-economic environment. STOs involved in exporting also require information at the micro level related to specific products or commodities. Micro-economic information required covers:

(a) Market outlook.

(b) Price trends.

(c) Major competitors' size of operations, products and their characteristics, and distribution and promotional policies.

(d) Marketing channels available and used by competitors.

(e) Freight rates and trends—past and expected.

(f) Licensing requirements, if any.

(g) Addresses of relevant chambers of commerce, importers, manufacturers and commercial banks.

Specific requirements and regulations: In addition, for consumer products. STOs will need to collect appropriate information on consumer preferences, including design, technical specifications, standards and other relevant information for export development and promotion. A number of countries have developed national specifications and standards to which imports must conform.

Some countries have similarly imposed product regulations in the interest of consumers. For example, elaborate safety standards and health and sanitary regulations have been prescribed by a number of developed countries. At times each incoming consignment is checked and inspected, according to the prescribed methods, to see if it meets specifications and standards. An STO intending to export to these countries should first collect information on any such regulations.

Packaging: Packaging and labelling is yet another type of information required by STOs. Both during transport and at the final distribution stage, good packaging is vital. Shipping companies and airlines sometimes prescribe required packaging standards, which must be adhered to. Appropriate packing also has to cater to consumer appeal. An STO must make it a point to remain abreast of international developments in packaging. including containerization.

Shipping: Information on shipping facilities available, port capacity, freight rates, loading and unloading facilities, and so on will enable an STO to assess the feasibility of exports and the prices which it should quote.

SOURCES OF INFORMATION

STOs have many different sources at their disposal to obtain such information.

Official sources: A large number of countries have central statistical offices which file with the UN Statistical Office, on standard forms, statistical information on national income, demographic trends, import-export trade and so on. This assortment of information is considerable.

Apart from information published by the UN and its various organs, a vast amount of material is published by national governments. In many countries, different ministries and departments publish annual reports, highlighting targets, achievements and policy changes on various activities. In fact, for making an assessment of the macro-economic environment of any country, the range of sources is so extensive and complete that a researcher may be able to collect all relevant information through desk research alone and need not undertake any field work.

Overseas representatives: Most governments have in their foreign embassies or missions a commercial wing whose task is to monitor commercial developments of interest in thier respective conntries of accreditation. Periodic reports submitted by them can provide a good source of information for STOs.

The commercial offices of foreign countries located in an STO's county are also usually able to provide good deal of information not only on general economic conditions, but also at a fairly micro level pertaining to the countries which they represent.

Some large STOs, with operations extending to many commodities and many markets, have found it useful to open offices in different strategic places in foreign countries. One of their tasks is to colled and monitor market information relating to that country as well as nearby markets.

Commercial sources: A large number of private institutions and agencies specialize in collecting information on a range of related commodities and products. The publish product directories statical series, annual surveys and trade journals which contain a wealth of information.

Many commodity brokers also publish market reports on the commodities they handle. Usually these reports are made available free of charge to their regular clients. However, others can obtain these for a small fee.

Somewhat on the lines, large transnational trading companies bring out newsletters which they make available to their trading partners, usually free of cost. Commercial banks involved in international financial business also put out economic reports or newsletters for their clients.

Up-to-date information on the latest prices, production trends and other commercial information is also available by commercial wire services. Two such services that operate on a global basis are those of Reuters (85 Fleet Street, London EC4I' 4AJ) and Unicom (72-78 Fleet Street, London EC4Y IHY).

FRAMEWORK OF COOPERATION

Collection of up-to-date and reasonably reliable market information and intelligence is fairly expensive. In may not always be a viable proposition for a single STO, with relatively limited trading responsibilities, to have all the required arrangements entirely on its own. Cooperation with other STOs would reduce costs for each STO considerably and at the same time would mean availability of adequate information at the desired speed.

4

Arranging Transport and Customs Formalities for Trade Shows

BRUCE BENDOW*

To ensure that your stand is ready for visitors on the opening day, make careful preparations for transporting the products and exhibit material. On the opening day of international trade fairs, one sometimes sees a pathetic sight: an empty stand, and embarrassed representatives standing around with nothing to show. The products to be displayed are still at sea, or have been damaged during transport, or are locked up in a customs shed, or are simply lost. Such incidents underline the need for careful preparations for transporting products and exhibit material to trade fairs.

It is highly recommended that all transport arrangements for joint participation be centralized and that individual

*Bruce Bendow is ITC's senior adviser on trade fairs and commercial publicity. This article is an excerpt from a handbook that he recently prepared, *Making the Most of Trade Fairs*, which is one of a series of guides being produced under ITC's technical cooperation programme with national chambers of commerce.

exhibitors be made responsible for delivering their goods to the group organizer or to his designated freight forwarder. This will help to ensure that goods arrive on time, eliminate confusion when the stand is being set up and result in savings on freight charges. Despite the centralized arrangements, these charges may be paid by the individual exhibitors.

The freight forwarder plays a key role in the smooth flow of transport arrangements. An experienced international forwarder should be chosen to handle most of the documentation, packing, customs and shipping arrangements.

A clearing and forwarding agent at the fair area must be carefully chosen to handle receipt of goods, customs clearance, transfer to the fair site and return shipment. Fair organizers often designate such agents. If not, the freight forwarder may be able to recommend one, or the assistance of the commercial attache posted nearest the fair site should be sought to find one.

To ensure trouble-free transport and customs clearance, information about official and shipping company requirements and other matters should be obtained as early as possible. One should take into account the waiting period for receipt of information and documents, possible long shipping times, and the need to inform exhibitors about their responsibilities.

The information to be obtained should cover the following:

1. Shipping schedules and rates.
2. Your country's customs and documentation requirements for exporting the products and the display and stand material, and for re-importing them.
3. Requirements of the host country's government; the shipping, forwarding and insurance firms; and the fair organizers, including:

   Nature and content of suppliers' invoices.

   Bills of lading.

Packing lists.

Distribution of shipping documents.

Identification and addressing of erates.

Import controls, duties and taxes.

Separation of consignments and the conditions under which equipment, printed matter, products and display materials will be cleared free of duty.

The desirability of re-usable packing cases.

Dimensions and weights of shipment that can be conveniently handled at the wharfs and by clearing agents.

It is especially, important to check whether the host government permits temporary duty-free import of exhibition samples and materials. It is also essential to check the rules and procedures for each type of product and material imported, that is, whether they can be sold, given away, destroyed, or have to be re-exported. If both the exhibitor's country and the country where the fair is to be held have signed the international convention on temporary admission of merchandise, an ATA carnet should be obtained from the chamber of commerce in the exhibitors country. Information about the carnet is available from the international Chamber of Commerce, 36 cours Albert 1er, F-75006 Paris, France.

Most of the about information on customs regulation can be supplied by the clearing and forwarding agents and the consulate of the host country.

One penalty for insufficient planning and follow-through of transport arrangements is that goods are not ready in time for shipment by sea and must be airfreighted. at high cost. Airfreight may be unavoidable for perishable goods or for goods that simply cannot be ready in time for surface shipment; however, an attempt should be made to minimize air shipments.

Each shipping case should be correctly marked not only to avoid mishaps during transport, but also to help to retrieve the cases from the mountain of shipments at the fair ground before opening day. Painting each case with a colour band will also be helpful.

Although this is inadvisable, individual exhibitors may, for some reason, arrange their own shipments. When they do so, they should be asked to supply the group organizer with a complete inventory and the bill of lading or airway bill numbers.

Adequate insurance coverage should be arranged for damage or loss not only during shipment but also during the fair.

The following list of pointers may be useful for companies entering trade fairs on their own. In joint participation involving several companies, when the group organizer arranges transport, specific instructions on documentation, the consolidation point, delivery dates and costs, packing and customs regulations should be provided to each exhibitor, accompanied by the appropriate forms.

CHART 4-*A*

Pointers on Transport for Companies Entering Trade Fairs on Their Own

---

1. Obtain transport times and shipping dates as early as possible.
2. Reserve space for the outward and return journeys as soon as possible.
3. Use a forwarding agent with a good repulation, and an agent in the country where the fair is to be held.
4. Obtain information on the customs regulations and documentation requirements of your own government and of the government of the host country.

5. Obtain on ATA customs carnet if possible.
6. List each item in the inventory. List the contents of each case, with a description and value figure for each item. Revise this list accurately for the return shipment.
7. Be sure the goods are packed so that they are not damaged.
8. Shippine cases should be clearly marked on at least two sides. Paint the cases with a colour band to facilitate identification of the fair site.
9. Cases should be small enough for convenient handling. They shoutd be capable of being opened and closed without tools and should be securely looked.
10. Whenever possible, avoid transshipments and consign the goods through to your stand at the fair.
11. Be sure your representative at the fair knows the bill of lading and airway bill numbers and has all other information on the shipping and clearing arrangements.
12. Arrange for storage of the shipping cases and their return to the stand at the close of the fair.
13. Arrange insurance coverage of the goods during transport and during the fair.
14. The shipment should contain items that may be needed to repair the exhibit, as well as stationery and office supplies, and inquiry and order forms, include sales literature if it is ready for shipment.

I

National

CAMILO JARAMILLO*

National trade promotion organizations can take many different forms. Each country should adopt the type most suited to its local conditions. A national trade promotion

*Camilo Jaramillo is ITC's adviser on the institutional aspects of trade promotion. This article is based on a study that he recently wrote on the institutional and managerial aspects of a national trade promotion organization.

programme consists of a package of trade promotion policies and measures carried out in close coordination by the various institutions concerned with the foreign trade sector.

The success of the overall programme is dependent to a large extent upon the effectiveness of each of the institutions involved. These institutions include the ministries concerned with economic, commercial and foreign affairs; planning authorities; trade promotion bodies; standards organizations; quality control agencies; packaging institutes; regulatory organizations; banks and other financial institutions; producer associations; and chambers of commerce, among others. These organizations should complement each other in their trade promotion activities to create a coherent and dynamic framework in which trade expansion can be achieved.

Trade promotion institutions have a central role to play in a national trade promotion programme. Over the last several decades a number of developing countries have set up such agencies as part of the government's efforts to accelerate export growth. The form and structure of these national trade promotion organizations (TPOs) vary substantially from one country to another, depending on such factors as the role that the TPO is to play, the priority assigned to trade promotion activities by the goverment, the availability of resources for the TPO's work, the existing institutional framework in the foreign trade sector and administrative practices in the country.

The discussion that follows outlines the types of TPOs most often found in developing and developed countries. Since no one standard formula exists for setting up a TPO, a country considering establishing one or improving an existing institution should select the form or individual features that are most appropriate to its own particular economic and commercial context and adapt them to local conditions. Some possible institutional alternatives are given below, including various possibilities for the governing body of the TPO and for the internal set-up of the agency. The discussion is based on research that ITC recently carried out on the institutional arrangements for trade promotion.

POSSIBLE TYPES OF ORGANIZATION

Trade promotion institutions can take different forms, as actual practice demonstrates. Some governments have set up autonomous or completely independent bodies as the country's focal point for trade promotion, while others have adopted the approach of creating a trade promotion department within an existing ministry. Some of these solutions are more effective than others in achieving trade promotion results, as discussed below.

Export promotion council: In many developing countries, export promotion councils have been set up by the government, composed of high-level officials representing various government departments and often business sector representatives. A council of this type is sometimes supported in its work by a technical secretariat, which could be a department of a ministry and which constitutes the core of the trade promotion organization. These councils are usually established primarily as bodies with policy-making responsibilities. In addition to adopting decisions on foreign trade, they may have a coordination role. They also sometimes provide certain services to the export community.

In some cases such councils are not as effective as they might be because, for example, their functions have not been fully defined, or their responsibilities for policy formulation and for implementing policy decisions have not been precisely laid down. In only a few cases has this form proved to be the best type of trade promotion institution for a developing country.

Department or section of a ministry: The designation of a division in a ministry as the national trade promotion focal point is a practice often followed by developing countries that are starting the export promotion process. The adoption of this alternative presents few problems, since it can usually be implemented by an internal decision of the minister concerned, and funds are in most cases provided from the overall budget of the ministry.

However, this solution can have several drawbacks, including the following:

The trade promotion department usually lacks the operational autonomy required to carry out its promotional activities. As an integral part of the ministry, it must follow the traditional bureaucratic procedures with respect to operations and staffing.

It is often difficult for the staff in the trade promotion division to differentiate promotional responsibilities from the traditional controlling functions that are common to ministries. The trade promotion focal point may, therefore, tend to mix both types of actions, often with negative results.

Given its involvement in the daily routine of the ministry, the trade promotion division in a ministry frequently loses sight of its original purpose, and in the long run the division may become largely or totally ineffective in its trade promotion work.

In cases in which a new trade promotion division is being set up, ministry staff that are not desired elsewhere may be transferred to the new division, thereby lowering the technical level of the trade promotion staff from the beginning.

Because of such drawbacks, this alternative is not always the best one for a successful trade promotion programme, which requires highly technical staff and the ability to mobilize resources and take action. Consequently, this approach could be seen only as a temporary solution, until a more adequate set-up is arrived at, as described below.

Autonomous institution connected with a ministry: This type of trade promotion organization is one that can be particularly effective for trade promotion activities. The creation of this kind of body may entail certain legal complications, but this alternative represents an approach that has proven to be advantageous in many countries. With a well defined legal statute, the institution can be fully autonomous, even though it is controlled to a certain degree by the ministry concerned. Success will depend, to a considerable extent, on the around of support that the body receives from the government and the degree of autonomy granted to it in actual practice.

Successful institutions of this type tend to operate almost like a business enterprise. They carry out their activities with total autonomy, based on a work programme approved by their board of directors and, in some cases, by the relevant minister. They are responsible for hiring and managing their personnel and usually operate outside the civil service framework, which allows them to employ the most qualified staff.

Totally independent institution: This organizational form is sometimes found in developed countries with a highly diversified foreign trade sector, but it is usually not a realistic possibility in developing countries, because the business sector is not generally in a position to support such organizations in their initial stages. Export promotion activities require considerable official financial support, and in most cases this must come from the government budget, or at least from official sources. The government will, therefore, require some type of authority over the way the funds are spent.

Although a totally independent organization might offer advantages from the operative point of view over an autonomous institution, this independence might also constitute a significant disadvantage, as the government might tend to leave the institution "to its own means," thereby lowering its possibilities of acting as a coordinating body vis-a-vis other trade service institutions in the public sector.

Semi-private organization: This is an alternative that exists in certain developed countries, but it is difficult to conceive of setting up this type of trade promotion organization in developing countries, where export "consciousness" is still usually low. The main advantage of this approach is that the export community feels itself totally involved in the activities of the TPO and can consequently make a significant contribution to its operations. However, in practice it is difficult to convince both the public and private sectors to launch such an agency and to make it operative, since a prerequisite for setting up a semi-private trade promotion body is a relatively high degree of export development in the country. The effective involvement of the business sector can be achieved through other means.

Marketing boards: In certain countries semi-private marketing boards exist that are in many cases engaged simultaneously in promotional and marketing activities. These bodies are usually organized on a sectoral basis, and they receive financial contributions from both the government and the business community. They perform their services for a certain product or group of products. They actively participate in the foreign marketing of these products and also undertake promotional actions, such as collecting information on foreign markets and disseminating it to their members. They can be effective institutions for solving export marketing problems in specific product sectors.

Other alternatives: In a few countries, due to the absence or weak performance of an official trade promotion organization, the business community has taken the initiative of organizing export promotion activities through some type of private organization, such as the chamber of commerce or the exporters' association. Such institutions can perform a very useful trade promotion role because of their close ties to the business community. But they often lack the financial resources to undertake the entire trade promotion effort themselves. The ideal solution is for them to work side by side with a national TPO, thereby complementing it in its activities.

GOVERNING BODY

The governing body or board of a TPO, equivalent to the board of directors of a company, has a very important role to play in the success of the TPO. It is responsible for producing the general directives to guide the activities of the TPO. It should also serve as a close link between the organization and the export community.

The degree of the governing body's involvement in the day-to-day operations of the TPO varies from country to country. In some cases, the governing board gives the TPO considerable flexibility, with the board's direction limited to approving the overall work plan and budget and with the executive responsibility left to the upper level of staff in the TPO. In other cases, however, it gets involved in the detailed scrutiny of each operation, which limits the operational flexibility of the TPO. The former approach is preferable, as it results in a more effectively operated TPO.

Selecting members of the governing body on the basis of their ability and experience in accomplish objectives of the board is important for the success of the board's work. The assignment of junior officials to represent ministries and business organizations, who lack the necessary authority and experience, should be avoided. Membership should be representative of the main government departments and export sectors.

Another key consideration is the size of the board. Experience demonstrates that large boards become ineffective, partly due to the difficulties of getting the necessary quorum to hold meetings. For this type of organization the membership should be kept to under ten persons. Convening meetings of the governing board at suitably frequent intervals is important to allow its members to handle the work before them.

Several alternatives are possible for the composition of the governing body. The approach chosen will depend, in most cases, on the role to be played by the TPO.

Totally official: This type of governing board usually consists of representatives of the ministries of finance, trade or commerce, industry, development; of the planning office; the central bank; and, in some cases, of the ministries of foreign affairs, agriculture and certain other sectors that have some bearing on the economic activities of the country. A completely official governing body is found most frequently when the TPO corresponds to an export promotion council that has been given certain responsibilities in foreign trade policy formulation.

If properly integrated and run, a governing board of this kind can develop the necessary coordination at the official level. However, if the trade promotion board is responsible for the functions of both trade policy formulation and trade promotion, a clear distinction should be made between the two types of activities to guarantee the necessary operational flexibility of the TPO.

In addition to the inconvenience that might result for the TPO from having these two types of functions, the fact that the governing body has members only from the official sector might lead it to act in isolation from the real needs of the business community.

Mixed official and private board: An alternative quite widely used, which could in some situations be considered as the best solution, is a governing board that has members from both the public and private sectors. It consists of representatives of the key government branches and selected members of the export community. The total number members of could vary, as could the promotion of officials to businessmen.

This type of governing board has the advantage of allowing the business sector to participate fully in the planning and direction of the TPO's work programme. Also this type of arrangement enables the board to be fully aware of the export development constraints of the business community and to present these to the government.

Totally private governing board: This alternative is not frequently found in developing countries. It has the advantage that since its members consist entirely of persons from the business community, its actions should ensure that the TPO carries out the most beneficial promational actions for the business sector. But the nature of its membership also precludes its action in trade policy formulation, an activity that should remain in the hands of specialized official bodies.

Absence of a governing board: There might be cases in which a TPO has no governing body, for instance when the TPO is merely a department or section in a ministry. In this situation the minister himself, or the director of the TPO, decides on what to do and how to do it. The disadvantage of such an arrangement is that the decisions taken may not always be in line with the requirements of the business community. This could be remedied through the establishment of advisory committees, wlth the participation of representatives of the export community, which could recommend work patterns and activities for successful operation of the TPO.

INTERNAL ORGANIZATION

The internal structure of a TPO depends to a large extent on the responsibilities that the organization has been given. As a general rule, however, most TPOs carry out the following types of activities: market identification and development, trade information services, specialized support services and promotional activities abroad, often including trade fairs and missions. In addition to these, a TPO is also sometimes responsible for training and for overseas commercial representation. Finally, it has certain administrative functions, which must be provided for in the structure of the organization. The way in which these functions can be organized within the trade promotion organization are discussed in the section below.

Product and market development: Some trade promotion organizations have a product and market development division, in which each staff member handles a given number of products or groups of products, is responsible for identifying their export potential and marketing problems, and for giving assistance in production and marketing matters. This integrated approach has the advantage of creating specialists in a given product, irrespective of the market to be penetrated. It allows the specialist to oversee the promotional activities in the most promising foreign markets and to direct requests from overseas buyers to the most suitable producers for exporters.

Other TPOs, on the other hand, make a clear distinction between the production and marketing functions by creating a division in charge of research and development activities for export products, thereby focusing on the export potential and export supply side of the trading process, with a separate division responsible for market research, on the demand side. In this type of set-up the first division is established on the basis of products, while the second is organized according to markets, on a geographical basis. In pratice, coordination between two such divisions may pose difficulties and may result in an overlapping of internal and external promotional activities.

Organizing the product and market development work along geographical lines as in this second approach is similar to the set-up in the economic division of a ministry of foreign affairs, in which coverage of a given country or region is important for the ministry's operations. In the case of a trade promotion organization, however, the final destination of export products is less important than the overall achievement of increased overseas sales, to whichever markets offer the best export possibilities.

One approach is not, however, necessarily better than the other. Success depends very much on the degree of internal coordination, the technical qualifications of the staff and other considerations. Each TPO should, therefore, decide which system best accommodates its needs. The second alternative might be preferable for countries with a high concentration of exports in a few markets, while the first might be more advisable for countries with a broad diversification of export markets and export products.

Trade information services: One feature that is common to almost all TPOs is a trade information service. The creation of this service has in many cases been the initial activity of TPOs in developing countries, because of the need of producers and exporters for information on foreign market possibilities. However, its location within the organization can vary considerably. In some cases it is attached to the division concerned with assisting exporters with their specific overseas marketing programmes, in others it forms part of the overseas commerciai representation division and in still others it acts as an independent unit. The exact location of the service is less important than the fact that exporters can make adequate use of the information and that the information is disseminated in the most effective way.

Specia'ized services: TPOs that have been successfully operating for a number of years and that have adequate financial resources usually provide some of the export support services required by the business community directly through their own staff. These services include assistance in documentation and procedures, transportation, marketing, costing and pricing, quality control, product adaptation, export packaging, export financing, publicity and legal matters.

The extent and scope of the services vary considerably from one TPO to another. Usually these services are grouped under one section or division within the TPO, but in some cases they are attached to the promotion division.

Training: Some TPOs have a specialized section dealing with training, not only for their own staff but also the export community. In other cases, most of a TPO's training is carried out by outside institutions, with the TPO limiting its role to sponsorship and to handling specialized training requirements.

Fairs, missions and commercial representation: Two areas in which the organizational structure of TPOs shows considerable variation from country to country are trade fairs and missions, on the one hand, and official commercial representation abroad, on the other. The differences arise from the degree of involvement of the TPO with these two activities.

When the TPO is responsible for organizing participation in trade fairs abroad and/or for trade missions to other countries, the TPO may have a fairly large unit to deal with these activities. Its involvement in fairs might include the organizational aspects only, or might extend to other areas, such as preparing the exhibiting facilities or issuing the publicity material. In certain countries a totally separate organization is responsible for trade fairs, and in those cases the role of the TPO is limited mainly to suggesting names of exporters to be included in the official trade fair delegation and helping select events for the annual trade fair programme.

In the case of official commercial representation abroad, the TPO's role varies depending on who is responsible for running the service. If the TPO has direct responsibility for it, it usually has a unit specialized in supervising and backstopping the activities for the commercial representatives. If, on the other hand, the service is the responsibility of some other unit within the government, such as the ministry of foreign affairs, the TPO might have only one person in charge of liaison with the commercial representatives.

Planning: Very few TPOs in developing countries have created a research and planning unit to systematically analyze foreign trade conditions, make recommendations to the TPO management and other governmental authorities on future activities, and help prepare work programmes for the TPO. The implementation of these activities is usually limited to TPOs in countries with a long experience in trade promotion.

Administration: A division or department usually found in TPOs is that dealing with administrative matters. It covers such functions as accounting, personnel management, finance and, in some cases, budgeting and training. The location of the administrative services is different from one organization to another. In some TPOs they are attached directly to the executive director or his deputy, but in others they are in a division that is at the same level as other divisions carrying out trade promotion activities.

DEGREE OF DECENTRALIZATION

Another organizational feature that varies considerably from one TPO to another is the degree to which the TPO's promotional activities are decentralized within the country. Some TPOs have a large number of offices, located in the main industrial centres. In such cases the TPO has usually established a local office in each city that offers significant export potential. There is no common practice regarding the activities carried out by the local offices. Some of them have a limited scope of action, while others are involved in such activities as research on export potential, trade information services and technical support.

In contrast, certain TPOs operate in a totally centralized manner, concentrating all their work in a single unit and communicating with producers and exporters in other cities by mail, telex, telephone and direct visits.

An example of an innovative decentralized system is that in Peru, where the TPO (the Found for the Promotion of Nontraditional Exports, or FOPEX) has signed agreements with the chambers of commerce in most of the major cities in the country. In accordance with these agreements, FOPEX finances the services of a professional staff member within the chamber, whose responsibility is to promote export activities. He provides market assistance to actual and potential exporters. He reports to the chamber that is directly responsible for his work. FOPEX has established a coordinating office that acts as a counterpart to these chambers and provides them with information necessary to efficiently carry out their duties. Each agreement contains a specific work programme, which fits into the national trade promotion programme.

ORGANIZATION AT THE EXECUTIVE LEVEL

Most TPOs are run by an executive director or a manager. In a few cases, the TPO's director is also chairman of the governing board. In some instances he is a full member of the board, while in others he participates in the board meetings without voting power. The autonomy that the top executive enjoys in the determination of the TPO's activities depends to a great extent on the amount of authority granted to him by the board. The statutes of the TPO sometimes clearly specify these powers, but the other cases it is up to the board to specifically delegate such authority.

There is no common practice with regard to the duties of the second highest official in the TPO. In some organizations the executive director retains a significant portion of the authority, while in others has deputies have a considerable degree of freedom to take decisions and manage day-to-day operations. When one or more deputy or assistant directors exist, the executive director has more time to handle important problems and can maintain close contact with other institutions involved in foreign trade. If he has to supervise most of the routine operations, on the other hand, this coordinating function with other organizations receives insufficient attention.

TPOs that have succeeded in carrying out their operations efficiently are usually those that have an executive director or general manager, supported by three or four deputes who are responsible for promotional activities, support services and administration. The top executive can, therefore, concentrate on key managerial issues.

Since many TPOs in developing countries are not in a strong position within the overall governmental structure, a large part of their successes or failures can be attributed to the ability of their executive director to convince other government branches to give the necessary support to their activities. Consequently the nomination of that executive should be made by the government with extreme care, considering the important implications that may have on the future operations of the organization.

Management team: In some of the most successful TPOs it is common to find, as in many business corporations, a management team composed of the chief executive, his deputies, and the directors of division of chief of section. This practice has proven to be quite effective, since it significantly improves the internal coordination of the organization and positively contributes to a better planning and implementation of activities.

The management team usually meets on a frequent and regular basis. The group discusses problems of a general nature, as well as subjects of a specific character that need to be handled by several executive units within the TPO. This management approach is highly recommended as a means to improve the operational efficiency of the agency.

II

Selecting an Overseas Agent*

Experience shows that many exporters who have a marketable, appropriately priced, product and who are able to develop and

*By James J. Ward, Bank of Irreland Professor of Marketing at University College of Galway in Ireland and a consultant on marketing training. He has carried out numerous training assignments for ITC in various developing countries and at headquarters. This article is adapted from material appearing in *Export Marketing Management*, one of a series of ITC training handbooks to be published in the near future. The article is based on materials used in ITC training programmes.

finance a marketing support plan encounter export difficulties in spite of all these advantages, because they select an overseas agent haphazardly.

An exporter needs to take four basic steps to solve the many problems inherent in finding the right agent for entry into a foreign market:

1. Determine his particular marketing requirements.
2. Establish contact with perspective agents.
3. Evaluate the list of agents and select a suitable one.
4. Appoint the agent.

DETERMINE THE MARKETING REQUIREMENTS

Before an exporter attempts to evaluate and select an overseas agent, he should determine his particular marketing requirements. Mere lists of known agents and references will be of little help to him. The final decision on the suitability of a potential agent rests with the exporter. He will need to consider the following points:

1. What are the principal types of users of his product? This information will make it possible for him to be selective in choosing potential agents with the right connections.
2. What are the special features and selling points of his product? Full information is required regarding quality, packaging and performance. The object here is to ascertain the points that render his product distinguishable from or superior to similar products, and therefore more readily saleable.
3. Are any trademarks or patterns in existence for his product? If the goods are branded or patented, it will be necessary to know if the trademarks, brand names or patents have been registered in the country to which the goods are to be exported.

4. What are the export prices? It is necessary for the exporter to have precise details on the prices of his products and whether these are FOB, CIF or other.

5. What is the delivery situation? It is important for the exporter to determine whether reasonable delivery times can be quoted; whether there is any seasonal fluctuation in supply; and whether he can make deliveries in reasonable quantities. The fact that his goods are readily available will obviously inspire interest and confidence in prospective agents.

6. Will the agent be required to hold local stocks? This may well be necessary to ensure prompt and regular deliveries to customers. If so, it must be determined who will finance such stocks.

7. What promotional support is the exporter prepared to offer? It will be necessary for him to determine if he is in a position to give support in terms of advertising, samples, material and participation in exhibitions, and how much he is willing to spend. In addition, it is important for him to decide if he is prepared to provide sales literature that has been translated into the appropriate language.

8. Has the exporter previously transacted business in the overseas market? If so, with whom, and what conclusions can be drawn?

9. Has he been represented in the foreign market before? If so, what was the date of termination of the previous agreement, the reason for its termination and the annual turnover achieved by the previous agent?

10. What officials of his export company will be responsible for the market under consideration? Will they be able to visit the market regularly in support of the agent?

ESTABLISH CONTACT WITH PROSPECTIVE AGENTS

The quality and number of sources of information on potential agents vary in each market, but it is important to explore as many as possible and not to take any decision on which agent to hire without considering all available details. Whatever its source, the information will largely consist of opinions, recommendations and advice of various types. The final decision on the suitability of a potential agent always rests with the exporter.

Some sources of information on agents are:

1. Government departments: Government departments in the foreign market are frequently in a position to provide lists of known and established agents. This information may not be entirely up to date, however, and should be taken simply as a guide to the pattern of agents in that market.
2. Trade associations: Frequently trade associations at home may be able to suggest potential agents as a result of contacts with their corresponding associations in the foreign market.
3. Banks: Most major banks have well established international networks, which can be a valuable source of such information. Banks can provide details on potential agents and, when necessary, will undertake specific inquiries to obtain further information.
4. Chambers of commerce: In many instances, chambers of commerce in the foreign market can also provide information on potential agents. However, the quality and quantity of information obtainable from different chambers varies considerably.
5. Commercial information services: Dun and Bradstreet and similar commercial information services supply on request brief reports on individual agents that cover in particular the financial aspects of their operations, their areas, of activity and their professional reputation.

6. Independent consultants. In most countries, consultants specializing in the selection and investigation of potential agents make their services available for a negotiated fee. Usually the services of these specialists also cover advice and assistance in contract drafting and contract negotiation, and sometimes supervision and control of the agent's performancc after appointment.

SELECT A SUITABLE AGENT

When an exporter has determined his precise requirements for an agent, he must give careful consideration to the following points in order to establish the suitability of a potential agent:

1. What is the agent's ability to cover the territory? It is of vital importance that he be able to service the entire area effectively. It would be wrong, for example, to assume that an agent appointed in London would necessarily be able to cover the whole of the United Kingdom.
2. Does he have the necessary staff to market the product effectively? It is not sufficient to accept oral assurances; the exporter must satisfy himself that the agent has the required staff with appropriate experience and product knowledge to market the product.
3. What is the business reputation of the potential partner? Inquiries should be directed not only to bank, chambers of commerce, trade associations and similar institutions, but also to local or potential customers in the territory.
4. What is the agent's company type and organization? An individual or a large company may be involved. The continuity of the operation must be assured in the event of death or illness of the principal responsible for handling it. After an exporter has appointed an

agent, he must constantly bear this factor in mind. The exporter may deem it advisable to bring some of the agent's personnel to the home office to be suitably trained so as to ensure continuity.

5. When a large agency organization is employed, the exporter should ensure that adequate staff are allocated to his product, so that it receives full attention and is not at a disadvantage because the organization is handling a number of other products as well.

A short list of prospective agents should be drawn up on the basis of the information gathered in the preceding step. Detailed and exhaustive discussions should then be held with them. A checklist for these discussions is given on page 119.

APPOINT THE AGENT

Most countries have specialized legislation covering, the rights and obligations of both parties in an agency agreement. An exporter planning to appoint an agent should always seek legal advice in the agent's country before entering into an agreement in order to be fully aware of the legal, financial and operational implications of his signature.

It is rarely possible to use a standard contract form for the agreement. Such a standard form must be seen rather as a basis for discussion, to be amended as local conditions require.

Any agency agreement should, as a minimum, cover the following points:

1. Type of agreement: exclusive or nonexclusive.
2. Geographic coverage: country, regions etc.
3. Product coverage: exporter's products included now or in the future.
4. Remuneration.

5. Exporter's obligations: prlce lists, brochures, samples, selling aids, training of sales staff, guarantees and repairs, sales promotion and advertising.
6. Agent's obligations: sales coverage, sales reports, strength of sales staff, warehousing and financing.
7. Duration and termination clauses.
8. Provisions for arbitration in case of dispute.

Experience has shown the benefits of complementing the agency contract with a separate document on operating procedures. A separate document has the advantage of allowing changes in the procedures as and when required, without the need for time-consuming and often difficult contract renegotiations. Some large international companies have detailed operational procedure manuals with hundreds of pages. But even a brief document, written and signed by the exporter and the agent, can significantly fecilitate collaboration.

Many agents tend to get upset at the principal's mere mention of the words control and supervision, because they feel that this will lead to unjustified and unnecessary meddling in their affairs. Every exporter is therefore advised to "defuse" this issue at the start by referring only to collaboration and mutual assistance in a general sense. In practical terms this means that the agent must be made to understand the following:

Regular sales and stock reports help the exporter schedule his production and shipment.

Sales forecasts ensure that the agent is supplied on time with the right products.

General market reports help both partners to recognize new opportunities and changes in time to plan accordingly.

CHART 4-B

Checklist for Choosing Agents

1. Size of the agent's company.
2. Date of foundation of the agent's company.
3. The company's ownership and control.
4. The company's capital, funds available and liabilities.
5. Names, age and experience of the company's senior executives,
6. Number, age and experience of the company's salesmen.
7. Other agencies that the company holds, including those of competing products, and turnover of each.
8. Length of the company's association with other principals.
9. New agencies that the company obtained or last during the past year.
10. The company's total annual sales and the trends in its sales in recent years.
11. The company's sales coverage, overall and by area.
12. Number of sales calls per month and per salesman by company staff.
13. Any major obstacles expected in the company's sales growth.
14. The agent's capability to provide sales promotion and advertising services.
15. The agent's transport facilities and warehousing capacity.
16. Agent's rate of commission; payment terms required.
17. References on the agent from banks, trade assoeiations and major buyers.

Reports on product performance, trade and consumer reactions provide valuable information for planning new products, product improvements, changes in packaging and presentation, and so forth.

Another potentially controversial subject between an exporter and an agent is advertising and sales promotion. Differences of opinion tend to arise not only on the size and use of the budget but also on the control over expenditures. The best solution-although it is not always feasible-is probably an understanding whereby the exporter sets down and controls the overall budget, and both partners decide jointly how it is to be spent.

The most important single factor for ensuring the successful operation of an agency agreement is not only observation of the letter of the contract, but also a full appreciation of its spirit and an understanding of the relationship between principal and agent. In other words, the two parties must always operate as a team: The principal must realize that the agent requires constant support, and the agent must understand the principal's needs for service and information.

Many customers in foreign markets have no direct personal contact with the exporter and therefore form an opinion about him and his products solely as a result of their contacts with his agent It is obvious that if the agent is to create the right image, and indeed promote the interests of his principal in the best possible manner, he must have full backing and support from the exporter at all times. This means that the agent must be kept constantly informed about the product, prices and deliveries.

When a new agent is appointed, arrangements should be made for him to visit the exporter to obtain firsthand background information on the product and on company policy and to establish personal contact with the executives concerned with his particular market. Such visits should be repeated periodically.

In the same way, valuable help can be given to the agent through visits to the foreign market by executives from the exporting company. No exporter can promote a successful operation abroad unless he is prepared to make visits to his markets to obtain firsthand information on the situation. Such visits are also appreciated by his customers, who will usually look upon them as a tangible proof of his interest in the market.

5

Trade Fair Participation

BRUCE BENDOW

I

Planning and Budgeting

Participating in trade fairs involves careful planning and budgeting. Some basic guidelines on how to organize such activities in a systematic way. Participating in trade fairs involves attending to many details Careful planning is vital. Unless each of the many persons concerned does his job properly, and on time, the participation can end in embarrasing confusion and cost far more than anticipated· Experience has shown that the following basic rules help keep these projects in the track:

1. One person should be made responsible for the entire operation as coordinator or project manager.

2. Each task and responsibility should be identified at the outset. The time necessary for each should be estimated, and their sequency determined.

3. **Based on this analysis, a consolidated work plan should be drawn up as early as possible, with clear deadlines.**

4. **The persons or outside contractors to be made responsible for carrying out each task should be identified.**

5. **Ample lead times should be allowed—the longer these are, the better.**

6. **Regular revision should be scheduled to spot any problems and to compensate for delays before they disrupt preparations.**

TIMETABLE

There are various ways of planning for an exhibition. Many organizations draw up rather complicated network analysis diagrams, which help shows the connections between the various activities and the critical deadlines. But whatever method is used, the basic procedure is to work back from the major deadlines, starting with the fair's opening day, and including such critical dates as the deadline for applying for space and shipping dates.

Once experience has been gained in several fairs, a standard checklist can be developed and the "start" and "finish" (or deadline) dates can be filled in.

Two timetables are shown on pages 126 to 133. The first is broken down by type of activity and covers many of the steps called for when an organization such as a chamber of commerce organizes a joint participation. When this timetable has been drawn up, its elements can be consolidated into a single sequential calendar giving the name of the person responsible for each step.

The activities of, and the trainiag required by, these persons will vary according to the fair organizer's deadline, the Institutional set up, the role of the government, distance from the market and shipping times, whether the stand is to be designed and constructed at home or abroad, how much money is available and so on.

For the first timetable, it is assumed that it will be possible to obtain all the necessary information about the market from the commercial attache posted there. For a privately arranged participation, this may not be possible and the responsible body may have to send its own staff members abroad to carry out the research.

Perhaps the most important point to note about the first timetable is that the lead times indicated are not uncharacteristic of the requirements for participating in a major fair abroad.

The second timetable should be useful for individual companies going into trade fairs in a modest way and on their own. It suggests only rough lead times and does not show many important activities for the sake of simplicity.

CHART 5-A

Trade Fair Checklist and Planning Form for Companies

Major deadlines	*Dates*
1. Opening day	———
2. Reserve space, shell stand, furnishings	———
3. Stand installation	———
4. Arrival of goods at part	———
5. Delivery to freight forwarders for sea freight	———
6. Order utilities, interpreter, etc.	———
7. Delivery to air freight forwarder	———
8. Mailing of invitations	———

BUDGETING

A detailed budget should be drawn up as soon as soon as possible after the decision is made to enter a trade fair. Although it will probably be necessary to wait for quotations and other information before all the items can be filled in with any exactness, a fairly close figure for the overall costs must be obtained in time to inform the companies to be invited to exhibit.

Each group organizer will have to decide how costs are to be shared. In most cases, the participating companies will share all costs, excluding perhaps the costs of time spent by the staff of the organizing chamber of commerce. Most costs will probably be added up and apportioned as a single fee to the individual participants according to the floor space they are to occupy on the stand. Other costs, such as freight, may be prorated; air tickets and hotel and living expenses for the companies own personnel may be paid direct by these companies, perhaps at a discount arranged by the chamber or trade association.

The planning timetable should provide for periodic review and revision of the budget in time for adjustments in case of cost overruns, It is a good idea to add about 15 per cent for contingencies to the estimates for the major items.

The budget planning guide on pages 133-135 can be used for planning joint participations and can be adapted for use by individual companies exhibiting on their own. (See timetables and planning guide on the following pages).

CHART 5-B

TIMETABLE I

Trade Fair Planning Timetable-group Participation Example: Fair to be Held 1-10 June 1983

Activity	*Start*	*Finish*
Basic Preparation		
1. Decision to exhibit	7.12.81	5 1.82
2. Book space; first payment	—	5.1.82
3. Planning meeting	—	24.5.82
4. Assign project coordinator	—	24.5.82
5. Send brief and questionnaire to commercial attache	—	26.5.82
6. Prepare preliminary budget	25.5.82	25.6.82
7. Prepare initial timetable	25.5.82	25.6.82
8. Deadline for information from commercial attache	—	25.6.82
9. Prepare detailed timetable	28.6.82	9.7.82
10. Prepare detailed budget	28.6.82	9.7.82
11. Second payment for space	—	1.10.82
12. First budget revision	1.12.12	15.12.82
13. Second budget revision	1.2.83	15.2.83
14. Third budget revision	1.3.83	15.3.83
15. Third payment for space	—	1.4.83
Design and Construction		
1. Select and appoint stand designer	8.6.82	7.7.82
2. Brief designer	26.10.82	30.10.82
3. Prepare stand design	1.11.82	30.11.82
4. Approve design	30.11.82	6.12.82

5. Second final design plan to fair organizer for approval	—	16.12.82
6. Reminder to exhibitors on information panel material	24.12.82	1.1.83
7. Prepare and issue tender calls for stand construction	6.12.81	4.1.83
8. Order electricity, plumbing, telephone	—	4.1.83
9. Order utilities services, furnishings	—	4.1.83
10. Appoint studio for panels	15.12.82	15.1.83
11. Deadline for information panel material	—	7.2.83
12. Appoint stand contractor	1.2.83	15.2.83
13. Preparation of panels	13.1.83	10.3.83
14. Stand construction (modular)	18.5.83	29.5.83
15. Furniture installed, displays set up	30.5.83	31.5.83
Fair	1.6.83	10.6.83
16. Dismantle stand	11.6.83	15.6.83
Shipping		
1. Appoint freight forwarder	15.10.82	22 10.82
2. Book shipping space, in and out	—	15.12.82
3. Appoint clearing agent (overseas)	30.11.82	30.12.82
4. Receive exhibitors' shipping lists for sea freight	—	19.2.83
5. Receive goods from exhibitors for sea freight	27.2.83	4.3.83
6. Shipping date for sea freight	—	15.3.83
7. Prepare shipping documents, send to learing agent	14.3.83	21.3.83
8. Receive exhibitors' shipping lists for airfreight	1.4.83	15.4.83
9. Book airfreight space	—	16.4.83

(Contd.)

CHART 5-B (Contd.)

10. Receive goods for airfrieght	9.5.83	16.5.83
11. Telex clearing agent airfreight details	—	17.5.83
12. Airfreight exhibits, printed matter	—	19.5.83
13. Delivery of exhibits, display material	—	30.5.83
Fair	1.6.83	10.6.83
14. Get exhibitors' disposal instructions	—	10.6.83
15. Return shipment	—	30.6.83
Staffing		
1. Appoint stand manager	—	31.12.82
2. Book local temporary staff	—	13.1.83
3. Brief staff	—	31.5.83
Exhibitors		
1. Announcement in chamber newsletter	—	17.1.82
2. Prepare list of prospective exhibitors	25.5.82	1.6.82
3. Prepare and print application forms and covering letter	2.8.82	22.8.82
4. Mail application form and covering letter	—	1.9.82
5. Second announcement in chamber newsletter	—	16.9.82
6. Personal recruitment calls	28.9.82	12.10.82
7. Closing date for appiications; first payment by exhibitors	—	19.10.82
8. Finalize list of exhibitors, products	20.10.82	25.10.82
9. Prepare exhibitors' manual and kit	30.11.82	30.12.82
10. Briefing meeting with exhibitors; issue manual and kit	—	5.1.83
11. Deadline for receiving names of exhibitors' stand representatives	—	17.1.83

12. Book hotels, airlines	—	17.1.83
13. Order passes and badges	—	1.2.83
14. Second payment by exhibitors	—	19.2.83
15. Prepare pre-opening briefing material	9.5.83	16.5.83
16. Additional payment by exhibitors for airfreight	—	17.5.83
17. Stand manager briefs exhibitors' staff. issues passes, badges, briefing kits	—	31.5.83
Promotion		
1. Prepare and issue first local press release	11.1.82	18.1.82
2. Prepare and send catalogue entry data to organizer	26.10.82	1.11.82
3. Obtain quotations for translation and printing	30.10.82	30.11.82
4. Prepare catalogue advertisement	15.12.82	30.12.82
5. Decide reception date	10.1.83	15.1.83
6. Book Reception room	—	17.1.83
7. Arrange for reception speakers	10.1.83	17.1.83
8. Prepare and translate first press release for overseas	7.1.83	28.1.83
9. Translate catalogue advertisement	17.1.83	31.1.83
10. Palace catalogue advertisement	—	1.2.83
11. Prepare brochure	17.1.83	5.2.83
12. Prepare second invitation letter and reception invitation	22.1.83	5.2.83
13 Appoint graphic designer for brochure	14.2.83	15.2.83
14. Book advertising space	—	15.2.83
15. Obtain mailing lists from overseas sourees	1.11.82	18.2.83

(Contd.)

CHART 5-B (Contd.)

16. Prepare overseas trade press ad	1.2.83	20.2.83
17. Translate brochure, second letter and invitation	7.2.83	21.2.83
18. Prepare first invitation letter	12.2.83	26.2.83
19. Get mailing lists from exhibitors	26.10.82	1.3.83
20. Translate first press release for overseas	15.2.83	1.3.83
21. Prepare second overseas press release and photographs	18.2.83	3.3.83
22. Mail first press release for overseas	—	8.3.83
23. Translate advertisement	24.2.83	10.3.83
24. Translate first invitation letter	28.2.83	14.3.83
25. Send advertisement material	—	15.3.83
26. Translate second overseas press release	22.3.83	5.4.83
27. Order guest tickets from organizers	—	5.4.84
28. Print first invitation letter	21.3.83	7.4.83
29. Mail second overseas press release and photographs	—	8.4.83
30. Mail first invitation letter	11.4.83	18.4.83
31. Print brochure, second letter and		
32. Books stand photographer	—	4.5.83
33. Mail brochure, letter, invitation and entiry tickets	2.5.83	9.5.83
34. Order catering for reception	—	24.5.83
35. Prepare second local press release	20.5.83	26.5.83
36. Issue second local press realease	—	27.5.83
Fair	1.6.83	10.6.83
37. Prepare third overseas press release	—	10.6.83
38. Issue third local press release	—	11.6.83
39. Translate third overseas press	—	11.6.83
40. Issue third overseas press release	—	12.6.83

CHART 5-B

TIMETABLE II

Individual Participation

Activity	*Months before fair (indicative)*	*Date*
1. Write to organizer for information application forms	18	————
2. Decision to exhibit	12-15	————
3. Decide total budget	12-15	————
4. Reserve space	12-15	————
5. Notify sales agent of plans	12-15	————
6. Assign project coordinator	12	————
7. Staff planning meeting	12	————
8. Request quotations from stand contractors, stand designers	12	————
9. Select products for display	11	————
10. Agree on product adaptation, production plans	11	————
11. Draw up detailed timetable	11	————
12. Draw up detailed budget	11	————
13. Appoint and brief stand designer	10	————
14. Apply for foreign travel, other permits, incentives	8	————
15. Book shell stand, furnishings, utilities	6-8	————
16. Appoint freight forwarder, agree on delivery times	8	————
17. Approve stand design	8	————

(Contd.)

CHART 5-B (Contd.)

18. Send plans to organizer	8	----
19. Send catalogue entry data to organizer	7	----
20. Decide on needs for printed matter	7	----
21. Appoint advertising agency to prepare printed matter	7	----
22. Prepare material for printed matter	6	----
23. Book hotel rooms	6	----
24. Decide on stand personnel	6	----
25. Book air tickets	6	----
26. Arrange insurance	6	----
27. Revise budget	6	----
28. Appoint contractor	5	----
29. Arrange translations	5	----
30. Prepare and plan advertisements for fair catalogues	5	----
31. Make up mailing list	5	----
32. Arrange for hostesses and interpreters	5	----
33. Complete display panels, sign-boards, etc.	4	----
34. Prepare and palace advertisement in trade journal	4	----
35. Obtain quotations from printers	4	----
36. Deliver goods and display matelial to freight for warder	3-4	----
37. Appoint clearing agent	4	----
38. Request passes, promotional aids from organizers	4	----
39. Agree on prices, quantities offered	3	----
40. Send brochure to printer	3	----

41. Mail invitations	1	————
42. Deadline for printing literature	2	————
43. Arrange for disposal and/or return of merchandise	0	————

CHART 5-C

Budget Planning Guide

Activity	*Planned costs*	*Actual costs*
1. *Space rental*	————	————
2. *Design and construction*		
(a) Designer's fee	————	————
(b) Production of signboards, display panels etc.	————	————
(c) Construction of shell scheme	————	————
(d) Display stands, window cases,		
(e) Carpeting	————	————
(f) Furniture	————	————
(g) Stand dressing	————	————
(h) Electrical fittings	————	————
(i) Electricity	————	————
(j) Refrigeration	————	————
(k) Water and waste	————	————
(l) Telephone	————	————
(m) Dismanting	————	————
(n) Contingencies	————	————
Total	————	————

(*Contd.*)

CHART 5·C (Contd.)

3. *Insurance*	----	----
4. *Shipping and handling*		
(a) Sea freight (outward)	----	----
(b) Airfreight	----	----
(c) Forwarding and handling	----	----
(d) Return freight	----	----
(e) Contingencies	----	----
Total	----	----
5. *Stand Service*		
(a) Cleaning	----	----
(b) Security	----	----
Total	----	----
6. *Staffing*		
(a) Interpreters	----	----
(b) Receptionists		
Total	----	----
7. *Promotion*		
(a) Brochure (design, translation and printing)	----	----
(b) Press releases, announcements, invitations (translation, printing stationery)	----	----
(c) Mailing lists	----	----
(d) Mailing and postage (foreign)	----	----
(e) Advertising (including catalogue entries)	----	----
(f) Public relations agency fee	----	----

(g) Reception room rental	----	----
(h) Reception catering	----	----
(i) Stand hospitality	----	----
(j) Stand photography	----	----
(k) Contingencies	----	----
Total	----	----

8. International travel and per diem

(a) Air fares	----	----
(b) Hotel and living expenses	----	----
(c) Local transportation	----	----
Total	----	----

9. Exhibition recruitment

(a) Printing of exhibitors' lists	----	----
(b) Postage	----	----
(c) Telephone	----	----
(d) Internal transportation	----	----
(e) Contingencies	----	----
Total	----	----

10. Miscellaneous

(a) Marketing consultant's fee	----	----
(b) Contingencies	----	----
Total	----	----

II

Preparing for the Fair

BRUCE BENDOW*

Successful trade show participation calls for adequate background information on the fair and the market, plus careful selection and briefing of exhibitors. Adequate information is one of the keys to participating in trade fairs successfully. A great deal of information should be collected before a decision is made to enter a fair. Once that decision has been made, priority should be given to obtaining much more information, which will be necessary to carry out a number of initial functions:

Planning the overall operation, and establishing a timetable.

Planning staff assignments.

Budgeting.

Visitor promotion.

Recruiting exhibitors.

Briefing exhibitors.

Preparation by exhibitors of their policies, products and staff.

Two types of information are needed information about the market, and information directly related to the fair itself.

*Bruce Bendow is ITC's senior adviser on trade fairs and commercial publicity. This article is an except from a handbook that the recently prepared. *Making the Most of Trade Fairs,* which is one of a series of guides being produced under ITC's technical cooperation programme with national chambers of commerce.

FAIR INFORMATION

This information, listed on page 141, mainly concerns the many physical and logistical arrangement which must be made. Most of it will be provided by the organizer with a set of contract forms sent to all prospective exhibitors. This can be obtained by writing to the organizer and expressing interest in participating. The organizer should also be able to supply the rest of it on more specific request.

MARKET INFORMATION

While it may seem obvious that information about physical arrangements must be obtained in order to arrange a successful trade fair participation, the need for market informations is often overlooked. The results can be disastrous: unsellable products being offered by uninformed attendants on a stand that attracts few visitors.

It is possible that an exhibitor can achieve some positive results by going into a trade fair blindly, but his chances for success will certainly be greatly increased if he has made preparation based on adequate information about the market. If a chamber commerce or trade association is organizing a joint participation in a trade fair, it will need some market information to make adequate preparations, and part of its responsibility is also to provide the market information needed by each exhibitor. When a company goes into a fair on its own, it may have difficulity in obtaining all of the necessary information, and should be able to look to its chamber or association for help.

Information on the following subjects, outlined in greater detail in the checklist on pages 145-146 is requred.

Market access: If trade barricrs make it impossible to export tc a market, the decision to enter a trade fair obviously should be negative. But even when the situation is not so hopeless, factors like tariffs and taxes must be taken into account in deciding on prices, and health and safety regulations must be complied with.

Market potential: Information on the size and growth rate of the market for particular types of products is useful to help convince companies that they should participate. identifying market segment—the various sectors of industry or the public which purchase the products—is important for selecting suitabte channels, planning the exhibition promotional programme, and even for adapting the product and packaging to make them more suitable.

Competition: Companies should know what they are up against before venturing into a market. If they know who their competitors are, the prices they charge and their strengths and weaknesses, they will be in a better position set their own prices realistically and to prepare their sales arguments—or, perhaps. to decide not to approach the market.

Product requirements: Information about product and packaging requirements is among the most important information needed by exhibitors should make every effort to show products which comply with what the market wants and demands. Sometimes a product or its package can be made more acceptable with a few simple changes. In other cases product adaptation may be difficult, time consuming and costly. Even if an exhibitor cannot adapt his product for a particular fair, he should be aware of the product requirements and in a position to assure prospective buyers that he can meet them. He will be better able to provide such assurance if he has studied these requirements beforehand.

Transport: Information on transport services to the market, and costs, is needed to plan and budget shipment of the displays, and to calculate CIF prices and delivery times, which exhibitors should be able to give to fair visitors.

Sales and distribution channels: This information is needed for deciding on the target andience for an exhibit, making up mailing lists, and planning the visitor promotion programme and follow up activities. Knowing how the sales channels work; who are the important importers, distributors or buyers; and how prices are marked up at each level, is also important for doing business on the stand.

Advertising and publicity: Many exhibitors wrongly assume that because they have a stand at a fair, the people they should meet will automatically visit it that at a large trade fan, business visitors often have on time to stop at one of several hundred stands; instead, they concentrate on visiting exhibitors whom they already are interested in seeing. If a company or country is not already well known in the trade and exhibiting regularly at the fair, it should therefore try to inform its target audience that it will be at the fair, and to interest these key people in visiting the stand. This can be done by mailing them invitations and material about the products being exhibited, and by advertising and press publicity. To carry out these activities, information about mailing lists and media must be obtained long in advance of the fair.

MARKET RESEARCH

If the exhibitors are already established in the market and have been participating in the trade fair, it probably will not be necessary to provide them with all of this information, although the chamber or trade association organizing a joint participation should bring it all together in order to plan and carry out the project.

Very ofen most of this information will not be at hand or known to the exhibitor, and market research will be necessary obtain it. Ideally, such research should have been carried out as a basis for deciding to enter the fair in the first place. If it was not, this should be done in the early stages of preparing for the fair.

A great deal of the required information about market access, imports and transport services should be available in the home country, perhaps in the chamber's or association's own library. But for practical information on such matters as trade practices, specific product preferences and the names of important people in the trade, research in the market itself will be necessary. It should be possible to rely for this on the commercial attache posted in the country where the fair is being held, if the participation is to be held under official auspices. But very often this is not the case, and the research has to be carried out by the chamber or association organizing a joint participation, or by an individual company planning to participate on its own.

Sending someone to the market to carry out research may seem like an expensive exercise, but it is far less expensive than exhibiting in a trade fair, and will greatly enhance the chances of trade fair participation being profitable. (For guidance on carrying out market research, see the ITC handbook *Inroduction to Export Market Research.*)

RECRUITING AND BRIEFING EXHIBITORS

Before a chamber of commerce or trade association commits itself to entering a trade fair with a government participation it should obviously have reasonable assurance that enough companies will participate to make it a success and cover the costs.

This is no great problem when the organization has been participating in the same fair over a number of years, but the situation becomes less certain when it plans to venture into a fair for the first time.

Informal contacts with potentially interested companies, and perhaps a discussion at a regular meeting, can help to indicate the level of interest. However, the decision to enter and the deadline for booking space will often be far before companies will be in a position to commit themselves firmly.

CHART 5-D

Fair Information Checklist

1. Place and dates.
2. Name and address of organizer.
3. Arrangement of halls and fair, Spaces available.
4. Cost of spaces.
5. Availability, description and cost of erected stands ("shell" stands).
6. Closing date for application for space.
7. Utilities available, Costs, Deadlines for applications.
8. Furnishing available Costs.
9. Availability and cost of local staff (receptionists, interpreters). names of designers constructors, decorators freight clearing agent, photographer, cleaning service.
10. Insurance and security arrangements.
11. Promotional material available from organizer.
12. Catalogue deadlines and advertising rates.
13. Availability of poster advertising in fair grounds.
14. Organizer's press publicity service, deadlines and requirements.
15. Packing requirements of the organizer.
16. Deadline for arrival of stands and goods.
17. Date of your country's day of honour at the fair.
18. Hotel locations and rates.
19. Reception facilities.

Nevertheless, very soon after the decision has been made, the organizing body should launch a recruitment campaign, designed to inform all companies that should exhibit about the planned participation, and stimulating their interest in doing so.

The recruitment campaign: The first "shots" in such a campaign might be an announcement in the organization's newsletter or other regular publication and a news story placed in the local newspapers and timed to appear shortly after the organization's own publication reaches its readers.

The purpose of the newspaper story is partly public relations for the organization itself and partly to inform member companies that might not see the organization's own publication. The article should state not only the facts about the fair, but the reasons for entering it, featuring such information as market potential and the importance of the fair.

Thereafter, the nature of the recruitment campaign should depend on the circumstances. If the participating companies are to be limited to the organization's membership, it can depend on further articles in its publication, letters and personal contacts. If nonmember companies are also to be included, and they are not easily identified, additional articles placed in the local newspaper should be used to help attract their interest.

It is one problem to recruit enough companies for a fain, the other, and sometimes more difficult problem, is to attract the companies that really should participate, and to weed out those that should not because they are not really serious about exporting, or dependable or cooperative, or because they or their products are not ready for the market. The presence of such exhibitors can damage the whole effort.

This problem is especially common when government incentives may provide the wrong motives for participating, and it is obviously more difficult for a private chamber or association to cope with when dealing with its own members than it is for a government agency which has discretion in dispensing incentives.

Nevertheless, in the interest of the companies that can successful participate in a fair, the organization should establish criteria for eligibility. The easiest criterion to establish and impose is suitability of the type of product to be shown Criterion concerning companies capabilities and motivations are more difficult to establish and may be impossible to actually enforce. The most practical approach would be to concentrate efforts on recruiting the most desirable companies as soon as possible, with the aim of filling up the available space before less desirable companies apply.

This is not to say that only the larger, successful companies should be encouraged to participate. A chamber of association can perform a valuable function by assisting less experienced but promising companies to enter export markets. But the extent to which a chamber or association can do this will obviously vary with its own experience and capabilities and on the attitudes of its stronger members.

In many cases publicity through newspapers or the organization's own publication, or even letters mailed to the heads of companies, will not be sufficient to persuade enough of the right companies to participate. Therefore a series of personal calls on key companies should be planned into the recruitment campaign. As important companies are persuaded to sign up, they should be made known to other prospects, to help create a "bandwagon" effect.

THE PARTICIPATION AGREEMENT

Any joint participation in a fair involves a substantial number of expenditures, preparations and activities which must be carried out either by the individual exhibitors or the group organiziers. To avoid mishaps and even legal problems, the respective responsibilities of the organizer and each exhibitor should be clearly stated in a contractual agreement, which is usually combined with an application form. The following items should be covered:

1. Payment of a fee to the chamber or trade association representing those costs that will be shared, with payment deadlines.
2. Supply of goods for display and of display imaterial.
3. Provision of information and transport arrangements and to meet the information requirements of the fair authorities.
4. Attendance of representatives on the stand.
5. Packing and shipping.
6. Insurance of goods during transport and at the fair.
7. Payment of duties and taxes.
8. Disposal of goods.
9. Arrangements with the fair authorities, including space rental.
10. Stand design and construction.
11. Promotion.
12. Transportation and hotel arrangements and costs.
13. Cancellation notice and refunds of fees.

In addition the application from should provide for the exhibitors to fill in the following informotion:

1. Items to be displayed.
2. Amount of floor space or modules of space desired.
3. Whether the products will be provided by a local representative or shipped abroad.
4. Whether the company will be represented at the fair by its local representative or by one or more people from company headquarters.
5. The names and addresses of the company's agents or importers in the market or markets coverd by the fair.

CHART 5-E

Market Information Checklist

1. Market access

—Tariffs and quotas.

—Internal taxes.

—Currency restrictions.

—Health and safety regulations.

2. Market potential

—Consumption; quantities, values, growth trends, geographic patterns.

—Imports: quantities, values, sources, trends.

—Idenification of market segments.

—Market outlook for the product.

3. Competition

—Domestic production: volume, growth.

—Domestic and foreign producers active in the market: names, market shares, strengths and weaknesses.

—Trademark and patent problems.

—Prices.

—Characteristics of leading products in the market.

—Other reasons for leaders's success.

4. Product requirements

—Product quailities: colour, taste, sizes, design and styling, technical specifications, trade standards and so on.

—Packaging: transport packaging; protective, information, display and size requirements for consumer packs; colour and design perference; legal requirements.

5. Transport

—Services available to the market.

—Freight rates.

6. **Sales and distribution channels.**

   —Normal channels for the product.

   —Relative importance, advantages and disadvantages of various channels.

   —Expected terms of sale.

   —Delivery time requirements.

   —Usual size of orders.

   —Price mark-ups.

   —Names and addresses of major importers/distributors, direct importors, agents, important buyers.

   —After-sales service practice.

7. **Advertising and publicity**

   —Availability, sources and costs of mailing lists; mailing costs.

   —Identicfiation, cost and deadline of suitable advertising media.

   —Sources and costs of translation and printing services.

This information will permit initial arrangements be be made. Later on, the exhibitors should provide additional information about:

1. **Their products.**
2. **Their companies.**
3. **Their specific purposes in exhibiting.**
4. **The business they already conduct in the market.**
5. **The type of business arrangements they are seeking.**
6. **Lists of people they wish to be invited to the fair.**
7. **The need for temporary staff.**
8. **Any special equipment reqantments.**

This information will be needed to prepare catalogue entries, promotional material, advertising and news releases: to carry out the mailing programme; to design the stand; and make other arrangements. One or more sparate forms should be provided for this information, and can be mailed to interested companies together with the application form.

BRIEFING THE EXHIBITORS

About six months before the fair opens, and after all the exhibitors have been selected, a briefing meeting should be held. A top officer of each company should be invited, would be appropriate for the meeting to be presided over by the head of chamber or trade association, with the project coordinator playing the key role. The stand manager, if he has already been appointed, should also be present.

The purpose of this meeting is to guide the exhibitors on how they should get ready for the exhibition, to give them necessary information, to encourage them to meet their responsibilities and deadines, and to start developing enthusiasm and a spirit of cooperation between the exhibitors, which is necessary for a successful joint venture.

A briefing list should be distributed at the meeting. This should contain whatever information forms have yet to be filled in, a report on the market, instructions on such matters as preparation of shipments, a schedule of deadlines, and any other available literature which would help the exhibitor, such lists of contacts.

In the course of the meeting highlights of the market report could be presented, stressing such matters as how the sales channels work and the importance of the fair in reaching them. The project coordinator, and if possible the stand manager, be introduced, and the designer's sketches of the stand should be shown. The project coordinator should outline the promotional plans and explain what information and material is needed, emphasizing the importance of deadlines.

It could be very useful to have an experienced exhibitor give some useful tips to the group, and for an English-speaking audience to show the films. "It'll Be OK On The Day" and "How Not To Exhibit Yourself" (available on a rental or purchase basis from Video Arts Ltd., Distribution Department, 205 Wardour Street. London W.I.V. 3FA).

Here are some of the subjects that could be covered at the briefing meeting, in addition to those already mentioned.

1. How exhibitors should establish their own budgets.
2. Importance of setting specific objectives.
3. Choosing and briefing their stand representatives.
4. Planning a business trip around the fair.
5. How to get the most out of the fair.
6. Following up after the fair.
7. Preparing sales literature in the local languages.
8. Preparing their products and packaging for the market
9. Checking their patent and trademark position.
10. Credit facilities government incentives and regulations which could affect terms of sale and delivery times.
11. The importance of establishing prices, terms of sale and delivery times.
12. The importance of each exhibitor carrying out its own pre-fair promotion.
13. Assistance to be provided by or available from the chamber or trade association.
14. Travel arrangements and hotel options.

On the afternoon or everying before the fair opens, the stand manager should conduct a briefing meeting for the company represent tives. The invisations to this meeting should be left at the exhibitors' hotels, together with a second briefing kit.

The briefing kit should contain the following information, in concise form:

1. Basic data about the fair and the stand:

   Date, daily opening and closing times.

   Stand and hall number.

   Stand telephone number.

   Name of stand manager and his hotel telephones number.

   Names of interpreters and hostesses.

   Location of special facilities at the fair; first aid, restaurants, private meeting rooms, post office, telex, photocopying service and so on.

2. Important telephone numbers:

   Your country's embassy.

   The clearing agent.

3. Dates and time of special events, such as the ambassador's visit, your national day, a press conference and so forth.
4. A list of the names and hotels or local addresses of all the exhibitor representives and the stand.
5. Time of daily end-of-day stand meeting.
6. Public transportation facilities between the hotels and the fair.

The kit should also contain exhibitors' passes, an invitation to the reception (if any), a copy of the fair catalogue, a set of inquiry forms, a map of the city, and publications on local attractions and entertainment.

The primary purpose of the briefing meeting is to answer any questions, introduce local assistants, explain any special procedures, and build up a team spirit. The representatives should be invited to elect their own leader and to arrange among themselves to cover each stand while individuals are away from the stand.

The opportunity should be taken to suggest that the representatives concentrate on achieving their companies main objectives, maximize their contacts by visiting other stands, make use of the inquiry forms and report on any "deals" which could provide the basis for publicity.

COMPETITION BETWEEN EXHIBITORS

One problem that can arise in a joint exhibit is friction between exhibitors showing similar products. Such a situation can undermine the entire effort.

One way to avoid such problems is to encourage exhibitors to show product lines which complement rather than directly compete with each other. When this is not possible, an extra effort should be made to encourage cooperation between the exhibitors, and their agreement on "rules of play" on the stand.

The situation should be discussed openly at the briefing sessions. Opportunities might be pointed out for companies to work together to secure purchase orders which would be too large for a single company to handle. And if out-right competition cannot be avoided, the group organizers particularly the stand manager, must make every effort to be seen to be even-handed in their treatment of exhibitors.

III

Measuring Exhibition Performance*

Trade promotion organizations should evaluate the costs and benefits of trade show participation in order to get the greatest

*By Percy Lovegrove, Promotions Manager of the Irish Export Board. He has had extensive experience in organizing trade fair participation for Irish companies abroad, and has also been involved in ITC's technical cooperation activities with developing countries in trade fairs.

return for their outlay. How much of your country's total trade promotion budget iu spect on trade fair participation? Thirty per cent? Forty per cent? Fifty per cent? More? Many national trade promotion organizations spend the largest share of their export promotion funds on participation trade fairs.

Whatever the amount, it is strongly recommended that an evaluation system be used to assess each participation. The necessity to evaluate the costs and benefits of the activity is be coming even more important with the rising costs of exhibiting.

The main purpose of such an evaluation is to assist decision-makers in national trade promotion organization to:

Decide whether to participate in the particular exibition again.

Decide whether the companies and products involved were the right ones.

Identity failings in the organization and arrangements for the participation, and determine in which areas performance can be imporved in the future.

Record business results and experience gained.

Such an evaluation system should result in a greater return for the outlay involved and a stronger impact on the country's trade expansion programme.

METHODS OF EVALUATION

Although the need to evaluate trade fair performance is widely acknowledged, in developed as well as in developing countries, in practice such appraisals are carried out with varying degrees of thoroughness and success. In theory, every aspect of trade fair activity is capable of being assessed either qualitatively or quantitatively in practive, the aspects to be exaluated must be selected realistically otherwise the task will become far too costly and time consuming. The subjects to be evaluated should be related to quantifiable objectives that are set down in writing prior to participation in the trade fair.

There is no magic formula for measuring the results of trade fair participation. Each organization should devise an assessment system that best meets its own purposes. The system should be reviewed critically on a regular basis, perhaps at the end of each annual programme, to monitor its effectiveness in providing information that is really useful and that will enable better results to be achieved from future participations.

The suggestions for trade fair evaluation and reporting that follow are not theoretical. They are based on actual examples obtained from national trade promotion orgaaizations that have many years' practical involvement in trade fair participation and from the author's personal experience.

KEY ELEMENTS OF A SYSTEM

Whatever system of evaluation is decided on, it should be:

1. Systematic—not haphazard.
2. Comprehensive—not restricted to only a few critieria.
3. Rigorous—not relying on merely a few opinions.
4. Consistent—not based on changing ground rules.
5. Continuous—not undertaken only occasionally.

An effective evaluation system is comprised of serveral different elements for assessing results. The following are some fairly standard yardsticks against which a group' performance at a particular fair can be measured:

Previously set objectives for participating in the fair.

Expenditure to participate in the fair.

Performance at previous fairs.

Specific types of measurements, such as the cost per trade contact made, or the cost per square metre of stand space rented. (These subjects are dealt with in greater detail in the discussion below).

The number of registered trade visitors out of total visitors attending the exhibition (this comparison is of questionable value because only a portion of the trade visitors will have a high interest in any particular product(s).

GUIDELINES FOR SETTING OBJECTIVES

An objective is a specific statement of what is to be accomplished to reach a particular standard of effectiveness. The objectives laid down for participating in a trade fair should be realistic and quantifiable if they are to be of use in measuring performance. They should meet the following criteria:

1. Be measurable.
2. Contain a time element.
3. Contain a quantity element.
4. Be attainable.
5. Contain priorities.

Some examples: The following examples illustrate how specific objectives that do not meet these criteria can be revised so that they do:

1. The objective "to increase my knowledge of exhibition work" is not measurable. But "to increase my knowlege of exhibition work by producing a planning schedule for exhibitions abroad" is measurable.
2. The objective "to produce a planning schedule etc." is *not* acceptable, as no time element is involved. But "to produce a planning schedule etc., by the end of December" is an acceptable objective.

3. "To obtain product publicity in the trade press" is too open-ended to be measured and is therefore *not* an acceptable objective. while "to obtain publicity in the three trade magazines catering for our products in the French market" *is* acceptable, as it indicates a specific quantity.

4. It is *not* acceptable to state as an objective "to introduce a new system of budgetary control for exhibitions." unless the authority to do so is vested in the person setting the objectives. This might be re-written: "To prepare by . . . . (date) and submit to . . . . (name) for consideration, a draft of a new system of budgetary control for exhibitions."

The relative importance of each objective should be indicated by giving it a priority rating.

THE TRADE PROMOTION ORGANIZATION'S OBJECTIVES

In proposing participation in a particular trade fair and in allocating financial and manpower resources to that project, it is essential that the national trade promotion organization have certain clearly defined objectives in mind. The pavilion manager or project leader should write the organization's "Activity Plan" for the participation. This should ideally cover the matters outlined in the box above.

THE INDIVIDUAL COMPANY'S OBJECTIVES

In practice, it is sometimes difficult to persuade individual companies to prepare written objectives for their participation in a trade fair. If necessary, this extremely important task can be under taken by the person in the national trade promotion organization who knows the company's capability and who has been responsible for selecting that company for participation. Ideally, however, the company should be strongly encouraged to set its own objectives.

CHART 5-F

Activity Plan: Trade Fair Participation

---

1. Background to the participation.
2. Criteria for company selection, and likely participants.
3. Objectives of the participation:
   (a) In relation to the industry sector covered by the exhibition.
   (b) In relation to the companies selected for participation.
4. The pavilion: space, theme, special facilities needed.
5. Publicity and proposed programmes for VIPs (high-officials and special guests).
6. Administration and staffing.
7. Proposed evaluation methods and follow-up action.
8. "Critical path" timetable (*i.e.* showing tasks to be completed and timing of each) to ensure complletion of stand to meet exhibition opening daadline.
9. Budget overall expenditure ond company contributions.

Examples: Obviously, objectives on the company level will vary from firm and from one fair to another. Below are a few actual examples selected at random from company objectives as notified to a national trade promotion organization prior to trade fair participation:

"To locate a main distributor in . . . . (country) market."

"To launch our product in. . . .(country) market and obtain buyer reaction from this and at least. . . . (number) other markets".

"To support our existing agents and evaluate their effectiveness."

"To meet at least . . . (number) of our existing customers is and obtain a minimum of. . . (number) new business prospects."

"To promote existing sales of our product in . . . . (country) and to obtain minimum-on-the spot orders worth. . . ."

"To assess our competitor" products with particular reference to packaging, presentation and price (if possible.)"

"Merely public relations."

All of the above are perfectly valid and measurable objectives except the final one. If a company's main reason for exhibiting is "public relations," the entire exhibition policy should be examined very carefully. It is not difficult to spend a substantial exhibiting budget for the purpose of achieving "public relations" benefits and other vague, ill-defined objectives. "Public relations" is often used as an excuse for not evaluating what has (or has not) been actually achieved. Perhaps it felt, that, like some forms of advertising, exhibiting results are not possible to evaluate.

Making useful contact: Each of the examples of company objectives listed above depends for its success (or failure) on the *need for stand staff to meet people of value to the business.* If an objective does not meet this criterion, the decision to exhibit should be critically re-examined.

When stand personnel actually meet useful contacts, realistic exhibiting objectives can begin to realized , and evaluating basic exhibiting performance becomes relatively straightforward—either the company actually meets a high percentage of potentially useful contacts at the exhibition, or it fails to meet them. This, then, is the main yardstick for exhibition performance measurement, and it should be given an appropriate priority rating in the setting of objectives.

REGISTERING VISITORS

The registration of visitors in an important link in the evaluation process. At a general or consumer exhibition, visitors include many persons who do not have any significant impact on the business of the companies participating. Registering visitors at such fairs is therefore of little use, as the possibilities

CHART 5-G

Expenditure Breakdown for Participation

Name of event: ——————————————————

Area in square metres: ——————————————————

Number of exhibitors: ——————————————————

Cost items:

1. Space ——————————————————
2. Stand construction ——————————————————
3. Shiping and handling (to and from the site) ——————————
4. Stand services ——————————————————
5. Advertising and publicity ——————————————————
6. Personnel expenses ——————————————————
7. Other expenditures in host country ——————————

Total cost ——————————————————

Amount recovered from exhibitors ——————————————————

Net cost to the national trade promotion organization ——————————

Total budget available for the event ——————————————————

Amount of expenditure above or below budget allotted ——————————

---

for making useful trade contacts are limited. However, registration of visitors is highly important at specialized trade fairs (for instance at food, textile or handicraft shows), to which only bona fide persons connected with the particular trade are admitted. Since every person who stops at a stand and talks to a staff member at a specialized exhibition is a potential business prospect, it is important to have a record of this encounter.

The "inquiry form" plays an important role in this record-keeping. It is drawn up in such a way that a "visitor" who is not a bona fide business prospect is quikly identified and is then courteously discouraged from taking more of the stand personnel's time. After the show the completed inquiry forms serve as the basis for drawing up the list of good business prospects resuiting from the participation.

A sample visitor inquiry form is shown on page 159.

COST ELEMENTS AND ANALYSIS

The costs involved in trade fair participation are important in the evaluation process. The main cost elements of participation are likely to be.

Rental of stand space.

Stand construction.

Shipping and handling of goods and display material (to and from the exhibition.)

Stand services (telephone, water, light, cleaning and so on).

Advertising and publicity.

Stand personnel and expenses (travel, hotel, meals and so forth).

Other expenditures in the host country, for instance hospitality.

A trade promotion organization should carefully monitor costs for each trade fair participation. This, in turn, will enable it to prepare a detailed table of total expenditures on each event, broken down as shown on page 157.

Given the total cost of the participation, it is possible to calculate:

The cost per business prospect contacted (number of registered visitors divided inio the total cost).

The cost in relation to returns (total cost divided into total value of business achieved). In an "order writting" exhibition, *i.e.*, one at which customers place orders directly for goods, a sales value that is eight to ten times the participating costs could be considered satisfactory. In other exhibitions where orders normally follow after the fair this evaluation would have to postponed for perhaps six months.

Quite apart from the advantages of having such information available for evaluating the trade fair concerned, it is possible, and indeed highly desirable to develop a historical record of the organization's trade fair activity, based on the information from each event, for planning the next year's programme. The following data can be readily calculated for each event (and subsequently for the entire year's programme) from the breakdown of total expenditure suggested below:

1. Total cost per sq.m. of exhibition space.
2. Ratio of stand construction cost to total cost.
3. Ratio of publicity costs to total cost.

EXHIBITION INQUIRY Code————

Name of firm————————————————Date————

Address——————————————————————

Business————————————————Telephone————

Name of inquire——————————————Seen by————

Type of business————Retailer————Wholesaler————Mail order

Interested in————————————————————

Information or literature required

——————————————On orders placed please complete

Literature supplied——————————Delivery reqd. by

——————————————Unit price

——————————————Exhibition

Example of an Exhibition Report

1. Introduction

Background to the participation as defined in the organization's "Activity Plan" (see discussion on page 155), as well as basic informa tion on the exhibition as a whole:

Total area of the exhibition.

Main industry ann product categories involved.

Total number of exhibitors taking part (host country and foreign).

Countries participating with national stands.

Total number of visitors (and a breakdown by host country and foreign visitors if possible).

2. Preparation for the exhibition

Stand design, layout, organization.

Advertising and publicity compaign.

3. Action during the exhibition

By the company representatives.

By the national trade promotion organization staff.

VIP visits.

4. Results

Business results of the companies represented (see exhibition inquiry form).

The suitability o' each company and product (related to the companies' pre-fair marketing objectives).

Results for the national trade promotion organization (related to its declared pre-fair objectives),

5 Post-exhibition action necessary.

By each company (in outline form).

By the national trade promotion organization.

6. Conclusions and recommendations.

   Participation statistics (see suggested list below).

   Conclusion in relation this participation.

   Recommendations on future participation.

To be included with this report: the exhibition floor plan, exhibition catalogue, publicity press clippings, copies of the companies' questionnaires, the brochure produced for the event by the national trade promotion organization, if any, and other relevant items of documentation.

CHART 5-H

Suggested List: Participation Statistics for Trade Fair Evaluation Report

---

1. Deviation from programmed budget.
2. Value of business written and projected follow-on orders.
3. Number of good business contacts made.
4. Cost per business contact made.
5. Cost per square metre of exhibition space.
6. Ratio of stand construction cost to total cost.
7. Ratio of publicity costs to total cost.
8. Ratio of personnel costs to total cost.
9. Portion of costs recovered from participating companies.
10. Number of registered visitors out of tolal attendance.

Note: The above points should be compared, when possible, with performance at previous fair(s).

4. Ratio of personnel costs to total cost.
5. Portion of total expenses recovered by the national trade promotion organization from participating companies.

THE EXHIBITION REPORT

An exhibition evaluation enables the responsible officer in the national trade promotion organization to produce a constructive report on the organization's participation. Such a report will vary in content from exhibition to exhibition and from one organization to another. An example of a report of this type based on the suggestions in this article and on actual national participation in specialized trade fairs is shown on pages 160-161.

FOLLOW-UP

Some of the national trade promotion organizations in developed countries that provided information for this article on their systems of trade fair organization and management indicated that they asked their companies to provide estimates of the value of "follow-up" business resulting from participation in an exhibition. How realistic can such an estimate be? The author had a study undertaken of actual business that resulted compared with projected "follow-up" business after a period of six months for two separate exhibition participations. The conclusion was that less than 50 per cent of the amount of business projected by the companies' representatives immediately following the exhibition had actually materialized.

Nevertheless, "follow-up" activities during the weeks and months after the participation in an exhibition are vitally important. It is the national trade promotion organization's responsibility to identify the main areas of post-exhibition action required and to ensure that not only its own organization but particularly the individual companies involved take vigorous action to ensure business prospect is supplied with whatever information he needs to translate an inquiry into an order.

Examples of follow-up: Listed below are actual examples taken from a project leader's report of recommended "follow-up" action for companies that participated in a national stand in a specialized exhibition in Canada:

"Company A, Company B and Company C will be writing to the most interested and exciting potential distributors with firm prices, supply schedules, contract terms etc. within the next four weeks. These proposals will be followed up by another visit to Canada after a period of three months to finalize distributorships. All other potential distributors who offered their services will be thanked for their interest, and end-users met will be advised of the newly appointed distributors."

"We (the national trade promotion organization that organized participation) will assist Company B and Company C in the follow-up action necessary, as they are both relatively new to the business of exporting."

"The necessary follow-up on the sales leads obtained by Company D and Company E will be organized through their respective Canadian agent."

"The two companies (Company F and Company G) represented by us (the national trade promotion organization that organized participation) will be encouraged to visit Canada later in the year provided they undertake initial follow-up work of the contacts made by us on their behalf." (In this particular case, five of the participants on the national stand —companies A through E—were represented by their own sales personnel and/or their agents; two—companies F and G—were represented by the national trade promotion organization that organized the participation).

CONCLUSION

To sum up, the main justification for time spent evaluating any project is to measure performance against previously set targets, to learn from the experience gained and to use that experience to improve performance the next time around. Complicated and highly sophisticated evaluation systems are not necessarily the best. In the course of providing background for this article, many trade promotion officials in highly industrialized countries gave examples of their evaluation questionnaires. It is significant that in almost every case simplicity was the keynote, and rarely did the questionnaires ask for international that could not be provided within a few minutes

IV

Designing and Constructing Your Trade Fair Stand*

A stand should be designed so that it attracts business visitors to the products displayed, as well as provides suitable conditions to do business. A trade fair is a physical event, of which the most prominent elements are the stands, with their structures, products, furnishings and decorations. Because of this, and because of all effort that goes into designing and building the stand and the activity that centres around it, the danger arises of placing too much importance on the stand and of neglecting other aspects of trade fair participation, which are at least as important.

It is well to think of the stand as the facility that aids exhibitors to achieve their objectives. It should perfom certain vital functions:

1. Attract the attention of visitors—those whom it is important to reach.
2. Display products to their best advantage.
3. Convey information or an idea, and create an impression.
4. Provide the physical conditions for doing business.

All the work of designing and building the stand should aim to achieve these functions, and to keep within the budget.

*By Bruce Bendow.

THE STAND DESIGNER

Designing a stand that will perform the functions listed above most effectively calls for a professional designer. Even when a simple shell stand provided by the fair organizer is to be used (this is discussed later in this article), professional design of the display can greatly enhance the stand's chances of succeeding. A professional designer is assential for a more ambitious stand, when several exhibitors have to be accommodated and when the stand has to be specially constructed.

A stand design service is often offered by the fair organizers or by the contractor actually building the stand. This can simplify contractual aarangements and supervision of construction. It has the added advantage of making available a designer familiar with local construction and exhibition requirements and with local tastes and practices. However, this designer may not provide individualized services and it will be difficult to give him a full picture of the exhibitor's requirements. The latter difficulty will also when dealing with free-lance designers based abroad.

A designer based in the exhibitor's country can obviously be more easily briefed and can be come more familiar with the products to be displayed. He will probably charge a lower fee than a designer in an industrialized country. A major factor in his selection should be his experience in trade fair work, particularly in the area where the fair is to be held.

DESIGN FACTORS

Many factors should be taken into account when designing a fair stand. The following should be explored before the designer starts to work:

1. The size of the stand.
2. The number of open sides possible. (The stand may be sandwiched between other stands along the wall or

located in an outside corner. It may extend through two aisles, jut into open space, or be an island encircled by space).

3. The stand's location in the hall in relation to traffic flows, stairways, entrances and so on.
4. Number, nature and mixture of individual exhibitors, and the relationships expected between them.
5. The products—number, variety, compatibility, size, weight, appearance and nature, comparative importance and attributes to be featured).
6. Number of representatives and staff expected to be at the stand at any one time.
7. The nature of the fair and the purpose of the stand. A stand at a consumer fair, with consumer publicity its objective, would probably be designed to accommodate large numbers of people. A stand designed for serious business discussions would have to provide one or more places for these to take place, and the degree of privacy required would have to be taken into account. The need to focus on the appearances the operation of the products creates on set of design problems; the need to tell a story about the exhibitors themselves creates another.
8. Whether their will be demonstrations or samplings.
9. The balance desired between group identification and focus on individual exhibitors.
10. The type and amount of drinks and snacks to be served.
11. The need for a central information and reception desk.
12. Whether audio-visual presentations will be made.
13. Whether a shell stand or a specially manufactured stand will be used.
14. Utility requirements: telephones, electricity, water and drainage, compressed air.

These and other requirements should be brought together in a written brief for the designer. A suggested outline for the brief is presented on page 171.

ELEMENTS OF A GOOD STAND DESIGN

Joint participation presents special design problems. It is customary to provide each exhibitor with individual booths of the same size or in modular sizes; a separate group information booth may also be provided. This system is simple and has the virtue of avoiding possible jealousy among exhibitors over the allocation of space. However, the result often destroys most of the impact that can be gained from a fullscale stand, especially if the booths are separated by full walls.

A stronger impression can be achieved with an open plan, which draws visitors through the stand, allocates space to individual products on a functional, flexible basis, and conveys information not only about the individual exhibit but also about the group, industry or country as a whole.

If an open plan is not possible, effort should be made to provide a design service for each exhibitor in order to keep the whole area up to standard and to achieve a common design element that will visually pull together the separate booths.

Some other pointers towards good stand design follow.

Focus attention on the products being displayed. Feature the important ones by such means as positioning and stop lighting. Do not divert attention from the products being offered by showing irrelevant ones (such as handicrafts at a food fair).

Use large picture panels on the walls and legends that can be read at a distance and that convey a clear, simple, factual message. Do not clutter up the walls with odds and ends, such as leaflets and small photographs. Keep the display simple.

Unless the promotion of tourism is the primary objective, do not use tourist posters; the space can be used more effectively to convey information more relevant to the exhibit's commercial objectives.

Do not use background music if it is inappropriate to the business atmosphere that the stand design aims at and interferes with business conversations.

Before trying to create an exotic national atmosphere, consider whether this is really consistent with the commercial image the stand aims at projecting. Are you selling your country, or what your country can offer to buyers?

If an audio-visual presentation is to be used, be sure that is does not interfere with business conversations and that people have a place to watch it without getting in the way of other visitors or blocking product displays.

The operation of models and demonstrations can be highly effective attention-getting devices and can convey a convincing, lasting impression.

Provide sufficient areas for business discussions. These should not necessarily be completely closed off from the rest of the stand. Half panels, perhaps topped by glass, can provide privacy without creating the impression of being cramped. They offer the added advantage of showing that serious business is being carried out.

Provide a place for registering business visitors, which is an important activity at a trade fair.

Provide for convenient storage and distribution of literature, but restrict distribution only to genuinely interested persons. Provide a place for hanging costs and keeping briefcases and other personal effects without cluttering up the stand.

Assign a single person to deal with the designer.

Avoid late changes in the design plans: They can create problems of, and delays in, construction and increase costs.

THE STAND CONTRACTOR

Several contractors, *i.e.*, the prime contractor or the builder, the electrician, the plumber and the decorator, often work together in setting up trade fair stands. However, if this is possible, it is best to use a single contractor able to provide a package of all the required services.

Generally, the fair organizer appoints an official contractor whose services may or may not be mandatory. In most cases, it is probably best to use this contractor because he is likely to be the most familiar with the exhibition grounds and to have close working relations with the organizer and the subcontractors. However, he may be overloaded with work or unable to provide the specialized construction services required.

If a decision is made to use an outside contractor, bids should be requested from three or four possible contractors chosen according to the following considerations:

Price.

Their ability to offer a complete service package, eliminating the need to contract several firms.

Their ability to carry out these services with their own personnel rather than by subcontract, a practice that increases unreliability.

Their financial status. Membership in the local exhibition trade association is usually an assurance of a sound financial position. One should remember that contractors usually require a substantial deposit from the exhibitor several months before a fair.

Their experience in fairs in general and at the specific fair site in particular, ana their standing with the fair organizer.

The agreement with the contractor should be in writing and signed by both parties. It should specify the following:

1. All tasks expected of the contractor, for example, pre-fabrication, construction, supply of furniture and fitting, installation of lighting and utilities. It is advisable to include maintenance during the fair, and dismantling and disposal.
2. No variations in the design or the specifications should be permitted unless agreed in writting; the hourly charges for such work should be included in the contract.
3. The responsibility of the contractor for conforming to all relevant rules and regulations.
4. Dates for completion, dismantling and removal.
5. Fees and terms of payment. Local practice must usually be followed, but it is wise to insist on withholding a third of the fee until all work has been completed, including dismantling.

All the contractor's responsibilities should be clarified. He should be told, for example, which items would be delivered to him, and which he should collect. He should be given the name of forwarding agent to arrange a delivery schedule. The exhibitor should have a representative on hand during construction to ensure that the work is carried out properly.

SHELL SCHEME

Fair organizers usually offer a shell scheme providing for the installation of a standard stand and basic furnishings. Shell schemes differ in the variety and individually achievable. The best ones can be as attractive and as effective as purpose-built stands, provided that they are well decorated.

A shell scheme has several advantages over specially built stands:

It can cost less than half a purpose-built stand.

It can cut construction time, and thus the time and expense required for supervising construction.

CHART 5-1

Outline of the Stand Designer's Brief

1. Name, location and dates of the exhibition.
2. Stand number (enclose floor plan of the hall).
3. Stand space.
4. Number of open sides (enclose organizer's detailed floor plan of the stand).
5. Details of shell scheme, if used.
6. Size and nature of fair audience.
7. Objectives of exhibiting.
8. Product types, quantities, weights, dimensions (enclose product brochures and photographs).
9. Planned demonstrations, tastings, distribution of samples, audio-visual presentations.
10. Products to be featured.
11. Proposed arrangements for receiving and handling visitors.
12. Number of visitors expected.
13. Requirements for administrative offices and meeting rooms.
14. Hospitality plans.
15. Telephone facilities.
16. Number of company representatives and staff on the stand.
17. Need for electrical power connections, water and waste disposal, compressed air, refrigeration.
18. Storage space needed for literature, samples, stationery and so on.
19. Wall displays, themes.
20. Rules and regulations of the fair organizer covering stand construction materials, dimensions, fire and safety regulations, dates for building and tearing down.
21. Names and addresses of official contractors.
22. Budget for design and construction work.
23. Deadlines for design proposals and final drawings.

It simplifies contracting procedures.

It reduces the liaison needed with, and between, designers and builder.

In many cases, therefore, the shell scheme may provide the best solution, although the suitability of a particular scheme for a joint stand should be studied with designer before a decision is made.

PREFABRICATION

To save on construction costs and reduce foreign exchange outlays, some exhibitors have their stands prefabricated in their own country and shipped to the fair site. It simplifies the designer's supervisory tasks. However, its many disadvantages usually outweigh its advantages. including high transport costs, the unavailability of suitable materials in the home country and the fabricator's possible lack of familiarity with the conditions and the labour situation at the site.

An often better solution is the use of readymade modular systems. These are particularly attractive to organizations that enter a substantial number of exhibitions because they are reusable; the better systems are highly flexible; and they are compact and economical to transport. But unless the system is to be frequently used, it will cost far more than a purpose-built stand. Some modular systems, however, can be rented for a single fair, and this possibility should be considered. With a good system and a designer familiar with it, a modern, attractive and efficient stand can be built at reasonable cost. Some systems form the basis of fair organizers' shell schemes, which adds to the advantages of using them.

THE SUPPLY LIST

The essence of supply planning is to tabulate the requirements of different departments or organizations and to phase them over the period of use or consumption.

Such a tabulation should separate capital equipment from supplies that are used or consumed on a continuing basis.

Thus the tabulation, or supply list, could be divided into the following broad categories of items:

1. Machinery, machine tools, power units of all kinds, generators and similar equipment, major hospital equipment, and any other items that are classified as capital equipment.
2. Motor transport of all kinds.
3. Spare parts for 1 and 2 above.
4. Bulk food grains, edible oils and fats, and other bulk foodstuffs.
5. Raw materials, chemical fertilizers, semiprocessed materials and inputs for manufacturing.
6. Departmental expendable supplies. (In this broad category, two or more departments may request similar or broadlv similar items to serve different purposes. For example, the department of works and the department of sanitation may call for various types of pipe. In all such cases an attempt should be made to reconcile variations in specifications so as to arrive at a degree of rationalization of supplies.)
7. Office equipment and furniture.
8. Common user items such as janitorial supplies, stationary and office supplies, and the like.

This list is not intended to be complete. Individual countries may identify other categories that should be included. The important point is to ensure that the list is as comprehensive as possible.

The preparation of a basic supply list presupposes the availability of certain information. First of all, specifications

CHART

Example: Format for a Basic Supply List

Item No.	*Item description*	*Unit*	*Unit cost*	*Quantity*	*Total cost*	*Local availability*	*Quantity to be imported*	*Delivery time scale*
21	Blankets, 140×200 cm all wool, with no more than 20 per cent reprocessed wool. Weight 1.25 kg. Packed in bales of 25 blankets in steel strapped, waterproof plastic pockets.	each	$ 3.00	100,000	300,000	23,000	77,000	Single shipment to arrive by 30.6.82.
22	Cisterns, water storage, capacity 500 litres. To BS No. XX XXX X	each	$ 50.00	1,000	50,000	1,000	Nil	To be called forward as and when required in minimum lots of 10 units on 30 days' notice.

23 Hose high pressure, 50mm ϕ. per Dunlop Cat. 14501, item ZPR444.	meter	$ 2.50	1,500	3,750	Nil	1,500	In two lots of 750 meters (75 reels) to arrive 30.7.82. and 31.10.82.

will have to be developed, if they do not already exist. Up-to-date costs of the items on the list are also required. Where technical equipment is concerned, the user departments will probably have access to manufactures' catalogues, sales literature or price lists and will be in a position to provide price data. Other items may be costed on the basis of previous purehases, plus a standard contingency figure for inflation or exchange rate adjustments. At this costing stage, it is usual to ignore discounts that may be applied to final purchases. (*See example of a list on pages 174-175*).

Once the list has been compiled, the next step is to consider which of the items will be available from local resources. This will be particularly important in certain categories, such as bulk grains and other foodstuffs, and will require that reliable methods for estimating local availability be developed. However the list may also be useful in assessing what might be produced locally, even if it is not already being produced.

The assessment of local resources is an aspect of materials management that is frequently neglected. It is sometimes claimed that a locally produced item is not of an acceptable quality or finish. The local producer is thereby shut out of the government supply processes and is seldom given the encouragement to improve quality and increase production.

Other uses: In addition to the purposes already indicated, a basic supply list provides data for subsequent budgetary control, aimed at keeping expenditure within prescribed limits, and conversely helps to avoid a year-end scramble to spend funds that have not been used within a given time limit and that might otherwise revert to the general budget of the government.

Finally, master supply lists become the input for supply planning. The supply plan can be expanded to incorporate procurement data, such as delivery time shcedules, thereby enabling the procurement departments to develop their own plans and materials managers to chart progress in fulfilling their materials requirements.

V

Stand Management and Follow-up

The success of trade fair participation depends to a great extent on how the stand manager performs his duties before, during and after the show. Although the exhibitors' active cooperation is necessary when planning and preparing for a joint stand, the organizing body holds a large part of the responsibility during this stage. The responsibility for success shifts more squarely to the exhibitor's reprsentatives when the fair starts. However, even then, the stand manager retains a number of duties, and the success of the venture will depend to an important extent on how well he performs them.

STAFF SUPERVISION

If the organizer of the joint participation has hired temporary staff, such as receptionists or interpreters, the stand manager will usually have the job of supervising them. They should be thoroughly briefed on their duties, and on the exhibitors, their products and their objectives, before the fair opens.

A duty schedule should be established, with allowance for rest breaks, and the stand manager should see to it that it is followed.

Each exhibitor should be encouraged to keep his display area tidy, but temporary staff should be gived the responsibility for this as will. Empty coffee cups or glasses, full ashtrays and printed matter left lying around will create a poor impression. At a busy trade fair, tidying up should be an almost continuous process.

MANNING THE STAND

The exhibitors should elect a leader from among themselves before the fair opens and either be or the stand manager should always be present on the stand. At peak periods both should be present, as should all temporary staff and exhibitors' personnel.

Correct behaviour of everyone on the stand is important. Lapses, such as inattention to visitors or habitual absence from the stand, can result in best business.

The stand manager may find himself in a difficult position because he has no authority over the company representatives at the fair However, the latter's inadequate performance can spoil the outcome not only for their companies but also for the group. The manager's only recourse is to point out the short-comings diplomatically and to suggest bow correcting them would rebound to the company's gain. Lapses should be minimized by advanced briefings and even by training courses on how to represent a company at a trade fair.

The manager should try to impose the rule requiring a representative planning to be absent from the stand to infrom the manager or receptionist when he expects to return, so that appointments with visitors can be made in his absence.

The list of pointers on manning a trade fair on page 180 could be distributedt o company mangers sending representatives to trade fairs, or to the representives themselves in their briefing kits.

HANDLING VISITORS

One of the stand manager's key functions, and that of any receptionist assisting him. is to inentify risitors' interests and to introduce visitors to exhibitors who may be able to do business with them.

The techniques for handling visitors depend partly on the stand's layout. When there is a single entrance with a reception desk, it is fairly easy to ask visitors to come up to the products they are interested in. Must stands however an open and are likely to attract visitors from various entrance points. If these visitors seem interested, they should be approached before they wander of the stand. The representative whose products the visitors are looking at should usually make the apporach. However, he is unable to attend to them, the stand manager should intervene.

Approaching visitors on a stand is an art in itself. The key is to observe a visitor long enough to get an idea of the products or displays of apparent interest to him to greet him, in a friendly manner and, finally, to ask him a leading question, such as "Are you familiar with our country's canned fruit products?" or to make a remark such as "This is just one of about a hundred models our industry produces".

The typical opening remark "Can I help you?" is to be avoided; all too often it prompts the reply "No", which can effectively stop all further conversation.

It is important to establish as soon as possible the visitor's identity, how important he is to the exhibitors' objectives, and what precisely he wants to know or whom he wishes to meet. When a visitor is established as "not important" in this sense, he should be dealt with politely but briefly, allowing stand personnel time to concentrate on "important" visitors.

A record should be kept of all significant visitors to the stand. Many fairs provide visitors with cards for this purpose which can simply be inserted in a device to print information including the visitor's name, that of his firm, his title and the trade or industrial sector to which his firm belongs. If such devices are available from the fair organizer, they should be obtained and used. Otherwise forms should be provided for visitors to fill out or for the receptionist and stand manager to use when obtaining information. This information is necessary for follow-up after the fair, for evaluating the effectiveness of the participation and making up lists for future fairs.

If the repsentative whom the visitor should see is busy, the latter should not be left simply standing around. He should be offered a seat and refreshment if it is available, and given

CHART 5-J

Manning a Trade Fair Stand

1. Company respersentatives should be knowledge about the company and its products, empowered to conduct business negotiations and clear on its objectives in exhibiting.
2. Never ignore a visitor to a your stand.
3. Approach visitors who seem interested in your display, do not wait for them to approach you.
4. Look interested. Do not sit about chatting with your collegues. Do not position yourself so as to hide your products or to block access to them.
5. Start the conversation with a positive remark about your product or a question that will generate discussion.
6. identify as quickly as possible the visitor's business and specific interest and his importance as a prospect. Always keep your objectives in mind.
7. Answer all questions as forthrightly and as factually as possible.
8. Remember to sell your company as well as your products, and relate your remarks to the visitor's interests.
9. Use the conversation to elicit information about the market and reactions to your products.
10. Carry negotations as far forward as you are empowered to, if you are convinced the visitor represents a solid prospect.
11. Use inquiry forms and supplementary notes to record details about the visitor's company, his interests and follow-up action to be taken.
12. Allow time after the fair closes to continue important discussions.
13. Provide promised information as soon as possible.
14. Observe fair hours, and never leave your exhibit unattended.
15. Use slack periods to make contacts at other stands, provided your own is manned.

CHART 5-K

Record of Contact

Event————

Date————

Title————

Visitor's name————

Company's name————

Address————————

Telephone-——————————Telex——————Cable————————

Product line——————

Type of business —Importer —Distributor —Wholesaler

Retailer —Agent —Manufacturer Other————

Agencies held————

Regions covered————

Sales staff———— Year establish————

Products interested in————

Nature of interest————

Action taken———

Follow-up required————

Order's placed————

Delivery required by————

Comments————

Seen by————————————

---

some material to read while waiting. If he does not wish to wait, an attempt should be made to fix an appointment for him.

Visitors can be important not only as sales prospects but also as sources of information about the market. Their comments about the products on display can also be valuable, and these should be elicited by the stand manager as well as by the company representatives, and incorporated in a report on the fair.

Above all, visitors should not be ignored.

STAND MEETINGS

At the end of each day, the stand manager should lead a meeting of all representatives, in order to air any problems, exchange information, reveal any developments that provide a basis for publicity and review progress to date.

FOLLOW-UP

The making of contacts at trade fairs is often only the start of a process that may lead to sales or to the appointment of an agent or importer. Unless these contacts are followed up, all the effort that went into exhibiting may end up entirely fruitless.

The foundation for follow-up is the basic information recorded about each visitor, the discussion that took place, the nature of his interest and the action to be taken. Special forms should be prepared for this purpose and a supply given to each exhibitor, who should be urged to use them conscientiously. A model of a record of inquiry form is given on page 181.

In some cases, when the group organizer has some responsibility for follow-up, forms should be made up with carbon copies for the stand manager. Exhibitors are often reluctant to provide such information; in any event, in most joint participations of the private sector, any follow-up must be carried out by the exhibiting firms themselves.

Speed is important. Any promises of information should be attended to as soon as possible. If the representative does not have the information, he should consider telexing his home office for it, rather than wait until he returns to his country.

After the fair, it is good practice to send a letter to all visitors to the stand, thanking them for their visit and offering to provide any further information required. This could be done by the group organizer.

CLOSING UP

When the fair closes, the stand manager must see to the following matters before he returns home:

He should obtain from the exhibitors instructions about disposal of the exhibits and a complete inventory of items to be returned to the company.

He must supervise the removal, packing and dispatch of the exhibits and the dismantling and disposal of the stand.

He should settle involvces and pay the temporary staff.

He should prepare and issue a press release for the media in the market on the positive results of the participation.

VI

Operating a Business Information Centre at an International Fair

A business information centre set up at an international trade fair can provide a useful service to foreign and local businessmen at the show. An international trade fair offers many

*Farid Nawas is a trade promotion adviser and project coordinator in ITC's technical cooperation project with the Government of Sudan. Dionisia Capaya is a UN Volunteer on trade documentation working with this project.

possibilities for contracting new business partners, getting information on the market and learning of potential areas for investment. But businessmen visiting a fair usually have only a limited amount of time to spend on the fairgrounds and, in the case of foreign businessmen, in the country hosting the show. Firms exhibiting at these events are also often working on a tight schedule, with little free time to leave their stands and explore new business leads. A business information centre set up in a central location at an international fair can help businessmen make the most of the opportunities that such an event offers. It can serve as a useful contact point as well as a source of information on such subjects as trade regulations, customs tariffs, export and import statistics, and investment laws.

The Trade Information Service of Sudan's Ministry of Cooperation, Commerce and Supply has organized a business information centre at several international fairs held in Khartoum. The techniques employed in Sudan to operate this service might be applicable in other developing countries wishing to stimulate contacts between their local business community and traders abroad.

THE SERVICES PROVIDED

The information centre organized by Sudan's Trade Information Service offers assistance in the following areas:

1. Trade contacts: Putting foreign and Sudanese businessmen in touch with each other is an important function of Sudan's business information centre. Names and addresses of Sudanese exporters, importers, agents, distributors and industrialists are given to inquirers from other countries, while Sudanese traders receive details on comparable business contacts in foreign markets. Such contacts can lead to new sales, on both the import and export sides, as well as to increased foreign investment in Sudan.

2. Foreign trade statistics: Foreign businessmen are provided with details on Sudan's imports and exports. Sudanese businessmen receive data on foreign markets of interest for their export products.

3. Tariffs and foreign trade regulations. Business visitors from other countries are informed of Sudan's customs tariffs for specific items and of its foreign trade regulations. Such information is also provided to Sudanese businessmen when it is available on foreign markets.

4. Price data: Sudanese exporters are given details on the international market prices of commodities of interest to them.

5. Investment opportunities: Possibilities for investing in the country are outlined to visiting foreign businessmen, in the light of the Government's Encouragement of Investment Act of 1980.

6. Meetings with Sudanese officials: Staff at the business information centre help arrange appointments for foreign businessmen and visiting officials with government offices in Sudan concerned with economic and commercial questions, including foreign investment.

PREPARATIONS REQUIRED

Three main types of arrangements are needed for organizing a business information stand at an international fair: physical preparations for the stand itself, publicity to attract business visitors and the training of stand staff.

The stand should be centrally situated at the fair to be of maximum benefit of businessmen. The cooperation of the fair authorities is necessary so that the best arrangements can be worked out for the stand's location. Their assistance is also required for obtaining furniture and other stand fittings, and facilities such as a telephone link-up. Sudan's Trade Information Service works closely with the Sudan Exhibitions and

Fairs Corporation (Sudanexpo), which makes a stand available free of charge for this purpose, along with certain basic facilities.

Publicity is another important element for a successful business information centre. The services offered on the stand need to be publicized both before and during the show so that businessmen use them to the fullest extent. Sudan's Trade Information Service producers a brochure in Arabic and English well before the exhibition opens that announces the stand's activities. The brochure is sent to the Chamber of Commerce, the Exporters' Association, government departments, state trading organizations and business associations in the country. Copies are also distributed to embassies in Khartoum. Shortly before the show opens supplies of the leaflet are delivered to all hotels for distribution to their guests coming for the fair. Finally, during the fair, brochures are hand-delivered to each stand. Posters are also placed in strategic locations at the exhibition to draw visitors to the stand.

Stand staff should be well briefed before the fair on how to receive business visitors and take the necessary action to follow. up their inquiries. They should receive detailed training in supplying the specific types of information that may be requested as well as in making contacts with appropriate business and government offices in the country for foreign businessmen.

STAND OPERATIONS AND EVALUATION

A systematic means saould be used for recording all business inquiries received on the stand during the fair. The Trade Information Serviee in Sudan has developed a standard form for all requests received during the event. It is distributed with the brochures before the fair and is also available on the stand. The form has space for noting the inquirer's position, the name and address of his firm, the type of business it is engaged in and the information the businessman is seeking (for instance

CHART 5·L

Business Information Centre
International Fair of Khartoum
Inquiry Porm

Inquirer:
Name ———————————————————

Title ———————————————————

Name of firm ———————————————————

Address ———————————————————

Telephone ————————Telex————————Cable————————

Type of Business:

Manufacturer — Agent/distributor

Importer — Other (specify)

Exporter

Type of Service requested:

Business contacts (specify)————————

Foreign trade regulations (specify)————————

Statistical data (specify)————————

Others (specify)————————

———————————————————

Follow-up action:————————

———————————————————

Inquiry recorded by ———————— Date ————————

names of contacts, details on foreign trade regulations, statistical data on other). Staff check that a visitor has correctly filled in the form when he comes to the stand. Afterwards they record follow-up action on the form. (*See form above*).

A final report should be drawn up summarizing the activities of the business information centre at the fair, and an evaluation should be made of the exercise so that any necessary changes can be made in the future. In Sudan the business inquiry forms serve as the basis for this report. The final report covers the number of visitors and their countries of origin, the type of information requested, follow-up action taken, business results achieved and recommendations for future participation. The report is submitted to the Ministry so that the authorities are informed of the effectiveness of the operation.

EXAMPLES

Sudan's Trade Information Service has been organizing business information centres for the past several years at international trade fairs held in Khartoum, as part of the technical cooperation activities that the Government is carrying out with ITC, financed by the Government of Norway, Stands operated at two of these events illustrate how a business information centre operates.

The most recent stand was organized at the Seventh International Fair in Khartoum early this year. Three staff from the Trade information Service and from Sudanexpo manned the centre during the 17 days of the exhibition. The types of information available on the stand included customs tariffs and trade regulations of Sudan; lists of exporters, importers and manufacturers in the country and abroad; international commodity price data: background on Sudan's investment laws; and brochures describing Ministry services.

Of the 132 business inquiries received at the stand, about half were from Sudanese exporters and importers and the rest from foreign visitors. Around four-fifths of the requests from Sudanese firms were for names of foreign suppliers of various products. The remainder of the Sudanese businessmen asked for names of potential importers abroad for their export goods.

Nearly 90% of the foreign visitors were interested in making contacts with Sudanese importers. Others asked for details on specific Sudanese export products, and several of the visiting businessmen sought information on investment opportunities. In a number of cases the stand staff made arrangements for meetings between businessmen and government officials in Khartoum.

On the basis of the services provided, particularly the contacts set up, several business transactions were completed. For instance, business deals were initiated between visiting businessmen and Sudanese buyers and agents of paper and paper products, agricultural and industrial machinery and equipment, building materials, furniture and appliances, chemicals and chemical products, transport equipment, textiles and garments, foodstuffs and various miscellaneous items. It was acknowledged by some of the visitors that their business deals with the Sudanese were concluded primarily through the assistance of the business information cenrre.

Another example is the business information centre organized jointly by Sudan's Trade Information Service, Sudanexpo and the UN Economic Commission for Africa (ECA) for the Third All-Africa Trade Fair in Khartoum in 1980. During that fair, the stand received 75 inquiries from visitors from nine African, three Asian and five European countries. Requests covered a variety of questions. As a result of the contacts arranged by the centre, business agreements were concluded between Sudanese firms and visitors from several countries in the region, including Ghana, Kenya, United Republic of Tanzania. Morocco and Egypt.

COSTS

The cost of operating the business centre, in addition to staff costs, has run to US $ 1,000 at the most each time. This excludes rental for the stand space, which is provided free of charge by Sudanexpo. The main cost items are printing and translating the brochure and printing the inquiry form,

Miscellaneous expenses include moving the furniture from the offices of the Trade Information Service to the fairgrounds for use during the show.

TRADE PROMOTION TOOL

In summary, a business information centre can be a useful trade promotion technique. Running such a service is a logical activity for a trade information service in a developing country that is seeking effective ways to disseminate the trade information at its disposal to key target audiences. If organized the right way, it can achieve concrete results through increased contacts and subsequently expanded trade transactions.

VII

How to Attract Visitors to Your Stand*

By failing to promote trade show participation, exhibitors miss making the contacts that can mean the difference between failure and success. Exhibitors at trade fairs make one of their most common and serious mistakes by failing actively to attract visitors to their stand. At a good trade fair, they can be reasonably sure of the presence of a large number of the businessmen of interest to them but they can by no means be certain that these persons will visit their stands. By failing actively to promote themselves, exhibitors miss making the contacts that can mean the difference between failure and success. Therefore, plans for entering a trade fair cannot be considered complete unless they include a programme for visitor promotion.

Promotional actively has a value beyond that of attracting visitors. It can intensify the impact of the exhibit on these visitors, make this impact last beyond the period of the fair itself, and generate inquiries even from businessmen who may not have visited the fair.

*By Bruçe Bendow.

The individual participating companies must contribute to the promotional effort for the joint stand. Although it will be wise for them to do all they can on their own behalf, the primary responsibility belongs to the organizer of the joint participation. Many exhibitors lack the means of the knowledge to carry out effective promotion on their own, and even if they had this ability, their individual efforts would never produce the impact of a campaign that promoted the group as a whole.

To be fully effective, a promotinal campaign requires expertise in publicity and knowledge of the ma-ket, which the staffs of chambers of commerce or trade associations may not possess. Ideally, the services of a public relations agency should be used, and this is the practice of some government agencies that enter trade fairs. A less costly alternative would be to use a free-lance publicity consultant, who might be identified through professional associations. If even this is too costly, the organizer of t! e joint participation should carry out the programme itself, buying such services as graphic design and translation.

The basic objective of a visitor promotion campaign is twofold:

1. Informing the target audience that the group will be exhibiting at the fair.
2. Motivating these persons to visit the stand.

The techniques for achieving these objectives include:

Target identification.

Preparation of promotional literature.

Direct contact through the mail.

Personal contact by telephone or by visits.

Press releases and contacts with the press.

Advertising.

Receptions.

AUDIENCE IDENTIFICATION

Identifying by name the members of the target audience is the foundation of a successful promotional effort. These are the persons wnose visit to the stand is important to achieving the exhibit's commercial objectives. They include direct business prospects or prospective representatives, and those who influence the development of trade. Depending on the exhibit's objectives and particular circumstances, the target audience could include the following:

Buyers at various levels of the trade.

Users of the products.

Agents, importers, distributors, wholesalers and retailers.

Persons who specify products to be purchased, such as interior designers, architects, engineers and caterers.

Prospective investors and licensers.

Repesentatives of chambers of commerce, trade and professional associations.

Travel agents and tour operators.

Consumers most likely to be interested in the products shown.

Journalists.

Compiling this list of names is time consuming. A good list for a specialized fair should include at least 6,000 names; the number for a general fair may be as many as 20,000. A variety of sources should be used, including:

Sales records of exhibitors in the group who already have contacts in the market.

Membership lists of chambers of commerce and trade associations in the market countries.

Commercial attaches posted in the market.

The government's trade information service.

Representatives of exhibitors in the market.

Trade directories.

Companies publishing mailing lists.

The previous fair's catalogue.

Advertisements in trade and industrial magazines.

PRINTED MATTER FOR THE FAIR

Printed matter should be prepared both for the joint stand as a whole and for each exhibitor. It has vital roles to perform before, during and after the fair.

The basic piece is a stand brochure, which should be malied before the fair, included in press kits and handed out to visitors during the fair. It informs prospective visitors and journalists of what is to be seen at the stand, stimulates their interest in seeing it, and serves as a reference and a reminder after the fair.

The cover should feature the name of both the exhibiting group and the fair. The stand number should be prominent. The cover should also contain the fair dates as well as location, although the latter would not be necessary for a major fair.

The heart of the brochure should be a profile of each exhibitor, consisting of a description of the company and the specific products it is exhibiting, its specific purpose in exhibiting and the name of its representative at the stand. The company's name, postal address, telex, cable and telephone numbers should be given.

Company profiles should be arranged alphabetically. They should be preceded by a fairly brief but factual note about the exhibiting group and the industry it represents. Brief, relevant information about the country's industrial and economic progress and its trade with the market or markets served by the fair may also be in order. A floor plan of the fair or the hall, clearly indicating the location of the stand, should also be included.

The most practical size for such a brochure is about 99 mm ×210 mm, which fits into standard business mailing envelopes and is convenient for visitors to slip into their pockets.

Because it plays an important role in creating an impression of the stand in advance, the brochure should be of high quality. It should be well printed on good paper, although it need not be lavish. It should be designed by a professional graphic designer.

The text of the stand brochure, and if possible of all other printed matter distributed before and during the fair, should be in the language of the markets from which the fair draws most of its visitors. As poor translations could lessen credibility, the texts should be translated, if possible, in these markets; translations done in the home country should be checked abroad.

Summaries in the appropriate language should be prepared for individual exhibitor's material when it is impractical to produce complete, translated versions.

Each exhibitor should have its own printed material, including leaflets about the company, detailed product information sheets, and, if appropriate, price lists. The quality of printed matter produced by companies tends to vary widely. Exhibitors should be shown examples of good company sales literature when they are briefed about the fair and they should be encouraged to meet the standards set. It may be possible for the chamber of commerce or trade association to assist exhibitors in producing sales literature as part of its package of services.

The process of producing, translating, clearing and printing advertising material is often lengthy, and printers frequently fail to meet deadlines. Therefore, it is wise to allow the process a generous schedule and to allocate a reasonable length of time between the printer's deadline for delivery and the date the material is actually needed.

CHART 5-M

Sources for a Visitor List

1. Sales records of exhibitors in the group who already have contacts in the market.
2. Membership lists of chambers of commerce and trade associations in the market countries.
3. Commercial attaches posted in the market.
4. The government's trade information service.
5. Representatives of exhibitors in the market.
6. Trade directories.
7. Companies publishing mailing lists.
8. The previous fair's calalogue.
9. Advertisements in trade and industrial magazines.

The stand brochure, and perhaps some of the company sales literature, should be distributed before the fair, by mail, and during the fair as well. As printed material is expensive, it should not be wasted. Certainly the supply should be controlled to last the duration of the fair. It is often best to place printed materials inside the stand to avoid their being snatched by passers-by with no real interest. The more elaborate and costly publications should be given out on request to persons belonging to the target audience.

MAILING

Mailing materials in advance to a selected target audience is one of the most effective ways of assuring the visit to the stand of a reasonable promotion of this audience. The materials may include letters (personalized if at all possible), the stand brochure and other printed matter, invitations to receptions or other special events (such as a demonstration or a contest), and free entry tickets to the fair, which can often be procured from the fair organizer along with other promotional material.

The mailing list should be divided into at least two or three groups, rated by how important their visit would be to achieving the exhibitors' objectives. Ideally, two or three mailings should be made, at least to the group with the highest priority. They should be scheduled long enough before the fair to build up interest with each mailing, of which the last should be close enough to the fair—about two weeks before—so that it will not be forgotten. One should obviously take the speed of mail service into account when drawing up a schedule. The first mailing may go to all the persons on the mailing list, and the second, containing the reception invitation, only to the group with the highest priority.

Clearly, the letters should be in the language of the addressees, they should be carefully translated and checked.

The individual exhibitors should be encouraged to mail their own materials to their business contacts. It is common practice to provide them with fair stickers for all their correspondence. These are often distributed by the fair organizers or are specially prepared to promote a particular stand ("Visit us on Stand 27 at the Nuremberg Toy Fair").

Companies entering foreign trade fairs on their own may find it difficult to carry out a mailing programme as ambitious as that described above, but they should be encouraged to do as much as they can.

PERSONAL CONTACTS

For a fairly ambitious joint fair participation, when the help of a public relaions agency or other source of assistance is available, the mailing programme should be backed up by a programme of personal contacts. These would consist of telephone calls or even of personal visits to as many persons as possible in the highest priority groups.

A programme of personal contacts to invite visitors of the stand should be carried out at least during the fair itself. Many of those exhibiting at other stands in specialized fairs may be prospective customers or representatives, and exhibitors should be urged to call on them to invite them to the stand. Such prospects can often be identified through the fair catalogue. Advantage should be taken of slack periods, particularly in the early days of the fair, to telephone importers and agents in the area, to invite them to visit the stand.

PRESS RELATIONS

Press coverage in trade and industrial journals. and in the less specialized press, can attract worthwhile visitors to the stand and increase the benefits of participating by publicizing the exhibitors and their products after the fair ends. Press coverage is particularly valuable because it can attract important visitors who may not have been included in the mailing list.

Placing a press publicity programme in the hands of a professional publicist or public relations agency greatly enhances its chances of success. If this is not feasible, the organizer of a joint participation should carry out some press relations activities itself.

A full-fledged publicity programme for a trade fair stand includes the following elements: a series of press releases, individual placement of feature articles, press conferences and other special events for the press.

The first step is to list the media agencies most likely to report on the show. The organizers of major fairs often mount their own publicity campaigns and announce the journals in which they advertise. Many or all of these journals may be included in the media list for publicizing a stand. Other sources of names of suitable publications are press directories and business contacts in the market who are likely to read the important specialized journals in their field.

Ideally, a series to press releases should be issued over a period of several months before the fair. This should start with a fairly general press release about the stand, including the types of products to be shown, background information about the industry and the main objectives in exhibiting. Subsequent releases should be more specific, featuring novelties, products of particular interest, or individual exhibitors that have already achieved some success on the market or that are important in their own country.

All press releases should prominently mention the name of the trade fair and the stand number, and the name of the person to contact for more information. High-quality, black-and-white glossy photographs of products to be exhibited should be sent with the releases. Even if press releases do not find their way into print, they serve to interest journalists in visiting the stand and in writing about it during or after the fair.

Press kits should be prepared for distribution at press conferences, to reporters visiting the stand and at the fair's press room. The kit should contain all the printed material and press releases that have been disseminated, and additional back ground on the exhibitor's country, particularly on its economic, trade and industrial progress.

The fair organizer will probably conduct its own publicity programme, and the project coordinator and stand manager should find out about it and try to participate in it, for instance by supplying the organizer's news bulletin with stories about deals made during the fair. The stand manager should also meet journalists visiting the stand. Every effort should be made to determine their special interests, to introduce them to appropriate exhibitors and to supply them with the information they need.

Although it would probably be difficult for a group with comparatively modest stand to attract many journalists to a press conference, key members of the press could be invited to a reception along with important business contacts.

At the end of the fair, significant deals made by exhibitors should be the subject of a final press release.

ADVERTISING

Advertising in specialized journals is another way of attracting visitors' attention. However, unless good-size ads are run in a series over a period, they are not likely to be very effective. Consideration may be given to placing full-page advertisements in the special trade fair issue of the most important journals, if the exhibitors agree to put up the money.

An advertisement placed in the fair catalogue is probably a better investment, because serious business visitors to a fair usually study the catalogue in advance and keep it as a reference afterwards.

Whether or not an advertisement is placed in the catalogue, it is important to supply the organizers with complete information in good time for the catalogue listings.

Posters and other means of advertising within the fair premises can also be worthwhile.

RECEPTION

A special reception early during the fair is a good way of initiating contacts with key persons. It could be held on the stand after regular fair hours, or at another place, such as a nearly hotel. It should be possible to arrange for your country's ambassador, the head of the chamber of commerce or trade association, or some other important person to serve as host and principal speaker. The exhibitors should be introduced and the reasons for exhibiting explained. But formal talks should be kept short, and ample time should be allowed for informal conversations. Identification tags should be issued to both the guests and the stand representatives.

6

Developing Your Own Case Materials

CLAUDE CELLICH*

Business schools in developing countries can enhance their teaching programmes by preparing their own case studies in international marketing. An increasing number of business schools in developing countries are using special eductional tools such as business games and case studies to enhance the effectiveness of both their regular degree courses and their executive development programmes. The application of such methods is particularly useful for training in trade promtion as they help to illustrate the realities of the international business world in the confines of the university classroom. Despite this move towards "participative" teaching techniques, which actively involve the students in the training process, most business schools in developing countries still use training materials prepared in industrialized countries, which are often not suited to the local export marketing context. This applies in particular to case studies –a tool that is considered to be one of the most effective for teaching business, especially certain export marketing and management subjects.

*Claude Cellich is chief of ITC's Training Section.

The lack of tailormade case studies can be overcome by preparing them locally. Most marketing professors in developing countries already have the expertise required to create their own export cases for classroom use. They also often have a substantial amount of potential case material at their fingertips, which, though additional research and adaptation, could successfully be developed for teaching purposes. By following the steps outlined below, they should be able to upgrade their courses in international marketing and management and thereby raise the level of trade promotion skill in their countries.

OBTAINING THE RAW MATERIALS

A case study used in export courses consists basically of a written description of a marketing or management problem faced by an export company within a given commercial and economic context. The solution to the problem is left open, as it is the subject of the classroom exercise for the students in the course.

Although an export case history can be developed from an imaginary example, case are usually more usually more useful and effective as teaching tools if they are based on the actual experiences of export firms. For this reason an instructor developing case material for his courses should base this work on actual export operations of firms in his country.

Each year business schools generate a wealth of written material that can be used as a foundation for developing marketing cases, in the form of doctoral dissertations, master's degree theses term papers and faculty research reports. Some of this research work usually relates to real business situations faced by firms at home or abroad. (Instructors could also make an effort to focus more research in this direction to add to case source material.) Papers produced within education programme for persons already in business, such as executive development seminars and in-company staff training, may be particularly appropriate as raw materials for case studies because they often deal with the actual export marketing and management problems of existing enterprises.

Publications in a business school's library may provide other sources of export case material. Specialized business magazines and economic newspapers frequently carry articles on company programmes and activities. The annual reports of major firms in the country, periodicals of national export promotion organizations and publications of the local chamber of commerce may also contain information that could serve as the nucleus for cases.

From the collection of materials at hand, a business instructor can identify those most suitable to develop into teaching cases through further research and adaptation. Cases should be selected that deal with export experiences typial of the local business community, that concern representative products exported from the country or that relate to major export markets.

DEVELOPING THE CASE

When the core material for the case has been selected, the next step is to do further research on each example to provide full background information on the export situation concerned. It is also sometimes necessary to adapt the material to the particular needs of the course participants.

Case outline: At this point it is useful to develop a basic outline for the case to assure that the final write-up is properly structured for teaching purposes. The outline will also show the instructor where the information gaps lie and therefore where research should be focused.

Such an outline could cover the following key points:

1. A brief introduction of the company: its product line, size, location, management structure, export operations, target markets.

2. The context within which the company operates at home and abroad: its position in the market, major competitors, export and import rules and regulations affecting its foreign trade operations, general trends in trade of the product.
3. The export marketing or export management problems facing the company: the background for those problems and the specific difficulties to be overcome.
4. The alternative courses of action being considered by the company's management to solve these problems. (This step might be eliminated to give students an opportunity for creative thinking.)

Supplementing the material through interviews: The process of developing the raw material into a classroom case can be undertaken by the instructor alone or by a team under his supervision including several graduate students. The most important source for supplementing the basic materials is interviews with the local export companies dealt with in the cases. Getting information directly from them adds to the authenticity of the cases (although the cases will not be issued with the company's name).

The manner of approaching a firm for interviews is important, as some of the details sought may be considered confidential, An introductory letter should be sent to the firm informing its officials of the purpose of the proposed visit, including how the case study will fit into the business school's overall programme. In some circumstances a personal introduction of the research team by a well known teacher from the school or another business executive might be advisable.

When the firm has agreed to receive the instructor and his assistants, the team should undertake background desk reserach on the compony and on its industry branch so that company officials' time is not wasted during interviews. It is advisable for the team to prepare and test the questions that they plan to raise during the interviews. The firm's organizational structure should also be studied in identify key persons to be contacted.

During the first meeting with the firm, the instructor and his team should carefully explain what a case study is and how it is going to be used, and, if possible, show an example of one that has already been prepared. The team should get permission from the appropriate officials during the first meeting to publish a case based on the information collected in the company. A with key decisionmarkers in the firm to get the required details.

Library sources: In addition to company interviews the case material can be supplemented through library sources. Trade statistics, market reports, product surveys and business reviews may provide data that can help to refine the material into an effective, up-to-date teaching device, For instance, through desk research, current trade statistics and tariff rates can be added to the text to make it applicable to the current international marketing situation.

Adaptation: The case material prepared should be adapted as necessary for the target group of students. If the case is to be used in an executive development programme for a particular industry branch, for example, the product in the case could be changed accordingly and the necessary adjustments made in the text. Or if a case is needed to illustrate a particular aspect of marketing, such as product design or packaging, elements of several basic might be combined to give the required export problem situation.

Final draft: When all of the field and desk research has been completed, the case text should be drafted in a simple. direct style. following the basic outline established at the beginning. The original (real) export situation should be adhered to as closely as possible to maintain the originality and outhenticity of the case (and thereby its usefulness as a teaching tool). However the characters in the case, such as the export manager and the overseas buyer, could be elaborated upon to make the case interesting. For instance, dialogue between the principal persons could be added to enliven the text.

In the final drafting all identifiable references to the real firm should be removed, such as the names of the company, its product brand and its officials. Secondary facts that are not necessary as background for the export situation described should also be eliminated. The temptation should be avoided to write lengthy cases covering many different aspects of marketing, of unnecessary details on the business environment. Otherwise the reader may become confused, thereby reducing the learning impact.

Finally, a disclaimer should be added to the case so that the business school will not be held responsible later on for recommending any of the techniques or actions described in the case. (Example: "This case was prepared with the intention of providing a basis for class discussion rather than illustrating either effective or ineffective management of a business situation.")

Company approval: The final draft of the case should be shown to the company supplying the information, and the responsible official there should give his written agreement for the case to to published by the school.

ACCOMPANYING TEACHING AIDS

Developing the actual case is only half of the job. Preparing material to guide the instructor in using the case for classroom purposes is also part of the case development exercise. (The person preparing the case may not necessarily be the one who will present it in a course.)

The instructor's guide gives a summary of the main features of the case that are useful for the teacher's planning. For instance, the marketing subjects covered in the case must be identified (such as product planning, designing a market strategy, participating in a trade fair, selecting an agent or other). The educational objective of the case should also be clearly stated in the guide (for example, to increase students' knowledge of the planning requirements for trade fair participation or to teach them how to determine the right export price). Indications should be given of the case setting (country, year and type of export firm involved), the courses for which the case is suited (such as export publicity methods, product development), the target audience (advanced business students or mid-career businessmen, for instance), estimated time for student preparation and class discussion, and recommended teaching equipment (blackboard, overhead projector and so on).

The instructor's guide should also contain a series of questions that the teacher can raise during the classroom discussion to help lead the students to a possible solution of the marketing problem. For instance, for a case dealing with a company's declining market share, some of the questions might be why was the share declining, what action could the company take within its financial limits and what types of assistance could it seek to reverse the decline.

A list of additional selected reading materials for students should also be issued as part of the guide. Many students have not had any professional business experience, and any relevant background material they receive in advance should help stimulate their interest and participation in the class discussion. Suggested readings could include magazine and newspaper articles, lecture notes, excerpts from export marketing handbooks and selected chapters of market surveys. ITC publications can be useful for this purpose, such as its trade promotion handbooks, market studies, monographs on trade channels, guides on trade functions and FORUM articles.

TESTING THE CASE

When the case and the teaching guidelines have been drawn up, they should be tested in an actural classroom situation to determine their effectiveness in teaching business skills. The usefulness of the case can be measured by the feedback obtained from the studedts after the case has been presented and discussed. For instance, the instructor might ask the students to explain the marketing principles involved or to review the reasons for selecting the solution agreed upon. If their replies are in line with the teaching objectives given in the instructor's guide, the case has been well prepared.

This testing process should be repeated several times by different instructors teaching different target groups to assure that the case and the guide can be used successfully on a general basis.

FINALIZING THE TEXT

On the basis of the testing further adjustment may needed in the case. For instance, additional background might be required on the company's product line, or the problem situation might need to be stated in more direct terms. Revisions might also be needed in the teacher's guide, for instance with added discussion questions. It is also useful to add examples in the teacher's guide of any erroneous analytical approaches taken by students during the testing process, for example in clearty identifying the problem or in reviewing relevant facts of the case.

After the final revisions have been added to the case, it can be made available for general use in business courses. It can also be offered in exchange for similar teaching material issued by business instructors in other developing countries.

PERIODICAL REVISION AND UPDATING

Most case studies should not be used for more than a few years because they rapidly become outdated. They therefore need to be either revised or completely rewritten on a regular basis. One solution would be to review the set each year and amend or discard those that are no longer valid.

For instance, a leading business school in North America prepares its own cases and uses them for a period of two years only. This practice ensures the development of case on a continuous basis. Frequent revision also keeps the faculty in close contact with the business community and ensures that they keep abreast of the latest business developments.

CASE-WRITING WORKSHOPS

ITC has run many case-writing workshops in developing countries as part of its training programme in trade promotion. The procedure used in these workshops is the following:

1. Lectures are given on the methodology of case research and writing and case presentation.
2. Participants carry out both desk and field research on individual cases, as part of their course work.
3. On the basis of the information that they collect, the course members prepare an outline for their cases and then write them and the teacher's guides to accompany them.
4. Major export problems illustrated by the cases are identified and solutions are proposed.
5. The cases are tested for their effectiveness as teaching tools.

This methodology could be used by training institutions in developing countries to encourage increased use of the case study method among new instructors.

RESOURCE MATERIALS

Various publications exist on case writing. One useful guide is *Case Method in Management Development* (published by the International Labour Office, 1211 Geneva 22, Switzerland).

ITC is preparing a compilation of selected case studies based on developing country experience, which will be published next year.

7

Complexity of Corporate Communications

OVERVIEW

After the successive managerial levels have learned the attitudes and opinions employees, the communication process can then be reversed in direction. Upward have come ideas, comments, reactions, attitudes, and reports through all levels from the very lowest. Now, downward must flow clarifications, interpretations, orders, instructions and policies.

This two-way flow completes the circle of a well-rounded communication process. Each direction of flow should stimulate and be stimulated by the other. In fact, several exchanges, up and down, may be needed to complete the education on some subjects. For this reacon; the phrase "sharing information" is perhaps a clearer term of best practice. Certainly, the downward flow is apt to be better designed and much more effective when it is based upon a clear understanding of what employees are thinking (or not thinking) about various subjects.

What is said in this chapter should constantly be viewed, therefore, in terms of what was said about the upward flow in the preceding chapter. In this discussion of the downward flow the subject will be taken up under the following headings:

1. Basic concepts of communication.
2. Communication through the several managerial levels.
3. Content and conveyers of education and communication.
4. Organizing the communication programme.
5. Rules of education and communication.

BASIC ELEMENTS

The discussion of various aspects of communication in this chapter will be more meaningful if some basic relationships and factors of communication are first described. Thus, in all cases of communication, there will be found to be a communicator, the person communicated to, the message, the communication channel or device, and the purpose of the communication. These can be simply displayed. Were this all there was to communication, interaction between people would not be unduly complicated nor difficult to understand.

A number of difficulties and complexities interpose themselves. First, the communicator must select words or signals to express the ideas of his message. These are filtered through or affected by his logical system, background, experiences, roles, status, feelings, and behavioural patterns. Second, the signals are filtered through, interpreted, or decoded by the recipient's intellectual system, feelings, loyalties, sedtiments, attitudes, position, background, experiences, and value system. Third, any communication channel is interfered with by—noises from messages from other sources which detract and distract from the clarity of the intended messages. Cases in point are others talking, competing messages, and technical inadequacies of the channel or device. And fourth, the result which the communicator had in mind may be in conflict with the goals or needs of the recipient, The communication system thus has to be expanded.

To cite a case in illustration, an executive seeks to convince a subordinate of the need to increase productivity. To the executive, the relation of productivity to profits, security, and high wages seems to be blatantly obvious. But in talking to the subordinate in these terms, the subordinate thinks in his mind (noises distracting his attention) how previous increases in output brought no raises, how he was called a scab for working hard (his filtering system), and so he is set against cooperating (cross-purposes).

This example also serves to illustrate the importance of having a feedback arrangement in the communication system. The communicator must observe or measure in some way the effect his communication is having, or has had, on the recipient. Then he can recast his message as it is being carried on or redesign future messages to be more effective. This may involve rechecking his own filtering system, becoming attuned to the filtering system of the recipient, clearing the noises from the communication channel, and reexamining his own desired results or the goals of the recipient.

COMMUNICATION AND MANAGERIAL LEVELS

If communication is to proceed satisfactorily, the leadership of ideas must stem from the top of the organization down through the intervening managerial levels. Hence, it is advisable to review communication practices through (1) top management, (2) middle management groups, and (3) supervisory levels.

1. Senior management groups: One of the most significant movements in recent years has been that concerned with top-level executive development. This is a most encouraging trend because good communications must be based upon an intelligent leadership.

Of particular interest here are the labour-related subjects which might well be included in top-level executive programmes. A variety of topics suggest themselves. Until top management seeks definite answers to questions such as the following, it can scarcely expect lower levels of management to know how to communicate intelligently.

(a) What are the social responsibilities of management?

(b) To what extent is business liable for the various risks which endanger employees?

(c) What is an optimum balance betweem reasonable profits and fair wages?

(d) Can workers be loyal to both the company and the union?

(e) What are realistic policies toward political activities on the part of the company?

(f) How do the roles of management and workers interact?

(g) To what extent, and how, should employees participate in mangerial decisions of importance to them?

These are significant questions. The trend of top executives to take counsel on these matters represents a wholesome advance in labour-management relations.

2. *Middle management groups*: Preparing middle management groups for their communication responsibilities usually involves the following three major areas of education:

(a) To learn precisely the educational plans of top management.

(b) To coordinate horizontally the educational responsibilities of various line and staff units.

(c) To transmit specific educational plans to lower supervisory levels, and ultimately to employees.

The nature of these educational responsibilities is readily apparent, so that brief comments concerning them will suffice here. Since the middle groups stand between the top and the bottom, they occupy a strategic position affecting labour-management relations. They must be adequately prepared to transmit accurately, and to control constructively, the plans, policies, and ideas of the top levels.

The middle management groups determine also the degree of consistency and uniformity with which employees in the various divisions of a company will be educated. Hence, coordinated educational sessions are particularly needful here, so that production and personnel units, let us say, take the same views on how the ideas of top management are to be carried out. When such units operate at cross purposes, even though with the best of intentions, the destructive effect upon employees is beyond measure.

This crosswise interchange of ideas leads some to conclude that organizational communications are essentially three-rather than two-dimensional: up, down, and across. Even though the main flows may be up and down, crosswise coordination is increasingly important as a company grows. The various functional and staff units must be brought into a common plan of thought if the top and the bottom are to work together effectively and harmoniously.

3. *Supervisory levels*: Whithout doubt day in and day out the supervisor is in closer contact with workers than any other management level or unit. In the formal organization structure, it is the foremen and supervisors who are management to the workers. And even informally, workers tend to feel that the supervisors determine how well they will or will not be treated as individuals. And when channels of communication are followed, it is through the supervisors that most information will be channeled downward and upward. Indeed, they may be bottlenecks, misinterpreters and deceivers—or the reverse—depending upon the kind of education to which they are exposed by upper managerial levels.

Granting the truth of these contentions, any neglect of supervisory education is to be condemned. Moreover, such education is greatly needed because few, if any, supervisors learn anything about the educational phases of their jobs before they become supervisors. They step into their managerial responsibilities with practically no knowledge of what is expected of them or how their obligations are to be performed. Therefore, it is manifest that this group must be educated not only in the various subject matters top management considers important but also in how to get such subject matters across to the worker.

CONTENT AND MODES

A key factor in communications is, of course, the message. Through the message the executive seeks to influence the employee. And thereby are to be changed the attitudes, opinions, the information, and—ultimately—the behaviour of the employee. But since message content must be transmitted through some agent (human or mechanical), it is important to give consideration to this aspect of communications. Hence the content and the conveyer are discussed together here, because they are so closely related.

In the space of this section, only excerpts and selected illustrations of communication content and conveyers can be given. It is not possible to examine the extent to which such content should be developed or the *pros* and *cons* of usage of various conveyers. It is hoped that the examples will serve to disclose typical content and usage. The materials in this section will be grouped under the following headings of typical subject matter, and incorporated under these headings will be examples of communication conveyers:

1. Major topics included in communication programmes:

   (a) Company history, objectives, and services

   (b) Company organization, finances, and operations

   (c) Personnel objectives, policies, and practices

   (d) Economics and the American system

   (e) Political and community relations

2. Major groups of communication conveyers:

   (a) Individualized personal contacts
   (b) Group personal contacts
   (c) Written media
   (d) Demonstration and displays
   (e) Radio, television, films and recordings

1. Company history: objectives and services. The significance an employee feels is in part due to the importance he and his associates attach to the company. If he knows nothing of a company's history, objectives and services, he can take little pride in his company. It is wise, therefore, to give him such information. A number of plans may be cited in this connection.

The induction programme for new employees is a common way of communicating the message of company history, objectives and services. Part of the personal confrrences of new employees with staff members of the personnel department and with their respective supervisors may be devoted to such subjects. At this time, too, some companies have used films to bighlight the story of how the company was founded, by whom and some of the early trials and tribulations. The story can be brought up to date to show the present position of the company in the industry.

Booklets are often used to cover these subjects. They are relatively inexpensive for presenting the story of a company's origin and growth. Moreover, they have a degree of permanence which films, for example, do not have, as far as ready reference to them is concerned. But to induce workers to read them is a problem. In this connection, well-designed, excellently illustrated and carefully worded copy is helpful. An interesting case of stimulation is provided by one company which developed a quiz game, based upon plant publications and meetings, to be played during the lunch hour. Winners were given free lunches for answering correctly questions about the company's history, products, and personalities.

Plant publications are also used to provide information about the background of a company. These cover such subjects as how management has sought to provide job security, the importance of quality production for company success, and reviews of various company operations internally and in relation to customers.

Product display boards are also used to help employees visualize their contributions to the final product. Cutaway models serve to show various parts of a product and something about their purposes. Some companies disply competitors' products so that employees may gain some insight into the task facing their own company in maintaining its position in the industry and in the market.

2. *Company organization, finances and operations*: This area of subject matter receives a great deal of attention from many companies. The reason is that it is necessary to help an employee see how he fits into the structure and operations of the company. Group meetings have been widely used to explain current problems of the company to employees. One company holds regular monthly meetings in which various executives take turns in explaining the cost and profit position of the company. Supervisors are briefed before the meetings so that they will be in a better position to carry on with the explanations in their own departments.

A variety of methods have been used to communicate information in this general area. Television, for example, has been employed to highlight a company's operations to a wide audience. The comic-book format has been used to present a company's annual report to employees. Some companies use the public-address system to inform employees about such items as new customer orders or cancellations, available training courses, and contemplated expansion programmes. And some companies have used conferences to discuss with employees various phase of company operations and plans.

3. Personnel objectives, policies and practices: Of immediate interest to employees is, of course, their financial and non-financial returns and possibilities. It is understandable, therefore, why many companies concern themselves with communications in this area. Practically all companies do some explaining of wages, hours and employment conditions during the induction process. But it would be foolhardy to stop there, because interest in these subjects continues throughout an employee's tenure with a company.

Every conceivable conveyer has been used for communications in these areas. Undoubtedly, the best one is the supervisor. He can give the personal attention practically everybody prefers to impersonal or mass media of communication. In one case, for example, each supervisor reviews with each of his subordinates his personal situation with respect to salary, available benefit plans, profit-sharing programme, vacations and holiday arrangements. One company uses staff interviewers to discuss safety practices on specific jobs. Interviews are used by another company to be sure that employees know all aspects of their jobs, how they are getting along on them, what the future has in store, and whether or not they are using all the help their supervisors can give them.

Use of other media in this area is also desirable. Booklets, for example, have been used to answer questions frequently asked about company retirement plans and pension arrangements. Employee forums—of large as well as small groups—are sponsored by one company at which subjects of interest are covered by company or outside speakers Another company uses informal dinner meetings at which written questions are answered by a panel of company executives.

Interesting examples of communications may also be cited in connection with questions of job security and union-management relations. Many companies have taken pains to show how job security is tied in with competitive leadership and high productivity, From the positive side, employees are told such things as: "The success of a company depends greatly on you." "Job security and job opportunity depend on satisfying the customer." "The security of your job is wrapped up in improvements of quality, reliability, and reputation." And when layoff are likely, some companies have been careful to advise employees regarding prospects for reemployment.

Communication can serve also to improve mutual understanding in union-management relations. For example, union and company officials have taken joint tours of their own plants as well as those of competitors to promote a better understanding of their own positions and problems. Other companies also use conferences and meetings with supervisors to gain their views and to clarify their undestanding of labour-management problems.

4. *Economic and the American system*: An interesting phase of communication has been along lines of increasing economic understanding. The movement has gained strength because of the belief that an employee who does not comprehend how our economic system works cannot feel confident about the fairness of his earnings, the reasonableness of profits, or the significance of the capitalistic system.

Interesting as these efforts are, space permits only the citation of a few examples of various types of efforts along these lines. For example, the Inland Steel Company and the Borg-Warner Corporation developed a series of four films which attempted to show the following:[1]

(a) How We Got What We Have

(b) What We Have

(c) How to Lose What We Have

(d) How to Keep What We Have

After each of the films is shown, a discussion period is deveted to an examination in detail of the particular subjects.

The Du Pont Company developed a conference method programme with a board type of presentation in this conection. This conference concerns itself with the features of the American economic system, its accomplishments, the place of competition, the place of individual freedom in the system and the place of the company in our system. A trained conference leader first conducts an appreciation sesssion over the whole subject matter. Then, he leads three 1½-hour discussion sessions, based on a broad presentation. He also trains others to conduct conferences on the programme. The technical aspects of the programme have since been made available for general distribution through the National Association of Manufacturers.

The Republic Steel Corporation also uses a conference programme, but on a more extensive basis. The conferences are built around lectures, visual aids, and discussions. It has as its objectives the following:

(a) Raising the level of knowledge and understanding about the economic system and how the corporation fits into it.

(b) Providing a framework for analyzing and appraising economic proposals and problems.

(c) Developing in individuals an appreciation of the role of the corporation and the economic system.

(d) Developing confidence in the corporation and the system

(e) Encouraging desirable changes in attitude and behviour both on and off the job.

5. Political and community relations: In addition, some industries have worked closely with various community agencies and groups to make education a community project. The instruction in such instances has been intended to clarify such subjects as collective bargaining, the importance of the American system of industry, the mutual interests of employees and management, and how various stages of the political system operate.

ORGANIZING THE COMMUNICATIONS PROGRAMME

These remarks about communications must include attention to two aspects of organizing the programme:

1. what organizational elements are involved in the programme and
2. where responsibility for programming should be placed.

From what has already been said, it should be apparent that in answer to the first point, every level and segment must concern itself with communications. In the formal structure, from supervisors to top management, and crosswise between line and staff executives, there must be acceptance of the educational obligation. But it would be unwise to overlook the flow of communications which takes place through informal channels. The informal lines of communication should be used, but with subtle care so that they do not go not go underground because of fear or misunderstanding. Also, the extraformal structures of union channels should be employed to communicate information upward and downward.

But when everyone is responsible, turning now to the second point, there is grave danger that no one will be responsible. Hence, specific delegation of authority for leadership of an educational programme is desirable. The personnel division is a natural choice here. It should provide leadership of ideas but should always submit programme proposals to the appropriate line executives for suggestions and approval. The latter, with line authority, will then spearhead the execution of approved plans using the help supplied by the personnel division. Moreover, the personnel division can seek out help on communications matters from management consultants, educational institutions, professional societies, and business and trade associations. Such an organizational setup would serve to insure proper design of programmes, minimum conflict between organization units, a strengthening of the work and support of line executives, and advantageous use of all communications resources and opportunities.

PRINCIPLES OF COMMUNICATION

From all that has been said thus far, it is obvious that good communication involves hard work. Attention is now directed to a number of principles and obstacles that further complicate the communication process. Among these are the following:

1. The factor of change—resistance to change
2. The educational process—difficults of teaching
3. The individual—obstacles in reaching people
4. Semantics—the mystery of words
5. Classes—obstacles of stereotypes
6. Degrees—questions of how much

1. The factor of change: The need for communication perhaps arises basically out of the dynamics of change. In the first place, if business operations did not change, there would be little need for communications. But they do change. So employees must be convinced to make and accept the changes. They must be convinced for a number of reasons. In the first place, there is the normal human resistance to getting out of a habitual way of doing things. Communications can be helpful in reducing the psychological frictions of this type.

Much more significant, in the second place, is the resistance arising from feelings of insecurity. Almost any change arouses questions of its possible negative impact upon job security, wage levels, social and organizational status, and personal prestige. To counter such feelings calls for considerable communication.

Usually, the practice in such cases has been to explain the nature of proposed change as already decided upon by management. This does not do too much in allaying fears. So explanations of why changes are needed and why they are desirable are communicated. This is of some help if specific attention is directed to advantages accruing to employees. Better still are communications which raise the need of change, without specifying a course of action, but instead inviting suggestions as to what should be done. This approach involves employees in managerial decision making, which few companies have been willing to adopt. If managerial resistance to this change in decision making can be reduced, undoubtedly much progress can be made in reducing employee resistances to change.

2. Educational process: Communication is thus for management a task of changing the thinking of employees—an educational process. Yet, frequently, management does not realize it is an educator. During a man's working life, he will learn something—if not from management, then from others. And what he learns elsewhere may not be to management's liking. Hence, it must be concluded that the role of educator must be accepted as a significant part of the job of every executive from the highest to the lowest supervisor.

As educators, management must be skilled in transmitting information and knowledge to subordinates. Each executive must therefore know the subject matter he must teach. This is not enough. A teacher must also be a preacher and a coach. He must be a preacher because convincing employees about the profit system, let us say, is more than a statement of cold logic. All of us learn best when the teacher is enthusiastic, transmits a feeling of convication, and employs various devices to bring human interest into his lessons.

As an educator, the executive must apply the best techniques of coaching. He must always keep in mind that the employees are to play the game, not he alone. So he must teach them how to act in the situations in which they will find themselves. This involves insight into the problems to be met and insight into the reactions that people will have in meeting them. Yet, many an executive fails to get across his ideas as he would like because he does not cultivate such insight. It is too easy to forget, once we have learned how to perform some act, how much difficulty we ourselves had in learning. Unless the coach keeps this in mind, the students develop obstructions to learning which make the executive's task even more difficult.

Finally, education has its problems because it is a thinking process. In all human activities, thinking ranks highest in difficulty. It is hard to concentrate for more than short periods of time. And sequential, logical analysis demands intense concentration. To get employees (or executives) to apply themselves, various, educational devices must be used. Simple doses, constantly repeated at properly spaced intervals, through the best of conveyers (such as pictures and diagrams), must be used. Much could be learned in this regard from the comic books and movies of Walt Disney. He educates extremely well in a most interesting and painless manner.

3. The iddivinual: This last point about the thinking process leads naturally to a consideration of the difficulties of reaching individuals simply because of their human makeup. We assume that we shall not receive a busy signal when we call up, that they will not be preoccupied with personal problems and interests. We assume employees want to know what our managerial problems are. And we assume that the people have the technical equipment and education to receive the message which is sent. These assumptions are rarely warranted. And so communications based upon them are often bound to be ineffective, as suggested.

4. Semantics: One of the most perplexing problems of communications arises in relation to symbols used to transmit messages. A given word, for example, may not mean the same thing to all who her it. But more important, the image a word creates in the mind, and the action the image initiates, may be far different than that visualized by the transmitter. Nonverbal sounds, too, such as a factory whistle, may connote one thing to the employer and another to the employee. Or a picture of a new machine the company proposes to install may not convey the idea of job security, as the company intends, but rather the idea of technological unemployment and job insecurity. And finally, the actions and trappings of executives may raise in the minds of employees ideas and actions far different than those in the minds or expectations of executives.

This area of the effect of symbols upon the minds and actions of people is entitled "semantics." It is concerned with a study of the meaning of symbols used in communication. Obviously, such study is appropriate to all areas of human endeavor. Onlv very recently, however, has it received the attention it deserves in the field of business.

The moral of all this to management is two fold: First, it should choose its words (and other symbols, too) carefully in preparing communications; and second, it should examine its own ractions and understanding of the words. This involves a good deal of study A good place to begin is with past communications. What words were used? Were they Simple or complex? Could they have been misconstrued? Then, some studies of employee reactions are called for. How do employees react to such words as *job, profits, boss, work, pay, order, service, and business*?

5. *Classes*: Another difficult in communications that must be overcome is the obstacle created by the class attitude taken by various groups. Thus, in many instances, workers feel that as a class, they are opposed to the class of executives. It is their duty, then, to refrain from accepting the views expressed by management. This is uniquely illustrated by the employee who gets a promotion to a supervisory position. While he is an employee, various fellow workers come to him because he is their natural informal leader. They believe whatever he has to say and take whatever action he suggests. After he becomes boss, the visits stop, and such messages as he initiates are

scorned or questioned. Yet, both before and after, the man in question holds—or so he thinks—the same feelings toward his fellow workers. But now he is in another class, and he takes on the characteristics, viewpoints, and motives of that class.

Such typing of classes occurs in the executive evlels, too. Staff people tend to categorize line executives as biased, relatively ignorant, and non-cooperative individuals. The line people return the compliment by classifying staff people as impractical visionaries, who are constantly scheming to take control of their departments. And upper level executives generally are suspicious of lower level supervisors, feeling that the latter are not company-minded, take the side of labour, and generally lack needed managerial qualities. The lower levels have their own picture of the upper levels, viewing them as a group which is simply profit—and cost-minded, with little or no regard for the daily problems of getting work done and for the human factor in the shop.

On top of these organizational stereotypes, there may be overlappings of political, racial, religious, colour, and job groupings. It is unwise to group all employees as being under the political influence of Democrats, Republicans, or labour unions. To address communications in terms of one grouping alone will certainly antagonize the others. And similarly, it is unwise to assume that all employees hold the same views on race, colour, and creed—even those of the same race, colour and creed.

The design of communications to minimize class distinctions must begin, therefore, with a revision of acts which tend to raise class barriers. Management, for example, must live so that employees will not consider executives as natural enemies. Similarly, staff people should not act as if they alone are repositories of all that is good; line people should have confidence in their own abilities and not reflect characteristic manifestations of an inferiority complex in relation to staff people; upper management should put more managerial responsibilities upon lower supervisors; and the lower levels should take a broader company view and seek to earn the confidence of upper executives.

Thus, good communications really begin with action. The way we live speaks louder than words. But if our actions are good, the words we speak—if carefully chosen—will effectively convey our messages to various selected recipients.

6. *Degrees and quality of communications*: But how much communication is necessary. Theoretically speaking, enough for an executive to make his managerial planning, organizing, directing and controlling of teamwork effective.

But there is also an ethical aspect to communication. For example, does management have the right to try to change or clarify basic economic, social, or political ideas? To illustrate, a programme may be undertaken to convince employees that private enterprise is better than any form of government ownership, that the profit system is superior to national planning, that union membership will bring no lasting benefits, and that management leadership is fairer and more democratic than union leadership or political administration of business. To some, such communications may be termed "indoctrination" or outright propaganda. Such views are based not upon the type of education, but upon its fairness, accuracy, and validity. And those who voice them may themselves indoctrinate or propagandize, but see nothing wrong in that because they believe the content of their programmes and messages is right and just.

Hence the right to indoctrinate or propagandize is not the basic issue. Since capitalists (management is too often used incorrectly as a synonym for this term) have so much at stake in a business enterprise, they should have the right to protect their investment by all legal and ethical means. But to go beyond the borders of fairness in such efforts by employing high-pressure tactics and partial truths is unjustifiable. The question, however, of what is fair, ethical and accurate is one that is difficult to answer in many cases. Nevertheless, this should not be reason to remove the rights of management (or for that matter, of unions, political groups, or other agencies) to indoctrinate—communicate.

To sum up, whether the communication is intended to provide information or change the attitudes of employees (even to the extent of indoctrination or propagandizement), the efforts of management are justified. But the premise of fairness, honesty, and ethical standards is assumed and must be maintained. Without this, counterforce will be built up that will result in loss of faith, confidence, and loyalty.

QUESTIONS

1. What are the major elements in the process of communication?
2. What makes up the filtering systems of the communicator and the recipient of communications?
3. How does feedback contribute to better communications?
4. With what subject matter is the education of top management primarily concerned?
5. Why is such significance generally attached to the role of the supervisor in employee-employer relations?
6. What are the major classes of content and conveyers of communication programmes?
7. What has the factor of change to do with communications?
8. What solutions would you suggest to the problem of semantics in communication?
9. To what aspects of educational nature must a good communication programme give attention?
10. On what grounds would management communication be justified? On what grounds would it be justifiably criticized?

CASE 7.1. PERCEPTIONS IN COMMUNICATION

While making the rounds of his department, the merchandising manager stopped at the display of men's ties. Without any preliminary introduction by way of leading into the subject, the manager said to the salesman on duty, "You could do a better job of rearranging your merchandise according to the current colour trends."

The manager was surprised and dismayed (but somehow kept it from showing) by the saleman's simple reply, "Since when?"

Not being sure of what the salesman meant, but thinking it might have been a lack of clarity on his part, the merchandising manager described what he meant by a better display and gave what he thought was a logical and clear explanation. But the salesman, the manager could see, was unconvinced.

The manager decided to explain again, even though he felt that his first explanation was logical, clear, and reasonable and even though he began to feel that the salesman was being somewhat thick-headed about it all. But during this additional explanation, the salesman began to feel a loss of self-esteem and an insult to his intelligence.

QUESTIONS

1. What has happened in this set of communications to cause it to deteriorate?
2. How might the original purpose of the merchandising manager have been attained?

CASE 7.2. INTERPRETING COMMUNICATIONS

Maury, a route manager, had a run-in with Stan, one of his truck salesmen. In the discussion, Maury told Stan that he disapproved of Stan's practices of loading his truck with merchandise not in accord with company practices, humming and singing on the route, carelessness in reporting inventories each day, and rendezvousing with other salesmen at lunch breaks.

Afterwards, Stan's views of the conversation could be summarized in his words as follows: "I knew how to load my truck long before he showed up around here. I knew him when he was one of us but he sure has changed. He has lost his friendly ways and just wants to polish the brass. He doesn't know how to manage us. Besides, he's just jealous that I could become a professional singer and am not dependent on him. Well, I'm working on acting lessons. Sure, the other men like to meet with me. I've been a natural friend of man and beast around here for years. Well, I know how to take care of that spying snake-in-in-the-grass if he gumshoes around here. I've talked this over with the boys and they agree that any more of this kid stuff and were talking to the business agent."

Any Maury's views could be summarized as follows: "I had to lay into Stan. I told him nicely a couple of times about the loading and the records. I know a thing or two about record-cheating, and I'll pounce on him. He thinks he's a swinging singer and it's gone to his head. The men just egg him on for a joke but he's trying to set them off against me. He's got to be more careful about public relations with that bellowing of his. If he doesn't straighten out, he's on the way out."

QUESTION

1. What has gone on here?

REFERENCE

1. These films have since been taken over by the American Economic Foundation for purposes of general distribution.

8

Communication : A Tool for Motivation

Dr. Niraj Kumar*

In a general sense, one can very easily say that communication means exchange of, or act of imparting thoughts, ideas, messages, experiences, wishes, emotions, moods, opinions, etc. Some social scientists have defined communication as an exchange of information. The American Management Association has defined communication as "any behaviour that results in an exchange of meaning." The Special Committee on Communication in Business and Industry (National Society for the Study of Communication, U.S.A.) has tentatively defined it as follows: "Communication is a mutual exchange of facts, thoughts, opinions or emotions. This requires presentation and reception, resulting in common understanding among all parties. This does not necessarily imply agreement." While delivering a series of lectures on the uses of communication by managers to the students in the Graduate School of Business at Columbia University, New York, Willard V. Merrihue has further defined communication as "any initiated behaviour on

*Reproduced from *Prabandh/October 1985-March 1980.*

the part of the sender which conveys the desired meaning to the receiver and causes desired response behaviour from the receiver." We can give a general working definition of communication as thus: "Communication is an interactional process in which meaning is stimulated through the sending and receiving of verbal and non-verbal messages." The key to the definition is process. More than 2,000 years ago, Heraclitus provided a basic insight into the extent of process when he stated that a man can never step in the same river twice (the very act changes the man and the river, *i.e.*, they both have been affected by the passage of time) Communication is not static for it cannot be properly understood as fixed elements in time and space. Perhaps all communication begin and end with the word "and." Communication is an irreversible and unrepeatable process. Mortensen states, "Communication does not necessarily stop simply because people stop talking and listening." By communication we mean here the broad field of human interchange of facts and opinions rather than working of the telephone, radio, television, telegraph, and the like.

Communication is, in the first instance, the process of transferring a particular information or message from an information source to a definite and particular destination. It sets employees in individual jobs, regulates their flow of work, co-ordinates their efforts, and secures better and higher work accomplishment. Management in action comes into existence as a direct result of communication. In other words, communication initiates human efforts and activities towards the successful execution of action plans. It is the essence of organised activity and is the basic process out of which all other functions are derived. Peter Drucker identifies four fundamentals of communication which show the nature of the process. These are briefly stated below:

(A) COMMUNICATION IS PERCEPTION

This implies that it is only the recipient who communicates, because if he does not perceive what is transmitted, no communication takes place. The effectiveness of communication is limited to the recipient's range of perception.

(B) COMMUNICATION IS EXPECTATION

People perceive only what they expect to. The unexpected is ignored or misunderstood.

(C) COMMUNICATION MAKES DEMANDS

Experiments have shown that words with unpleasant emotional charges or threats tend to be suppressed while those with pleasant associations are retained longer. In other words, communication makes a demand on the recipient in terms of his emotional preference or rejection. It also demands him to become somebody or do something.

(D) COMMUNICATION AND INFORMATION ARE DIFFERENT

Informational is logical, formal and impersonal, while communication is perception. The less tied up information is with human factors, the more valid and reliable it becomes. However, both these are interdependent.

THEORY OF COMMUNICATION

As early as 1938, Chester Barnard observed that, "in an exhaustive theory of organisation, communication would occupy a central phase, because the structure, extensiveness and scope of the organisation are almost entirely determined by communication techniques." If this is the case, it is apparent that central to the study of organisation is communication. It is the one aspect that allows an organisation to be an organisation. Think about it. If we removed all forms of communication from the organisation, would there be an organisation. Recent research studies indicate that depending upon your position within the organisation, it can range from 50 per cent to 95 per cent of your working day. Can there be any doubt that "organisation man" depends upon communication?

The message may be transmitted as spoken or written words, pictures, or in some other form. In oral communication, the transmitter is the voice-box, in telegraphy, it is the telegraphy key (Morse Key) which codes the message into dashes and dots. The receiver decodes the transmitted message in an understandable form to the Information destination. The receiver may be, for example, the mechanism of the human ear, which converts sound waves into a form which can be recognised by the brain; a television receiver decodes the electromagnetic waves into recognisable visual representations.

BERLO'S TECHNICAL MODEL

Communication process involves an apparently simple procedure consisting of only a few steps. Berlo has provided one technical model for understanding the communication process. His model contains the following elements:

1. A Communication source.
2. The Encoder.
3. The Message.
4. The Channel.
5. The Decoder.
6. The Communication Receiver.

These elements are not necessarily always separated and exclusive, since a person can send a message to himself, and, therefore, he would be both the source and the receiver and do both encoding and decoding. They are mutually interdependent, and the whole process is a unity in conveying a meaningful information. Furthermore, the elements are not restricted to people only, since machines may be used in the communication process.

SIGNIFICANCE OF COMMUNICATION

Since managing is getting things done through others, it is obligatory on the part of the manager to communicate with the members of the organisation, Research studies conducted in the field of inter-personal communication have revealed that a manager spends 90 per cent of his time in communicating with others, either sending or receiving information. Without effective communication, the superior-subordinate relationship cannot thrive.

George R. Terry, in describing the importance of communication, writes: "It serves as the lubricant fostering the smooth operation of the management process." In all positive or negative actions, managers have to resort to communication in their dealings with human beings. Personal and social interests of employees can be merged in, and harmonised with, organisational interests through the permeating effect of communication.

Barnard has given serious consideration to communication in large-scale enterprises. He views it as the means by which people are linked together in an organisation in order to achieve a central purpose. Group activity is impossible without information transfer because, without it, co-ordination and change cannot be effected.

"Evil communication corrupt good manners." Good communication persuades human beings to make greater efforts towards their work performance. Communication creates understanding and acceptance on the part of employees. "In short, effective communication increases understanding of employees, gains their willing acceptance and leads them to greater efforts."

Bavelas and Barrett have stated: "It is entirely possible to view an organisation as an elaborate system for gathering, evaluating, recombing and disseminating information. It is not surprising, in these terms, that the effectiveness of an organisation with respect to the achievement of its goals should be so closely related to its effectiveness in handling information."

Actually, communication is the only key that unlocked the door to increased personal effectiveness, enhanced job satisfaction, and improved on-the-job performance. It is also an important tool is raising productivity, preventing conflicts and strikes, cutting costs and contributing on the whole to the growth and profitability of any business.

Peter F Drucker impelling the need more and better employee communication, as a for significant factor in organisational climate, states: "To measure work against objectives requires information......Management must try to convey this information not because the worker wants it, but because the best interest of the enterprise demands that he should have it. The great mass of employees may never be reached even with the best of efforts. But only by trying to disseminate information to every worker can management hope to reach the small group that in every plant, office or store leads public opinion and moulds common attitudes.

Now it is evident that silence was not golden, misunderstanding flourished in an atmosphere of secrecy. Business, like other institutions in a democrecy, can only progress rapidly, if it is able to carry on its task in accordance with the wishes of its peoples whether those people were acting in their capacities as voters, as employees, as shareholders, as suppliers or as neighbours.

The following are some specific areas where communication plays a significant role:

1. During union negotiations, to gain solid support for the company's efforts to reach an agreement without any strikes.
2. When strikes occur, to get employees back to work with a minimum of hostility toward the company and the least financial loss to themselves.
3. To maintain active participation in all employee's benefit plans and gain the goodwill inherent in the company's contribution to these plans.
4. In elections of union representatives to give all employees full information on which to base a sound decision.

5. To increase productivity and reduce losses.
6. To develop team work, by spending the flow of information at all levels.
7. To promote health and safety and to improve safety records.
8. To help protect management's right to manage the business.
9. To gain the confidence and support of community neighbours.
10. To improve and maintain cordial employer-employee relations.
11. To maintain and improve the business climate.

Presently, the main stream of communication embodies the significant contributions of both sociologists and psychologists and the use of these for the welfare of the enterprise. Purpose and goals are uppermost in the minds of those who manage enterprise. With a view to achieving these ends, they seize upon the social principles and technique of many contributions including communication experts.

During and after World War II, management was seized with the problem of effective communication. At that time the trend of thinking went something like this. "The efficiency of our operations can be increased if we can only improve the morale of our employees. We can do this by improving communication with them. So let's communicate."

Further, more mutual trust and confidence between management and worker can be increased by the help of communications of what the manager wants and what the employees perform. A clear-cut understanding provides job satisfaction to the employees, creates their confidence in the loyalty towards the enterprise. Evidently, therefore, effective communication satisfies the personal and social wants of human beings and stimulates their job interest and co-operation,

A study of Purdue University which addressed a series of questions to fifty Presidents to obtain their views on in-plant communication reveals briefly as:

1. A definite relationship exists between communication and employee productivity;
2. Labour disputes and strikes are definitely linked with breakdowns in communication;
3. A number of factors contribute to communication breakdowns; but the greatest single factor is inadequate use of communication media.

COST OF MIS-COMMUNICATION

Numerous management problems arise due to failure in communication or mis-communication. Industrial relations problems and frequent conflicts between management and workers are very often traceable to communication failures. The cost of mis-communication in terms of time factor and money involved is, undoubtedly, very high but what is more alarming, is the cost arising as a consequence of hostility, inefficiency and mis-understanding which ultimately leads to indiscipline and low morale resulting in poor productivity the cost of which is quite prohibitive to an organisation. An employee may fail to inform the production manager about the shortage of a vital material for the next few weeks or he may forget to notify the marketing manager about the non-availability of a new product of the company as previously scheduled; a promising junior executive accepts an attractive offer in competitive company because his boss totally ignored to give him any credit for his excellent work performance; a grievance is pending because the foreman has completely overlooked a worker's grumbling need for a guard on his machinery; a departmental head's report prepared after strenuous efforts which could have been of tremendous importance in deciding the major issues vital for averting a lock-out goes unread because his supervisor wanted a brief summary of the case. The cost of mis-communication can, to a great extent, be avoided by improving the executive's personal skill as a sender and receiver of communications, developing his sensitivity to language and emotional content of the message and his ability to overcome communication barriers and tap the ideas and experiences of others.

MIS-CONCEPTIONS ABOUT COMMUNICATION

None of us gave any thought to the process of communication. We just do it. The process of communication seems so simple, natural and spontaneous to us that we hardly give any time, thinking about the art and science involved in the effective presentation and exchange of ideas, thoughts etc. People tend to regard communication as both a natural function and as one in which they are usually able to convey an accurate and exact message through choice of the right words. But unfortunately, this does not hold to be true.

MIS-CONCEPTION NO. 1

COMMUNICATION IS A NORMAL HUMAN FUNCTION

Generally, what most of us regard as a very normal human activity is not a natural function at all. It is a learned one. In ancient days, about a century ago, an European King decided to try an experiment to find out whether communication is a normal and natural human activity or a learned one. For this, he isolated a number of newly-born babies in a quiet and calm room and instructed those who were taking care of them not to speak even a single word in the infant's presence. When the babies began to talk, the king thought that the world's languages were the one natural to man. The records of these experiments showed that not even one of the unfortunate infants ever said a single word in any language. In fact, most of them died. Communication, to become most effective, requires deliberate effort and deliberate thought. Quite often one finds himself in great predicament because he has not been deliberate enough in thinking about communicating effectively.

MIS-CONCEPTION NO. 2

COMMUNICATION IS EASY

Everyone can think, a number of times they were misunderstood and may very often get into hot waters by merely saying something to which some one took it in the wrong way. It may have been perfectly clear to the speaker but was not understood by another person—the speaker mis-communicated.

To rule out any misunderstanding on the part of the person spoken- to, it is advisable to impart a correct and precise message. Communication has secured when the person receiving the message understands it completely, even though he may not agree with the sum and substance of the message thus delivered. But if the communicator is certain as to the correctness and precise nature of his communcation but the person receiving the message does not understand, the communicator mis-communcated.

A correct and careful selection of the words can help us to be more precise. Any way, all of our efforts still must yield to the fact that communication is, at best, a rather inexact and an imperfect tool.

MIS-CONCEPTION NO. 3

If we can talk and write well, with clarity, and expression a language that will be comprehended by the receiver, then we are thoroughly conversant with all the basic skills of communication.

To be really sensitive and understand what the communication is, we must be aware of and be able to interpret meaning and various gestures that can add to, change or sometimes even negate a verbally communicated message. Just as a person simply by nodding his head, frown or lifted eyebrow conveys a rather precise message without uttering even a single word, the executives in the business world too can communicate an attitude or response without speaking a word on the subject through these behavioural signals.

COMMUNICATION AND MOTIVATION

Motivation is concerned with the 'why' of human behaviour. Questions such as "Why does one man work diligently and another attempts to avoid work?" and "Why does one man find pleasure in performing a job while another dislikes it?" represents to attempts to understand the motives of human behaviour. Motivation is an internal feeling in the individual. It is an internal need, that is satisfied through an external expression. It is the willingness to exert toward the accomplishment of some goal. Motivation focusses the attention of those inner drives that activate or move an individual to action.

It is observed that effective motivation of workers in any industrial organization depends mainly on:

(i) thorough orientation at the outset, and

(ii) perceptive follow-up, to ensure that the individual worker is employing his talents to the best of his ability, and the company or organisation is not only aware but is also assured of his future progress.

Initial orientation of employees, which also includes briefing of safety rules, working conditions, benefits, pay policies etc., and on-the-job instructions by the immediate superiors, is normally a part of industrial practice. But performance appraisal of employees cannot be evaluated on this score alone. Personal discussions with employees on job performance are perhaps one of the most important channels for two-way communication on all aspects of the job-relationship. They are also the key to harnessing skills, attitudes and motivations. A Manual issued by the General Electric Company, New York, supports this view:

'Man to main discussions with employees are one of the best tools available with management to aid in developing the organisational unit into a better working team. If such discussions are held properly, it has been said, 75 per cent of industry's employee communication problems can be overcome".

The two-way communication aspect of performance appraisal discussion has also been emphasised in the same Manual which gives the following suggestions: "What you should try to do so that the employee can accomplish:

ANNEXURE A

1. Build a better working relationship by getting to know the men better by letting him know you respect him, and are sincerely interested in his progress and his opinions.	1. Express his opinions freely, tell you his personal problems and aspirations, the reasons for his actions. Get help in solving any special problems he has encountered on the job.
2. Let the man know what is expected of him. Review the position guide and standards (Accountability Factors) by which he is measured. Tell him of your personal performances about the way he performs the job.	2. Benefit by a realistic reappraisal, if necessary, of importance of his contribution etc.
3. Give the man recongnition and praise for good performance or abilities. This will build up his self-confidence and make him willing to do still better.	3. Make more effect use of his special abilities and be encouraged to suggest improvements in the job.

4. Point out tactfully those areas in which his performance falls short of the job requirements on your expectations.	4. Tell you the reasons why it is difficult or impossible to do the job as you want to get it done.
5. Explain salary and other administrative matters as they affect the employee and his job.	5. Discuss and reach a clearer understanding of what he might expect in terms of salary and promotion on his pre sent job. Overcome misunderstanding and confusion about authority and responsibility.
6. Work with him in developing a programme for his self-improvement for future progress.	6. Have your help and encouragement in overcoming his limitations and improving his abilities so that he can qualify for future increases in pay and responsibilities.
7. Find out how you are doing as a supervisor in terms of availability, understanding, organising, delegating, and the like.	7. Point out the barriers to his doing a good job imposed by your methods or supervision.

A motive is inferred from the behaviour of men. It is not a directly observable fact. It is assumed to exist as an internal factor that integrates a man's behaviour. "The concept of motivation has been variously identified as an indisputable fact of behaviour, and as a mere explanatory fiction. The common and unifying element in these diverse conceptions is that motivation is an agency or factor or force that helps to explain behaviour. Motivation is a hypothetical cause of behaviour". According to one of the experts in motivation, Fedrick Herzberg, "employees do have a will to work".

Communication provides an opportunity in the hierarchical system of management to exchange ideas, to pool experiences, to develop attitude and through an inter-personal reaction, to influence action pattern and behaviour of the men at work. In the book "Business Organisation And Operations". W.R. Spriegal has very rightly stated that "Most of the conflicts in business are not basic but are caused by misunderstood motives and ignorance of facts. Proper communications between interested parties reduce the points of friction and minimise those that inevitably arise". Peter Drucker has very rightly observed, "the manager has a specific tool; information. He does not 'handle' people to do their own work. His tool—his only tool—to do all this is the spoken or written words or the language of numbers. No matter whether the manager's job is . . . manufacturing, engineering, accounting, or selling his effectiveness depends on his ability to listen and to read, on his ability to speak and write. He needs skill in getting his thinking across to other people as well as skill in finding out what other people are after".

Hence, we can conclude: communication not only offers excellent opportunity for better motivation, but it also contributes tremendously to the development of management thought.

BARRIERS TO COMMUNICATION

The term 'barrier to communication' indicates what in the nature of the individual component of the communication process serves potentially to prevent or reduce effective communication between one person and another. The problems of communication directly retard the performance of managers towards realizing the enterprise goals. No management, however efficient it may be, can plan and control its activities properly if messages are inadequately transmitted or if the action is not effective.

Effective communication will encourage the improvement of information transfer, for 'improvement' is all that can be realistically expected. However, there is no such thing as perfect communication. Good communications form the basis for achieving any said purpose. Executives recognise that employees are extremely sensitive about certain topics. They maintain "zones of silence" as indicated by these typical comments:

(a) "If we speak up, our message will be called propaganda",

(b) "The union would not like it",

(c) "Let sleeping dogs alone—discussion is too risky. Employees will ask questions, we can't answer the way they want them answered", and

(d) "That's a topic that always gets the person into trouble when he talks about it".

"Never wrestle with a pig, you will both get dirty".

Hence, the failure to communicate effectively can destroy an organisation. In recent times, recognition of this basic and fundamental fact has been engaging the serious attention of the management to the frequent causes of communication breakdowns in an organisation. With a view to making communication more effective and meaningful, it is essential for the management to recognise the potential barriers which considerably reduce its effectiveness and perceptivity.

Some of these barriers can be associated with the nature of persons themselves; some, with the technical processes of encoding and decoding and some with the message itself. These cannot be treated in complete isolation from other; and it can advantageously be argued that since the things and actions are the products of human will, they are all, really, to be associated with one or both the persons involved.

In a survey of over 750 company members whose general level of responsibility placed them in the management category, the National Industrial Conference Board asked, "What are the barriers to communication within a company? ' The barriers cited by these management representatives could be categorised into the following three major groups:

1. Barriers arising from the fact that the individuals are involved in communications and individuals differ. These might be called "prexisting barriers to communication" which a company inherits because they are common to society.
2. Barriers arising from the company's "climate" or "atmosphere" which tend to stultify communications.
3. Barriers that are largely mechanical in the sense that they stem from lack of proper facilities or means of communication.

MECHANICAL BARRIERS

Communication barriers which involve surmounting the idiosyncracies of human personalities or complex inter-relationships of people in groups are not easily amenable to correction. Consequently, some companies are averse to such problems, and they primarily devote their attention to removing the mechanical barriers to communication. These mechanical barriers belong to the categories mentioned below:

1. DEFECTIVE PLANNING

In an organisation, formal channels of communication are generally followed in communicating orders and information. It has been observed that sometimes confusion arises on an important issue as to who will do the communicating on one occasion or another. It is necessary, therefore, that management should give its special consideration to the simple mechanics of who will initiate the communication process, proper timing for such initiation, as well as the consequent handling of such matters in future. With a view to removing such type of a mechnical barrier to communication, proper planning and co-ordination of activities are sine-qua-non for having a presentation that will be complete in all respects and in accordance with the objectives and total operations of the organisation structure.

2. AMBIGUITY (GOBBLEDYGOOK STYLE)

Gobbledygook style which consists of using longer phrases, complex sentences, words of long and multiple communication. Management should, therefore, avoid such a style, which is fairly common in government undertakings. It has been observed that many organisations have considerably improved their communication system by avoiding ambiguity in communication, and have developed techniques of reading written material more easily and legibly.

3. MEDIA

The media-selection often acts as a barrier to communication. It has been observed that management has sometimes to send information to such persons who are not on a regular mailing list, or the adoption of a particular type of communication media may not suit the persons concerned. In such cases, the communication might seriously suffer.

4. FORMAT

In an organisation, the format for written communication may also act as a barrier. It is a natural tendency for a human being to consider mimeographed document as not being as important as the one that is individually typed. Consequently, individuals pay less attention to such documents. Thus, it acts as a barrier to effective communication.

5. MISUSE OR OVERUSE OF A MEDIUM OF COMMUNICATION

The misuse or overuse of a medium of communication may cause people to ignore what comes over it. People begin to form such impression and attitude as it is not worth important. They may anticipate that it may be just more of the same. Consequently, it acts as a barrier to effective communication, and this tendency should be dispensed with altogether.

In addition to the above-mentioned barriers there are many others which arise from specific situations. There are obstacles due to emotional reactions, due to deep-rooted feelings and prejudice, physical conditions, heat, noise or cold, and many other barriers of diversified origin. All of them act as serious barriers to clear communication and unless they are known to the sender, he is in no position to overcome them.

ANNEXURE B

Barriers to Communication

Speaker should	*Barriers*	*Listener should*
1. Speak at level of listeners' status interests and experiences	1. Different status position, self-experience	1. Think in terms of speakers' status interest experience
2. Adapt to listeners' prejudices	2. Prejudices	2. Dispel prejudices
3. Use common ground and 'You' attitude	3. 'I' versus 'You' attitude	3. Develop 'You' attitude
4. Make changes seem attractive	4. Resistence to change	4. Be open-minded
5. Organise clearly for under-standing	5. Refute rather than under-stand	5. Listen to understand, not to refute

6. Develop ideas for listeners' interest	6. Extra time to listen	6. Use listening time constructively
7. Use listener level language	7. Language	7. Analyse speaker's language
8. Think logically	8. Crooked thinking	8. Think logically

GOOD COMMUNICATION GATEWAYS

Researchers in communication have suggested ways and means by the adoption of which leaders, executives or workers can avoid pitfalls or considerably reduce the adverse effects of above-mentioned inhibiting factors. The following check list presents some cardinal rules for overcoming barriers or obstacles to effective communication:

1. PLAN AND CLARIFY YOUR IDEAS BEFORE COMMUNICATING

Many a good communication fails on account of inadequate communication planning. An effective communication should possess clarity and it should be expressed in a language and transmitted in a way that can be comprehanded by the receiver. Such clarity requires a literate approach to language and familiarity with language patterns of subordinates, peers, and superiors. Adherence to this principle will overcome several barriers to communication, badly expressed messages, faulty translations and transmissions, unclarified assumptions, and the need for follow-up clarifications.

2. CREATE THE CLIMATE OF TRUST AND CONFIDENCE

Communication thrives best in a climate of trust and confidence. Distrust of a superior for any reason necessarily restricts communication effectiveness. Heightened emotions make it much more difficult to understand with an opponent. Our experience makes it clear that a neutral, understanding, catalyst type of leader or therapist can overcome communication barriers and create a climate of trust and confidence which is a sine-qua-non for planning effective communications in organisations.

3. TIME YOUR MESSAGE CAREFULLY

Every communicator must recognise the fact that when he is trying to communicate with his subordinates something, other things are also being heard simultaneously that may distort his message. For minimising the distortion, it is always better to communicate the information before other beliefs and attitudes aiming at distortion take hold of the listener.

4. RE-INFORCE WORDS WITH ACTION

The meaning of words are not in the words, they are in us. Words by themselves are suspect. The most persuasive kind of communication is that which we do, and not what we say. Actions speak louder than words. If the verbal announcements are reinforced by action, many communication barriers would be removed. Morever, knowledge of the subject and the audience and projection of one's warmth and sincerity are essential for making effective and persuasive communication.

5. USE FEEDBACK

Feedback ensures that the flow of information is actually having a reciprocating effect on behaviour. A communicator must always be on the lookout for clues, indicating whether or not he is being understood. Receiver's responses to the communication can be judged by observing his non-verbal signs such as expression of comprehension, or bewilderment, a facial expression, such as raising a eye-brow or a frown. This kind of feedback is possible only in face-to-face communication. Further, the receiver may be encouraged to ask additional questions, express his opinion and comments without any fear and prejudice which will make feedback more effective. Feedback is also obtained by simply observing whether the subordinate behaves in accordance with the communication, and if direct observation is impossible, the communication has to depend on reports and results. The speed and efficiency of communication increases manifold if an organisation permits considerable feedback.

6. COMMUNICATION MUST BE DIRECTED TO A PURPOSE AND A PERSON

For overcoming barriers, communication must be directed to a purpose and a person. Managers should consider the pros and cons of the communicated information. Attitudes, feelings, experience and expectations of the individual or group should be taken into consideration before communication. Every individual brings to the communication process certain personal equipment-experiences, attitudes, feelings, expectations, and these essential attributes must be considered if we are to achieve understanding with him.

7. SIMPLE AND MEANINGFUL LANGUAGE

It goes without saying that complexities in language distort and lead to misinterpretation. Undoubtedly, words are intelligible and simple but they should be preferred to multi-syllabic, circumlocutory or metaphorical language.

8. MIND THE OVERTONES

It has been observed that whenever we communicate, our tones and pitch of voice, our expressions, specially facial expressions, our apparent receptiveness to the response of others, our mood and way of communication etc., all have a far-reaching consequence on those we are communicating with. These subtleties of communication often affect the listener's reaction to the message even more than its basic content. Our voice, tones, facial gestures and body language communicate as much or more meaning than words. Effective communications are person-oriented, not word oriented. We know from personal experience that although one word may have many meanings, people always give their own meanings to all words.

9

Organisational Effectiveness through Management Information Systems

B. B. SAKSENA

"We shall all have to be concerned about the future because we will have to spend the rest of our lives there."

—*Charles Ketering*

There is a whole truth condensed in the above quotation. Since every man's innate desire is to live the future in happiness, in comfort, in congenial surroundings, etc., every one of us has necessarily to contribute in this direction. Man's happiness is, among other things, a substantial derivative of his pay packet which has to be not only reasonable but also assured. The former depends on how well the organisation is faring in an intensely competitive world. The latter, however, depends on the organisation's ability to continue as a going concern. This, in turn, depends on the combined effectiveness of the people constituting the organisation.

Thus, even from a purely selfish view point of our own future happy existence, we have to look to the future well-being of our respective organisations as these two are inextricably linked together. Managers' within an organisation commit resources and if the decisions in respect of these commitments are optimal, the organisation's operations will be cost effective and efficient. A prerequisite for sound decisions or better decisions, among other things, is information supply and its timeliness. A look at the decision-making processes reveals that coping with a decision-making situation requires;

(a) Collection of relevant information typical to the situation,

(b) formulation of alternatives,

(c) evaluating the alternatives, and

(d) deciding on the alternative to be adopted.

Thus, information is an important prerequisite for decision-making. It does not mean that the mere supply of information will necessarily result in right decisions. It does, however, improve the odds of making a better selection from the available alternatives, and in consequence, the chances of the decision turning right.

With this role of information in improving the quality of managerial decisions being placed in proper focus, it becomes clear that it should be the endeavour of every organisation, or rather every organisation should endeavour to install effective information systems and place this task in its proper notch in the whole organisation system. It is to be realised that information system is an important sub-system in a business system and is quite important to organisational effectiveness as it supports decision-making. No amount of structural re-organisation would help in the emergence of a truely effective organisation unless, with the structural changes brought about, the information sub-system within it is also buttressed or fortified. Failure to do so may result in partial realisation of the total goals sought to be achieved with the structural changes.

Essential qualities of a vibrant information system are that it should satisfy manager's needs for information in respect of accuracy within his limits to tolerance, timeliness, relevance and format. The elements of information systems are inputs, storage, processing and retrieval and output. The inputs to the information system are the returns, statements, status reports in respect of the organisation's operations as also data culled out from journals, periodicals, publications relating to the industry, etc. The outputs are the information reports that are worked out for the users thereof, *viz.*, the managers, from the input data. Between the two stages of supply of raw data and the final product in the form of analytical reports is the element of processing that is involved. This could be manual or with the help of machines. The raw data, however, after processing and generation of information reports is available for reprocessing if the same is carefully stored to facilitate retrieval. Since storage is a sub-element of an information system, it follows that a carefully worked out procedure for storing the data should be built in any such system. This approach, in fact, converts, at once, information into a powerful resource of the organisation. No longer will it then be necessary for managers to call for bits of information required by them and use it as their own exclusive property. A common pool of data is created wherefrom information is generated by skillful manual or machine manipulations to meet the varied needs of different levels of managers. It achieves both a lateral vertical and integration of the operations within the organisation. It also helps to reduce proliferation of returns and costs. Like all other systems, information systems are also operated by people. It is only when there is a realisation by everyone that he or she has an important role to play in the success of the information systems activity, can a truely robust system be developed, become operational and immensely useful to the organisation system.

INFORMATION SYSTEMS MANAGEMENT—AN INDUSTRY WITHIN AN INDUSTRY

Only the discerning perceive information management as an industry within an industry. In fact, information systems are very important sub-systems in the total business system. With ineffective management information systems, the organisation's own effectiveness is, in jeopardy. In other words, a sick MIS results in a sick organisation heading towards a comatose stage.

From what has been stated earlier, MIS consist of inputs, processing storage and retrieval and outputs. Similar are the operations in any industry. It is not difficult to visualise what the plight of an industry will be if it is plagued with problems of non-availability of raw materials as required or by the availability of sub-standard materials. Either the production of finished goods comes to a grinding halt or slows down or results in finished goods which are sub-standard with no public demand therefor. So is the case in information systems. If there is no input in the form of returns, statements, etc., which are the raw material for information systems, or the same are inaccurate, there would either not be any finished products of information reports or the same would be undependable and unreliable with no useful purpose to serve. On the contrary, if any one relied on them and took decisions based on them it may as well spell disaster for the organisation. Again in any industry, there is processing involved before a finished product results. So is the case, in information systems. Use of unskilled labour or using insufficient labour or equipping skilled labour with inappropriate or faulty tools could adversely affect the final product and slow down the manufacturing process, throwing delivery schedules away. Fall in company sales is a forgone conclusion. No different is the situation in information systems. In the absence, of proper equipments for processing data or inadequately staffed MIS Department, which if inexperienced could worsen matters, important elements of a good information system, *viz.*, relevance, timeliness of reports or accuracy thereof would not be met. A fall in users credibility in the system is certain and results in their withdrawal from the system.

Also, an industry should have proper storage and inventory control systems, to indicate what is in store, both raw materials and finished goods, how much of them are in store and where they are stored. In their absence, cost effectiveness may be a casualty with telling effects on its operations. Again, no different is the situation in information systems. Not only is adequate storage of the inflowing data is necessary and facilities that will be able to retrieve the same quickly are needed, but also what precisely is in store and how long it is in store require to be carefully catalogued.

Finally, any industry succeeds only when it can keep up the demand from its customer for its product. In the case of information systems also, its success is to be judged from the number of users of information reports and their demand for the same for improving the quality of their decisions. A regular demand from users for information, which is the product of information system can be ensured only if the four essential attributes for a virile and robust information system are met, *viz* , timeliness, accuracy, relevance and format of information report. It has also to maintain the users' captivating interest in its products. This comes out of a closer working between information systems people and the users, assessing their needs and meeting them. It may be added that not all users of information are from within the organisation although majority of them are the people from within. External users could also draw from the system.

From the foregoing, it is clear that managing information systems requires as much skill as is needed to run a business. It is no different from running a business. However, one thing is certain that the success of the latter is dependent on the success of the former which, in fact, operates as a small industry within the business system.

Just as consumer education of the products, besides attactive packaging, is essential to create interest in them and, therefore, a demand, so is the case of information reports which are but products of data processing. Not all users of information reports are initiated into the use that could be made thereof. Therefore, a very useful exercise in this respect is explaining to the users how the reports can be used for quicker and better decisions by them.

The chances of a manager using information increase if the information that is supplied is that which he needs at the point of time when the demand is felt to cope up with the decision situation encountered. Thus, generally as a rule, information should be provided when asked. However, among the several decision situations faced, there are many which are routine and required to be taken frequentty. There are still some situations more particularly those arising out of special studies, which require typical information for the analysis in hand. In the former, decision rules are clearly defined and because of the need for frequent access to such information, standard output reports can be worked out, generated and provided to the user at predetermined intervals. The user, however, has to keep before him his responsibility areas in mind and the information needed for each of them.

As an illustration, in the area of staff management, a Regional Manager may have the following responsibilities to discharge:

(a) Appointments, *i.e.*, filling up vacancies,

(b) Development of personnel,

(c) Adhering to policy decisions in respect of transfers, and

(d) Extension in service of officials and retirements.

A decision situation relating to appointment may arise out of a vacancy having been created either on account of a transfer, retirement, promotion or sanction of a new post. The requirements of the job it clearly expressed. say, in terms of grade, length of service in the grade, experience in any specific activity, age, training undergone, number of years spent in current assignment, etc., could help generate a report short-listing people in the grade satisfying the criteria for selection of personnel. Similarly, in the responsibility area of development of personnel, the information needed may relate to identification of officers in certain positions such as Field Officers or Divisional Managers, who have not been exposed to any formal training in their present task. For this situation, a list of such officers could be generated providing therein, besides the names of such officers, their grades, the date since when they have been in the present position, etc. In the alternative, a list of all the officers who have not undergone any training along with their essential bio-data could be used in conjunction with the report of the type referred to above. This will help in selection of officers who will benefit from the training by ensuring post training continuance in the job. Any deputation made from the list for training could be recorded in the report so that at any time the list is updated and can be used for a certain time, span. Once a year, however, a fresh output duly updated could be generated and supplied.

Again, there are policy decisions to be adhered to. For instance, there may be a need to know the officers who would be completing, say, 4 years in one place or in a specific assignment during the next year and the date when they would be doing so. This list, if arranged in the ascending order of the date of completion of 4 years, could help in advance planning for transfers and postings and proper deployment.

The responsibility for extension in service of employees requires information relating to those employees who would be completing a specified number of years of service, say, during the next year. A report showing an appropriate list of such officers along with their grades, the positions held, the date of birth, the date of completion of the specified period of service, the number of years spent in present assignment, etc., will help in initiating timely steps in the responsibility area. A similar list of officers/employees retiring in various grades during the next year will also be useful to the Regional Manager in timely placement decisions. The nature of the decision of the type referred to above is routine and of almost daily occurrence. Output reports can, therefore, be generated at the beginning of, say, each year for use during the whole year. Decisions taken could be recorded on the respective reports so that at any time an up-to-date position is available. However, at the beginning of each year, a fresh set of reports can be generated for use during the year.

If, however, a special study is on hand, information required may not conform to a predetermined format. Such studies may require information typical to the analysis being undertaken. It need not be furnished on a regular basis but made available on demand. For instance, the training college/centres may want to study about the post-training utilisation of skills that is being made in the organisation or how the training facilities are utilised. For such studies, perhaps information reports, say, for training imparted in each of the last 3-5 years, showing the officers or the number of officers who have undergone various training programmes during each year and which of them/or the number that have not been posted for a period of say, 3 years following such training, in assignments in which the training could have been used, would be useful. Useful findings of the extent to which post-training utilisation is taking place could be made for improving decisions on training.

As another example, a study relating to the changing profile of the employees in respect of age, qualifications, length of service in each grade or the number of officers eligible for promotion in each grade for each year for the next, say, 5 years will require information of a different type for a review of the promotion policy. A matrix of age vs. service range in the grade (for each grade) would reveal the level of frustration that is building up in the organisation. Such reports are specific in nature and need to be furnished only when the demand for this information is made by users and not otherwise. In any case, the users should have an idea of the data elements collected in each information system so that they can determine whether a report required by them can be generated from the system. Since information is a product of data processing, it will suffice if the users in the organisation are fully acquainted with the data elements in the system, *i.e.*, the data collected through the input formats, the periodicity of updating thereof and the period for which the data is stored. This will enable them to determine what precisely would be the reports that could be generated therefrom, how recent would be this information content, etc., and indent accordingly.

How Users Should Indent for Information Reports: Since relevance of format, besides timeliness, largely determines whether or not the output report will be used, it is necessary that while indenting for information reports, users very specifically and precisely indicate the criteria, if any, to be applied in generation of the report, the particulars to be reported therein and the order thereof. Whether the information should be listed in descending, ascending or in alphabetical order, etc., wherever this is required, should also be clearly mentioned. The essential data required in a report must be also unambiguously stated and what is desirable or optional should be indicated as such. A clear specification of the needed report leaves no ambiguity and results in reducing the lead time between indent for and supply of information as also in an output in an acceptable format. There are greater chances of such reports being used in decision-making. In a computer based information system, as there are limitations on the print positions to 132 characters, the report asked for would not be able to accommodate in one line elements which cover more than 132 characters. This aspect also has to be borne in mind by the users while indenting information.

CONCLUSION

Organisational effectiveness can be increased if managers move from the culture of taking decisions by hunch or intuitive guess work to that of taking information-based decisions. In this, information sub-system in an organisation, which in fact operates like a typical industry, plays an important part and requires the support of all people in the organisation. While periodic restructuring of the organisation is a means to an end, it alone cannot achieve the envisaged goals. The structure has to be adequately supported by well developed information systems and the structure for handling data flow from the grassroot level to higher levels also carefully worked out at each organisational restructuring that is being contemplated, Also, consumer education plays a useful role in managers moving towards the culture of taking more of information-based decisions to the overall benefit of the organisation.

10

Writing Effective Business Letters

ANN RAINE THOMSON

Why are effective letters essential to importers and exporters? You write business letters for two main reasons: to get results and to provide a record. Whether you write to introduce your company, to ask for information or to give it, to make a complaint or to apologize for a mistake, your letter must do the job you want it to do.

YOUR REPRESENTATIVE

A business letter should work for you like a representative for your organization. A good "rep" will promote good relations, help create markets, smooth out problems and contribute positively to transactions. He will get closer to his clients, build up confidence and mutual understanding. A good letter can do all these things.

As an importer or exporter, you will write mainly to people whom you never meet. When you meet people face-to-face, they respond to you. They form impressions and make judgements about you from the way look and behave, from what you say and how you say it. You in turn will be sensitive to their reactions and modify your behaviour and conversation accordingly. You adjust to this immediate feedback. If you have expressed your-self badly, you can see that you have been misunderstood and try to put the situation right.

When you write you have no such opportunity to adapt and explain. Your letter must represent you on its own. How it is presented and what it contains will be all the receiver has to go by. If it's brief, clear and to the point, he will read and understand it as you intended. If it's long-winded and illogical he may not take the time to read it at all. If he does read it, he may misinterpret the message— which could be worse.

As your representative, a letter will also convey an impression of you, the writer, and of your organization. An efficient letter will reflect an efficient organization; a confused and ill-written letter will flash up "keep off" signs to the receiver. These may be hard to switch off later! Reputations are slow to build but fast to fall.

In the competitive world of international trade, survival (let alone growth) may depend on the quality of an organization's business communications. The business letter has a specially important function which no sophisticated telefax or electronic mail system has yet replaced. You will write to introduce your organization to new clients. You will write to promote your products. You will write to consolidate relationships. Telex and telefax have an importanl place in keeping day-to-day business moving, but they cannot do some of the more subtle things that an effective letter can do.

SHORT, CLEAR AND SIMPLE

To whom do you write letters? Mostly you will write to foreign clients—people whose language and customs may differ from your own. The chances are that you will communicate with them in English, now the lingua franca for international commerce.

Because so many people for whom English is not their mother tongue communicate with each other in English, a new clear, simple use of the language is now the accepted style. This international English is a functional language which crosses cultural barriers. It has no place for obscure vocabulary or complex sentences. Elaborate conventions are excluded as they may be significant only within certain cultural groups, sounding strange or even ridiculous elsewhere.

To bridge the gaps of distance and culture and to reach the *person* to whom you are writing, write as you would speak, from one person to another. Letters which are formal, aloof and addressed from "one area of possible mutual interest" to another will have little impact. The receiver will not feel involved. He will not feel. "This is for me."

Remember too that the people you write to are pressed for time. They are daily bombarded with requests and information about products. If you want your reader to take notice of any new information, your message must be instantly clear to him. It must be appealing, short and easy to read. Otherwise it will join the pile in the wastepaper bin.

These guidelines for initial letters apply equally to follow-up business. Correspondence continuing through a transaction must also be short. clear and simple. In the first place your receiver will not thank you for having to spend time reading a wordy text. In the second place, if it is not clear, he is more likely to misunderstand its precise meaning, which could be disastrous all round.

MAKING LETTERS EFFECTIVE

What makes a business letter effective? Here comes the good news! Effective letters are simple letters. One simple structure can be applied to all letters. Simple language and simple sentences communicate better. You don't need an enormous vocabulary—it is reckoned that 5,000 words is sufficient for effective business writting. So forget all the elaborate words and complex sentence structures that won you high marks at school. Reserve these for leisure. They have no place in commerce. An effective letter is a functional letter. Remember, you are writting to get results, not to win a prize for literature!

Here are four simple rules for effective letter writing:

1. Be Clear:

   Clear presentation and layout. Good margins, space between paragraphs, good type. Make it attractive. You wouldn't want your representative sloppily dressed!

   Clear, logical structure. This type of letter is easier to follow and to refer to later than one that is confused.

   It shows that the writer has thought it out. It inspires confidence and show that you are competent.

   Clear sentence structure. A sentence composed of subject+verb+object is the easiest to understand.

   Clear linked paragraphs—one idea for each.

2. Be Concise:

   Keep it short and to the point. Tell the reader what he needs to know, not everything you know.

   Aim for one page only. If you have to include a lot of information. It may be better to set this out separately and attach it. Other people may need to see this, but not necessarily the whole letter.

   Write short words, short sentences and short paragraphs. Long words and long sentences confuse the reader; large chunks of unrelieved print will tire him before he starts.

   Leave out unnecessary words and cluttering "official sounding" phrases. They obscure meaning and their impersonal tone will alienate the reader.

ANNEXURE A

Letter A: Exporter's Letter Introducing his Organization

EVER LEATHER EXPORTS

Motijheel C.A. Dhaka-2, Bangladesh

Tel: 231234 72 Telex: 642333

Your Ref. :
Our Ref. : RL/88/SR

26 October, 1988

Mr. Guido Rossi
Italia Leather Products,
Biella,
Vc
Italy

Dear Mr. Rossi,

We are exporters of high-grade dried and tanned leather and would like to make ourselves and our products known to you. As you have recently moved to a new factory which promises much greater production, we feel you will be looking for further suppliers of good quality leather.

With this letter we are sending some samples which we hope will interest you. They represent the range of quality and colours that we offer. Enclosed too is a brochure which tells you more about Ever Leather Exports and sets out our scale of prices and terms. On the back page you will find a list of manufacturers with whom we already do business. The Bruno Company in Turin and the Bianchi Company in Milan have been customers of ours for over 12 years.

I shall be in Milan in six weeks' time for the Leather Industries Trade Fair and would like to visit you at your factory during my stay. I wiil telephone you when I arrive in Italy to see when if would be convenient.

I look forward to meeting you in Biella next month.

Yours sincerely,
Shafi Rahman
Export Manager
Encl.

Layout Black Style, Justified Right Margin

Letterhead: usually printed

Reference: initials of sender/year/typist's initials

Receiver's name and address

Address Mr. Rossi by name

Opening statement
Says who they are and why they are writing

Background
Mr. Rossi's possible needs

Recommendation
Offers catalogue and samples

Basis for recommendation
Directs reader to more information
Mentions important clients

Action
Visit—when and where, will, telephone

Politeness
"Yours sincerely" matches "Dear Mr. Rossi"

Enclosures
Samples, catalogue

---

3. Be Correct:

Make sure your facts are accurate.

Use a layout which conforms to accepted patterns.

Address the reader correctly. If you know his or her name, use it. If you don't know it, find out the name if you can.

Check for errors in grammar, punctuation spelling and typing.

4. Be Complete:

Include all necessary information. Before you write, think out what your reader needs to know.

The importance of tone: As your representative, your letter should convey a tone that is natural and friendly, as you would be if you were to speak person-to-person. To follow the four simple rules for letter writting will help. It will also help if you are in line with some of the trends in acceptable writing. If you know what the acccpted style is and the reasons for it, you are more likely to strike the right note.

Trends in business and official writing: The trends in official and business writing can be summed up in four points: simple style, personal approach, the introduction of new jargon and the stronger position of women.

Simple style: The most remarkable—and the most practical—trend has been to simplify the language. (You must have guessed by now!) This has been partly due to the international use of English as a vehicle of commercial communication. However, it is also the accepted style within English-speaking countries because it is a more efficient way of exchanging information. This is one reason why multinational companies and other organizations train their staff to write effective business letters.

Personal approach: The second change has been to make business and official writing more personal. Except in the most formal situations, where protocol still sadly inhibits it or in legal documents (desperately needing to be made more accessible), writing is directed to the reader as a person. Where possible, he is referred to by name and certainly addressed in the second person as "you." Even governments have changed their style of official writing to make themselves more easily understood and to give themselves a more human—and therefore more acceptable—image. Official letters from the U.K. Government now talk to the reader as "you" and not as "persons who have resourse to . . ." etc. A motto given to the British Civil Service for its written communications is "Be short, be simple and be human." This is not a bad one to follow.

Danger of new jargon words: A third trend has been the appearance of new words. Some of the language arising out of technology and social change may be bewildering to the unintiated. Think of your reader before you use any specialist or jargon words. You may know the jargon of your business, but does he?

Position of women: Another trend, I am pleased to say, is that women now have a much stronger positition in many societies. When you write letters to a company for the first time, the manager may not necessarily be male. Try to find out whether the person you are writing to is a man or a woman. If you are unable to do so, you can use the opening "Dear Sir or Madam" if you do not include the family name in the inside address. If you do refer to a family name, for instance "J.M. Smith," it is customary to open the letter with "Dear Mr. Smith," even if you are not certain that the person is a man.

HOW TO PREPARE AN EFFECTIVE BUSINESS LETTER

Before you write a business letter ask yourself. . .

ANNEXURE B

Some Common Pitfalls

Here are some "DO's" and "DON'Ts" for writing business letters. Follow the "DO's" and your letter will look professional and be more effective. It will be more attractive, easier to read and understand and have a more personal tone. It will be an acceptable and more efficient means of communicating with your client. If will be a good representative for your organization. In short, it will get results—fulfill its purpose.

DON'T present your letter poorly.	DO make your letter look attractive.
NO	YES
Large blocks of close print.	Wide margins and plenty of while space.
Miserable small margins	An accepted layout
Blobby type	Crisp type
Scruffy paper	Good quality paper
	Short, spaced paragraphs

NB. Saving paper is not an economy if your letter is never read!

DON'T while things down as they come to mind.	DO give your letter a logical structure.
NO	YES
Illogical sequence	Plan what you want to say
Fail to outline first	Ontline your points
	Use the suggested structure
	Consider how the reader will react

DON'T address the person or sign off incorrectly.	**DO use the right conventions.**
NO	**YES**
"Dear Mr. John Smith." . . ."Yours faithfully"	**"Dears Sirs," (to an organization or company) . . ."Yours faithfuliy"**
"Dear Sir,". . . . . "Yours sincerly"	**"Dear Sir" (Madam) (to a person's position, *e.g.*, the Export Manager) . . ."Yours sincerely"**
	Use the receiver's name if you can if your letter is a reply you will know the name already.
DON'T use elaborate courtesies	**DO be clear and direct.**
NO	**YES**
***To inform*:**	***To inform*:**
"It is with great pleasure that I musl inform you that". . .	**"I am pleased to tell you". . .**
***To ask for information* :**	***To ask for information*:**
"We would be highly obliged if you would be so kind as to". . .	**"We would be pleased if you would". . .**
***To apologize*:**	***To apologize*:**
"We wish to convey to you our most humble and sincere apologies for" . . .	**"We would like to apologize" . . . "We are sorry that" . . .**
***To complain*:**	***To complain*:**
"We feel we have no alternative but to bring to your attention the fact that" . . .	**"We are disappointed that" . . . "We are sorry to inform you" . . .**

DON'T use official sounding words and phrases.

DO keep your language natural.

NO

"Please advise us of your requirements"

YES

"Please let us known when, where or how to" . . .

Avoid words like "afterment-ioned", "undersigned", "here-under", the "said" document . . .

If your letter is clear, "this" or "these" will suffice.

"Please find enclosed . . ."

"We enclose/Enclosed is". . .

"Re."/"per"/"inst."—Do not use old-fashioned officialese.

"Thank you for your letter of the 5th inst." (instant)

"Thank you for your letter of 5 November".

DON'T use "textual litter"—unnecessary phrases which add words, obscure meaning and sound formal.

DO keep your sentences simple and concise.

NO

"It was interesting to note in this connection that both types of packing were satis-factory".

YES

"Both types of packing were satisfactory".

"It is our considered opinion that there is no justification for the increase in interest rates".

"There is no justification for the increase in interest rates".

DON'T hide behind dull, im-personal phrases.

Avoid using the passive form of the verb.

DO take responsibility for what you say.

Use the active form of the verb (much more impact).

NO	YES
"It is suggested that" ...	"We suggest that" ...
"It has been decided that"...	"The department has decided that" ...
"It is proposed that" ...	"I propose"...
DON'T separate the subject of your sentence from the verb—it's hard for the reader to follow.	DO use simple sentences.
NO	YES
"In order to give you further information, a comprehensive list of our products, together with their prices, terms and conditions of sale is enclos ed".	"We enclose details of our range of products, a price list, terms and conditions of sale".
DON'T end vaguely.	DO be precise about the action you want.
NO	YES
"We look forward to your favourable reply". (When? ...	"We will telex you on 24 October to find out what quantities you need. Please let us know by (date) which of these samples you prefer".

---

1. What is the purpose of this letter? To clarify the mind, write it out in one sentence. (If there's no useful purpose, forget it.)

2. Who is to receive this letter? How much do I know about him? About his expectations and attitudes? What does he know about the topic already? What does he need to know? What does he not need to know? Be selective.

3. What do I want to happen as an immediate result? What will the next step be? How shall I follow it up? What do I want his next step to be? When? Where? How?

Planning a logical structure: This simple structure can be used for any business letter. Set out the structure first, then make notes about what you will say at each stage. You should end up with a logical sequence of points which will be easy for the reader to grasp:

Opening statement: Sets out the subject and purpose of the letter. The reader knows at first glance what it is about. The subject may be put at the top of the text as a title. Sometimes this will suffice. If there is no subject line the opening sentence(s) will make the opening statement.

Background: Any background information. Reference to previous correspondence, more details about the subject or reasons for writing.

Recommendation: The most important sentence. This will say what you have to offer—a solution to the problem, offer of product etc.—or state what you want.

Basis far recommendation: Reporting information: detail reasons for recommendation.

Action: State clearly what the next steps will be. The reader must know what will happen next. He must know what he should do and/or what you will do next.

Polite signining off: For people you know "with best wishes" or "kind regards" will do. Elaborate courtesies are out of place, even if you haven't written to the receiver before. They are too formal these days and will make you second old-fashioned.

Writing the letter: Throughout, have your reader in mind. He is a busy person: make it easy for him. So set it out in a clear and pleasing way, keep to your logical structure, make your paragraphs and sentences short and your vocabulary simple. tn fact, stick to the your rules for good writing.

Revising and editing: Before sending the letter, it's good idea to put it aside for a while before taking another look. You may see it with clearer eyes second time. So stand back and try to see how your reader is likely to react. Will he understand the points you have made? Is anything ambiguous? Is it too wordy? At the same time check it for accuracy.

Follow up the suggested action: If at the end of the letter you have said you will forward some samples or send him a telex on a certain day, do it. You must support the letter with the action promised or lose credibility.

EXAMPLES OF BUSINESS LETTERS

Some examples of letters used in international trade are given on pages 268-269 and 278-279. These letters illustrate the following points, discussed in the preceding sections:

The most acceptable forms of layout.

How the structure can be used.

Modes of addressing the receiver (usually referred to as the opening salutation).

The correct form of complimentary close to match the opening salutation.

Introduction: Letter A is an exporter's letter to introduction his organization. It illustrates:

Loyout: Block style with open punctuation. This letter has been written on a word processor where it was possible to "justify" the right margin. This gives a neat appearance.

Opening salutation: Mr. Rahman has found out Mr. Rossi's name and addresses him personally. This makes a better start to the relationship.

ANNEXURE C

Letter B: Importer's Letter to Supplier Asking for Information

AGRICULTURAL CO-OPERATIVE SOCIETY

Market Town, Mozambique

Tel: 6759990 Telex: 123456

28 October, 1988

Agricultural Supplies,
98 South Street,
Wellington,
New Zealand

Dear Sirs,

We have seen your feature page in this month's edition of "Agriculture International" and would like to have further information about your smaller back hoes for trenching.

We are a co-operative wholesale organization supplying about 50 farms in this region. One common problems has been draining the land. We have decided to invest in some basic mechanical equipment which could be rented out with a crew of operators to local farmers.

Please would you send us details of machines which meet the following requirements:

1. Machines must be suitable for working in heavy clay soils as well as sand and silt.

2. They must be simple enough for an unskilled crew.

3. Our maximum price per machine is $10,000.

We would appreciate any advice you could give us about the anticipated life of each machine and a routine for maintenance.

We have our next monthly meeting of members on 24 November and would like to present your suggestions on that day.

Yours faithfully,
J. Perez
President

Layout: *Indented Style*

Letterhead: usually printed

Addressed to company
Punctuated for indented format

Opening statement
Says why he is writing in first sentence

Background
More information
Why they want back hoes

Recommendation
Says what he wants

Basis for recommendation
Numbered points for clarity
Further information to suppliers

Action
Gives date by which he needs a reply and why

"Yours faithfully" matches "Dear Sirs"

Name of sender
Position/designation

Complimentary close: He signs off "Yours sincerely" which is correct when the receiver's name is used.

Tone: Warm and friendly. Natural language.

Inquiry: Letter B is an inquiry from an importer. Its main features are:

Layout: Indented style with full punctuation in the receiver's address.

Opening salutation: "Dear Sirs" for a letter to an organization where you don't know the position or the name of the person to whom you are writing.

Complimentary close: "Yours faithfully", used when the receiver is not addressed by name.

Numbered points: Mr. Perez has numbered his main points. This makes them stand out for the receiver. They can also be easily referred to in the reply.

From these two examples you can see that writing business letters is easy. All you have to do is follow the guidelines above. You can then be assured that your letter is an effective "representative" for your export or import business.

11

Commercial Reporting: Obtaining and Relaying Market Information Effectively

J.M. Knowles*

Among your tasks as an official commercial representative is informing your head office and your exporters at home of new market developments. As a commercial representative, you have four principal export promotion activities, each demanding a thorough knowledge of the markets for which you are responsible. These activities are finding specific trade opportunities, identifying trade barriers, monitoring other factors that influence trade, and promoting your country's goods and services. To perform these tasks, you must be able to:

- **Assess how particular products will sell, that is, is there a market for them?**

Reprinted from ITC Forum J.M. Knowles is ITC adviser on commercial representation abroad. This article is based on an ITC handbook that he recently complied and edited. *Commercial Representation: Handbook for Official Trade Representatives.

Convey clearly to your exporters at home your findings on the market prospects for their products.

Advise them on what steps they should take to pursue any market opportunities that you have uncovered.

First and foremost, however, it is essential that you be thoroughly familiar with the goods and services that your country has available for export. Your trade promotion organization (TPO) or ministry should ensure that you are given the opportunity to learn as much as possible about your country's actual and potential exports, and should keep this knowledge current by supplying your office with a continually updated exporters' register, supplemented by any other available product information, such as company brochures.

MARKET INTELLIGENCE

For your work, market intelligence is commercial information on the market potential and the marketing requirements for your country's products, and the interpretation of such information for the interpretation of such information for the guidance of your exporters. Obtaining market intelligence involves two processes:

1. Estimating sales potential in the territory covered by your post for specific export products of interest to your exporters, on the basis of research. To do this you will have to evaluate and interpret relevant commercial information related to such matters as market access and distribution channels. You will also need to analyze local and foreign competition, general market conditions and the competitive position of your country's exporters who are already selling to the market?
2. Assessing the various possible methods of approach to marketing those products successfully in the territory covered by your post.

Your primary source of commercial intelligence on your post territory should be your personal contacts with knowledeable individuals in your country(ies) of assignment. Nevertheless you must also have adequate documentation on the market(s) you are covering, as well as suitable material from home on the export supply situation.

Basic documentation: The basic reference material you will need for this work is trade and production statistics, industrial studies, directories of importers, directories of manufacturers and exporters in your home country, an economic year book, and information on foreign trade regulations, foreign exchange controls and investment policies in the market(s) you are covering. Buyers' guides on export products from home will also be useful.

In addition to reference material, you will need current economic and commercial information. The incoming flow of such published data must be sufficiently up to date and extensive to enable you to detect new trends, spot new opportunities and report on any developments of interest as they occur or as you are able to predict them.

Other information that you acquire in the course of your daily contracts and research will likewise be useful sources of documentation for your work. Examples are unpublished reports, correspondence and clippings from newspapers or periodicals.

A small, but select, commercial library that is carefully planned and managed is the best way to keep such material in an organized way. You will not be able to set the library up overnight. It will evolve over time, as you learn what kinds of information you need and what sources are available to you. Ensure that, even though the volume of documentation in your library may be small, the material you have is useful and is kept up to date.

(See Appendix A on pages 290-294 for suggestions on the sources to include in your library.)

Computerized foreign trade data: In addition to basic documentation, computerized trade data can be a usefnl tool for your analysis of the market. ITC provides trade ministries and TPOs in developing countries with computerized foieign trade data for their research on world markets and their formulation of national export promotion strategies. These stratgies, which outline trade promotion priorities, are the framework within which you should be operating abroad.

You should seek a briefing from your ministry or TPO on the extent to which it, or other institutions at home, can draw upon the computerized data available through ITC. It is provided in the following forms:

Import Tabulation System (ITS): Tabulations of foreign trade statistics on microfiche using the Comtrade databank of the UN Statistical Office.

Profilimport: Printouts of import data of various countries that enable the user to compare the export performance of his or her home country in a given product with that of other developing countries.

Statistical trade analyses: Printouts are prepared on request. They may include what are known as country profiles, import or export screening tables trade diversification tables and import or export estimation tables. If you need anr of this information, you should ask your TPO to obtain oy provide it.

The above statistical material can be supplied on magnetic tape or diskettes. Details on formats and costs are available from ITC.

Import promotion offices: About two dozen countries, including most of the industrialized ones, have set up import promotion offices that provide marketing support to exporters in developing countries. The nature and extent of their services vary from one organization to another, but in most cases they offer:

Advice to the newly arrived commercial representative on useful official and business contacts.

Marketing seminars organized specifically for commercial representatives of developing countries posted to the country.

Statistics on the country's markets; information on import regulations and procedures; lists of importers, distributors and agents.

Information on, and assistance in, participating in trade fairs.

ITC issues an annual directory of such offices (Import Promotion Offices: A Directory of Import Promotion Offices and Similar Organizations That Provide Marketing Assistance to Exporters in Developing Countries), which is probably available in the library of your ministry or TPO at home. Copies can also be obtained direct from ITC. In any event, the existance of such an office in your post territory will usually be made known to you through your first contacts with government officials in your post.

Make it a point to call on the import promotion office as early as possible and o familiarize yourself with the services it can put at your disposal.

COMMERCIAL REPORTING

Going hand in hand with your information gathering activites is the function of commercial reporting. Your task is to transmit that information to its potential users.

In general you will be expected to provide all government ministries and parastatal organizations in your country that require commercial intelligence with up-to-date background information, to enable them to follow economic and commercial trends and to consider the impact of specific developments on your country's trade position and policies. At the same time, your ministry or TPO will wish to have any information that will help existing exporters find solutions to their marketing problems or encourage new exporters to enter the market.

Commercial reporting is of two kinds. The first covers reports that you initiate on such subjects as new market opportunities and changes in the conditions for your exporters' access to the market. They also include basic country reports, market reviews and other pre-written, multi-purpose reports. The second concerns reports that you write in response to trade inquiries from your TPO and your exporters back home.

Basic guidelines: Commercial reporting can be extremely time-consuming. Do not be led astray into relaying information home at the expense of your main objective, which is to promote your country's export trade. Report only on matters that are likely to have a significant effect on your country's commercial interests. Be alert to all political and policy changes in your territory, and decide what is pertinent nent to your country's trade promotion strategy and its export community.

Ask yourself the following questions before you undertake any report in response to an inquiry, as well as when reporting on your own initiative:

Who are the main users of market intelligence?

What types of information does each target audience need?

What information is really useful, and what is not?

What will be the adverse effects if I fail to provide a particular item of information?

What direct contribution will this report make to an essential decision or a desirable action?

When deciding how much of your time you should spend on reporting, you should take such factors into account as:

Your position at the post, and the extent to which some of your colleagues may have been charged with economic and commercial reporting.

The nature of your country's export community and the prospects of these exporters in the market. If your country has a large number of exprienced traders operating in your territory, you might decide to report on items of general relevance rather than on matters of use only to individual firms. However if you have identified a small number of products that have substantial export prospects in your territory and have decided to promote them actively, your reporting should be concentrated on information that can support specific promotional efforts.

Basic reports: You should systematically report basic information on key sectors of your country's foreign trade. By periodically furnishing this information you help your trade officials at home formulate your country's trade promotion strategy, and you provide support to the international marketing efforts of your export firms.

Preparing such reports on a regular basis can also save you time later on. When you receive a request from your TPO or an exporter for a particular piece of market information, or for a report on a marketing problem, you may find that you have already done most of the research for your periodic report. All that you need to do is update what you have on hand by making one or two telephone calls.

Urgent reporting: There are many circumstances in which urgent reporting is vital to your country's economic and commercial interests. You must obviously report immediately any action or anticipated action that threatens to prevent of limit the access of any of your country's export products to the market covered by your post. Information on changes in the political climate, labour disputes affecting transport, new import restrictions, tariff revisions, variations in exchange rates and any of a vast range of other developments should be transmitted as soon as they come to your attention.

Details on new openings for your country's exports should also be relayed home immediately. To the degree possible, export opportunities should be sent direct to identified exporters listed in your exporter's register, with a copy to your TPO or ministry both for follow-up purposes and to ensure that all potential exporters are given the opportunity to submit their offers. In international trade it is usually the first acceptable offer received that wins the order. Always treat new trade opportunities as "urgent."

Major export inquiries: As the services that you provide become more familiar to and appreciated by your head office and exporters at home, demand for these services will grow. You will inevitably receive requests from exporters from exporters for assistance that you cannot respond to without extensive desk and field research. If you judge that responding to such a request would seriously disrupt your work programme, you may consider one of the following actions:

Send an interim reply to the exporter, explaining the nature and magnitude of the research required and why you cannot report before a fixed future date.

Propose that the study be undertaken immediately by one of three or four reputable marketing consultants, at the exporter's expense.

Notify your ministry or TPO of the request and ask it to take up the matter with the exporter to find a solution. If you are then required to prepare the report, your ministry or TPO should decide, in consultation with you, on any additional resources that should be provided to your post and on any modifications in your work programme.

PRE-WRITTEN MULTI-PURPOSE REPORTS

Preparing to receive business visitors and officials from home, either as individuals or in groups, will probably take a considerable amount of your time. You can lighten your workload to a great extent if you have a few standardized, multipurpose reports that you update regularly for distribution to them. Such reports should contain basic information, about your host country and its markets that is likely to be useful or even indispensable for their visit. The material for such reports is generally readily availabe.

Keep a sufficient stock of these reports on hand, ready for incorporation into the personalized brief you prepare for each visitor. To this you can add, as necessary, an ad hoc report tailored to your visitor's specific interests and requirements. including an itinerary.

Examples of pre-written reports are a basic country survey, a market review, product surveys and a visitors information brief.

Market review: In the market review you analyze and interpret the statistical information in your country survey and present the most significant aspects of the market in a form that your readers can easily absorb. Your main objective is to identify areas in which your suppliers are likely to be competitive and thereby to encourage them to enter the market.

Your market review should contain an assessment of current market conditions and prospects and an explanation of why the market is of interest. Take into account such factors as the size and growth potential of the market as a whole and of specific import categories. Indicate your country's market share in total imports. State which of your products sell well and why (for instance because of their price, delivery or quality), and which are doing poorly or losing ground, and why.

APPENDIX A

Setting up Your Commercial Library

As a commercial representative, you should assure that the library in your office contains timely information on the topics of prime concern for your work.

Some of the main categories of publications, documents and files that should be available in your library are given below:

1. *Trade, production and other economic statistics*: You can subscribe to these through the government statistical office. Be selective, as it will often be possible to consult certain types of statistics at the source or in public libraries of institutions.

2. *Customs tariffs*: It is not usually necessary to maintain a full set of customs tariff documents. They are frequently so voluminous and complex that only a full-time specialist can interpret them with any degree of accuracy. Investigate other ways of obtaining the product classification and rates of duly (or other fiscal charges) applicable to individual products.

   One common source of such information is customs brokers or forwarding agents, who will supply the required information, probably without charge, if it is likely to lead to future business with your exporters. Another source is buyers who have long experience with customs treatment of the goods in question.

   The most up-to-date and authoritative source of such information is the customs administration itself. However, final rulings are made only when the goods reach the part of entry.

3. *Import regulations*: Your commercial library should receive all official notices published by the government

concerning foreign goods entering the country, covering such topics as:

Import licensing.

Import quotas.

Prohibited imports.

Other compulsory measures.

Import procurement.

Preferential trading arrangements.

This information appears in your host government's official gazette, journal or bulletin that formally announces all laws and regulations. The ministries concerned (*i.e.*, trade or finance) may issue monthly or quarterly periodicals that give a more detailed explanation of the nature of any new measures or changes announced.

4. *Other laws and regulations*: Your office should receive all official publications covering regulations on food and drugs, animal and plant health controls, safety and standards, and labelling and marking. Many of these regulations may be issued by the ministry of agriculture or the ministry of health. As with customs information, they may be complex and require the interpretation of experts.

State, provincial and regional governments often have their own laws and regulations affecting imports, particularly on health, safety and other aspects of consumer protection. Their published statistics may also be useful for market rerearch.

5. *The press*: The following are among the newspapers and magazines that you should obtain for your library and consult regularly:

Daily press: A leading national newspaper and a major national business newspaper or, alternatively, an international newspaper, such as the *Financial Times* of London.

Weekly press: A leading local economic or business magazine, if available, and/or an international weekly such as *The Economist*.

Monthly or quarterly periodicals specializing in subjects such as trade, marketing, agriculture, industry, transport and shipping, capital projects, banking and consumer goods.

6. *Trade and business directories*: These are specialized directories that may be available in your territory, listing different types of companies or organizations:

Manufacturing firms in general

Companies in specific manufacturing sectors (*e.g.*, food, clothing)

Construction firms, contractors

Transport firms,

Banking and other financial institutions

Publicity and advertising agencies

Trade fair and exhibition organizers

Importers

Wholesalers

Distributors

Jobbers

Commission agents

Retailers in general

Department stores

Supermarkets

Chain stores

7. *Institutional of business association publications*: Your office may wish to subscribe to the annual or other publications of selected professional and research institutions or business associations, chambers of commerce and the like. Their periodicals often contain useful market intelligence for your exporters.

8. *Company publications*: Most companies will provide annual reports and published bulletins of newsletters on request. Arrange for your office to receive such periodicals regularly.

9. *Exporters' register*: Among the most important sources of information from home is your country's official register of exporters, if one has been set up, supplemented by product catalogues issued by various companies. Make sure that your office has a copy of the register and receives regular updates to it. Use this register in responding to trade inquires from home and from your territory and in undertaking product-specific promotional activities.

10. *Index of your firms' local representatives*: An index of local firms that are already agents or representatives of your country's exporters, or are interested in becoming so, can be set up in your library on the basis of questionaries sent to all such firms in your post territory. This index should help you to establish contact rapidly between your potential exporters at home and possible agents or representatives in your territory.

11. *Importers' and exporters' lists*: Set up and maintain, on a product-by-product basis, lists of direct importers and exporters in your post territory to be supplied on request to your exporters and importers at home. The lists should concentrate on products for which your country has a demonstrated capacity to export or a clear need to import. Establish the lists on the basis of

direct inquiries from importers and exporters, as well as information obtained from trade directories, chambers of commerce, trade associations, personal contacts and so on.

12. *Contact register*: Maintain a register of useful professional and social contracts. Base it on a compilation of calling cards, and organize it alphabetically. Jot down pertinent information on each contact on the back of each card.

13. *Other company information*: Catalogues, price lists and other material on the goods or services of companies and organizations are an important source of information in your commercial library. They should be filed alphabetically by name of firm or oganization. Those originating from home should be separated from those obtained locally. If you receive more than one or two copies of catalogues or product pamphlets distribute the extras to potential agents or buyers.

Basic Guidelines on Commerical Reporting

Identify your target audience.

Decide what their information needs are.

Be selective and concentrate on reporting that will help to increase exports.

Supply information on new market developments through ad hoc and period reports.

Report urgently when justified.

Maintain a balance between reporting and other export promotion activities.

Emphasize the prospects for improving your market share in different lines of goods. Examine product categories that have sold steadily or progressed quickly after their introduction and those supplied by other countries with which your products (perhaps with some adaptation) should be able to compete. Mention criticisms of your countrys' products, together with your views on how to overcome them.

Include any other important topics relevant to your exporters such as competitors' marketing methods and advantages, markèting trends, distribution systems, promotional techniques. purchasing groups and authorities, financial considerations, and market and economic projections.

End your report by recommending specific steps to enable your exporters to enter the market or to expand their shares in it.

Update your market review at least once a year.

Product surveys: Any market surveys on particular products that you have writien in response to specific requests from your ministry or TPO or on your own initiative should be standardized for distribution to other users. Surveys provided to individual exporters at their request can be similarly adapted by removing any commercially confidential information. These surveys can serve many purposes and save you a great deal of time in preparing new reports.

Such surveys identify the possibilities for marketing particular products and any problems that may be involved. They should usually contain basic information on import statistics, local production, current competition, market requirements, import duties and regulations, prices, trade channels, and your conclusions and recommendations for action. Update item before each use to ensure that all information is still valid.

Visitors' information brief: A visitors' information brief is a general-purpose document for persons coming to your post country for a short period of time. It can include details on:

Requirements for passports, visas and vaccinations.

Foreign exchange regulations; customs concessions for visitors.

Official holidays; office hours; working days; the time difference between your home country and your post country.

Recommended hotels and restaurants.

Main banks, airline offices, tourist bureaus, travel agents, post offices and so on.

Communication charges.

Business services available including interpretation, translation and secretarial help.

Medical facilities; health considerations, such as potable water.

Suggested format and text for visiting cards; special customs and courtesies; tipping practices.

Climate; recommended clothing.

Electric current voltages.

Free-time activities—sports facilities, cultural sites, shops, cinemas, theatres and so on.

Where appropriate give names, addresses, contact persons, telephone numbers, costs and your recommendations. Some of this information will be available in brochures.

The other standard documents that you should provide are maps of the country and of major cities, and a selected list of your office personnel with their telephone numbers and home addresses.

Brief for business visitors to your country: If you are able to do so, and if there is a demand for such a document, you may wish to prepare a visitors' information brief, for business persons and trade officials from your post territory going to your home country. It should cover the same type of information as the brief on your post territory. It can facilitate the visit of such persons, who are important for your country's trade relations.

12

Radio As a Trade Promotion Tool

BILL McCABE*

The South Pacific Trade Commission's radio programme, "Pacific Sunrise," has effectively stimulated business and trade development in the region. The South Pacific Trade Commission (SPTC), which works to promote business development in and trade from the island members of the South Pacific Forum, realized several years ago that there was a lack of current trade information in these islands (the Cook Islands, Fiji, Kiribati, Niue, Papua New Guinea, Solomon Islands, Tonga, Tuvalu, Vanuatu, Western Samoa, Federated States of Micronesia, Palau, Marshall Islands and Nauru). Wishing to promote the activities of the Commission and the assistance it can provide, we developed ideas for a weekly radio programme and supporting activities such as a monthly newsletter and a limited advertising campaign. We called the project "Pacific Sunrise" and set out to sell the idea to Radio Australia.

*Reproduced from ITC *Forum*. Bill McCabe is a Senior Trade Commissioner of the Australian Government in charge of the South Pacific Trade Commission in Sydney. He has served nearly 20 years as a Trade Commissioner with the Australian Government.

SETTING UP THE PROGRAMME

"Pacific Sunrise," from the beginning, was to be a new kind of programme, one to be produced by the "hard information" section of Radio Australia, namely the "News and Current Affairs" department. It was to be produced by that department precisely because of that office's ability to deliver balanced, accurate, factual information that is editorially independent of any vested interests, including those of the South Pacific Trade Commission. So, although the SPTC was to be an important source of information and talent (not to mention paying the bills) for the new programme, it was to be put under the same scrutiny as the other regional and national trade and business organizations. The same applied to Australia's interests in the region. (Radio Australia is a Government-funded, independent organization working under the Australian Broadcasting Corporation; the SPTC is an internationally funded Commission ultimately responsible to the South Pacific Forum).

The South Pacific Trade Commission thus came to Radio Australia with a proposal that complemented Radio Australia's desire to provide relevant and effective information services to the South Pacific islands. We also came prepared to fund the programme on a semi-commercial basis, which fitted in well with Radio Australia's newly formed business plan: The SPTC was prepared to buy Radio Australia's services but not its editorial independence.

The arrangement that was worked out was that the radio programme would be produced by the SPTC utilizing staff and facilities leased from Radio Australia. Specifically, the programme would be prepared by a staff journalist from the "News and Current Affairs" section of the radio. The SPTC gave permission to Radio Australia to broadcast the programme and was given free access to all of the information collected for it. (This is now used with additional material to produce a monthly newsletter). The budget for the programme was negotiated between Radio Australia and the SPTC and was to be paid to Radio Australia monthly.

It has been a credit to the flexibility and sensitivity of both sides that an agreement was not only negotiated but has also been successfully implemented. It has now been in operation for over a year and a half. The relationship between the two organizations is unusual and provides a model that others may be able to apply or adapt to their own circumstances when starting a new radio programme of this type.

KEY FEATURES OF THE PROGRAMME

One of the first principles that we set down for the programme is that it is "market driven." That is, the information broadcast must fill a vacuum for business listeners in the Forum island countries and territories and be packaged in a way that is consistent with current listening styles are radio conventions in the South Pacific. For the former, Radio Australia has relied on the SPTC, and for the latter, the SPTC has relied on Radio Australia.

"Pacific Sunrise" is a 15-minute weekly programme presented by an announcer from one of the islands with experience in information programming. Fifteen minutes was judged to be the appropriate length, one reason being that business people are busy and unable to listen regularly to a longer programme going on the air at the peak breakfast or evening broadcast times.

The use of a local announcer is important to help listeners to identify with the programme, although this is not without complications. Although these islands share many of the same trade and business problems, they do not have a common ethnic, cultural or historical background. Choosing the wrong presenter, or using him in the wrong way, could easily turn listeners away.

The theme music was chosen with the same attention to market preference and local sensitivities. Indigenous music is not used since it could put off a significant part of our listeners, given their diverse backgrounds. Music that has political undertones is also avoided.

Apart from the obvious imperative that the programme has to be acceptable to the market to be effective is the added factor that it is produced and broadcast under Radio Australia's name—an independent information service. It cannot give even the impression—let alone make reality—that its independence is negotiable. Such an impression would destroy the credibility of the programme, The programme also has to be acceptable to local radio stations, many of which are government run.

The language of the programme is English only. This decision was made largely for economic reasons. At least a dozen indigenous first languages are used in these islands, but the expense of providing companion programmes, editorally sound and reliably delivered to the various countries, is beyond any possible budget that the SPTC could provide. Fortunately, English is spoken by most decisionmakers of the region and is the language of business. We encourage local stations to translate any items that interest them and re-broadcast in local languages.

DELIVERING THE PROGRAMME

Delivery of "Pacific Sunrise" has proved to be the most difficult problem we have faced, and it remains a difficulty. One of the key reasons for the lack of information in the region is that communication systems are not highly developed. Satellite communications are limited, there is little use of tax, and there is no regional radio station (Radio Australia tries to fill this role), no regional newspaper, no television and few magazines. Because of the infrequency of (lights into some of the islands, even postal service is slow.

Ironically, the element that provides our market opportunity also provides our biggest challenge. We need to deliver the programme quickly to maintain the information edge that up-to-date material provides. We decided, therefore, to broadcast the programme during the period of Monday evening into

Tuesday morning, on Radio Australia's South Pacific shortwave service, in the hope that local stations would record it and re-broadcast the programme by the end of the week. Many of the target islands were already doing this for a number of Radio Australia's programmes, most significantly the "News and Current Affairs" service. We therefore broadcast the programme three times to reach all of the locations at peak listening times and also to provide more than one opportunity to record if shortwave conditions are giving unacceptable quality.

CONTENT OF THE PROGRAMME

In terms of content, we have divided the programme into three parts. The first item is a reportage and analysis of current developments in business and trade. This includes news on visiting trade delegations or trade shows; regional policy on airlines, hotel development or fisheries; scientific developments allowing for the growth or improvement of new industries; and so on.

The second item is on commercial and banking developments. This covers such subjects as exchange rate changes; bank lending policy; other new developments in the banking sector; take-overs or changes in multinationals affecting trade; and macro-economic issues.

The final item might loosely be called an educational or motivational item. Successful business people are interviewed to provide role models for success; also items have been included on personnel management, the challenges of quick growth of a business, the problems for collectives in approaching banks and so on.

In all of these items we have attempted to take the following attitudes:

1. The aim of the item is to inform and explain—not to criticize or "break a story" for its own sake.

2. In developing areas where resources and skills are scarce, the objective is to encourage their development where they exist, not to emphasize the cases in which they are lacking. Failure in key areas is not ignored, but is kept in perspective.

3. Problems are regarded as challenges with perhaps as yet obscure solutions—not as reasons for discouragement; individual failure is looked upon as a valuable learning resource.

4. Since the region is likely to understand its own problems better than Australian-based experts, the majority of the items are collected directly from the region or the people concerned—such as the foreign investor. (This exacerbates the delivery problem by shortwave since most of this material has to be collected by telephone from the region, placed into the programme, broadcast shortwave, recorded off-air and finally re-broadcast locally. The original phone quality needs to be very good for such a process).

5. Where the item is provided by one of Radio Australia's own correspondents or an Australian expert, the information is either treated as a "straight" piece of reportage or is presented as part of a current debate, not the "answer to all the region's problems." Pieces that seem too didactic or over-opinionated are avoided.

6. The programme does not regard trade as existing in a vacuum—as something apart from political, cultural and social processes. Nor does it regard export business as somehow separate from domestic business activity. The programme therefore looks at all areas of business activity and, where they affect business, also at the political, social and cultural processes. The emphasis is no *process* rather than *event*, since the programme is conscious that any one item can take only a tiny slice

of time. Thus continuity of themes and conscientiously following up stories is an important aspect of the programme. This is another reason why the programme is weekly and why the associated "Pacific Sunrise" newsletter is very important.

INFORMATION COLLECTION

The information is largely collected by the person serving both as the journalist and the producer, and to a lesser extent by the presenter, who is encouraged to have as active an involvement in the programme as his time allows. It is collected from the following sources:

1. The South Pacific Trade Commission. The SPTC is both a source of information and the object of various items, as circumstances dictate.
2. Individual contacts in the region of the producer and Radio Australia's specialist South Pacific correspondents based in both Australia and the region.
3. Regionally and nationally based newspapers and trade and business magazines.
4. The major international news agencies and also Pacnews, the South Pacific News Ageney, both of which are subscribed to by Radio Australia.

EVOLUTION OF THE PROGRAMME

The programme has evolved slowly. We believe that our basic assumptions on the approach and content of the programme have proved to be right. However there has been a "learning curve," particularly for Radio Australia, in terms of the correct level for the programme. We have found that the basic business, commercial and economic concepts need to be explained carefully, as much of the business community in the target audience has had little or no formal education in business or economics. Thus the amount of material we cover in one item has to be well disciplined and limited. This pushes us further toward a thematic approach and running follow-up items or series.

The structure of the programme has evolved so that the entire programme, not just the last item, has become implicitly educative (we hope). The first item mentioned above, that of a reportage and an analysis of current developments in business and trade, while remaining a piece of current information, now tends to look more at the larger issues affecting trade and business at a regional or national level than it did in the beginning. For example, this might include regional policy on tourism, or national balance-of-trade figures.

The second item, originally conceived as information on commercial and banking developments, now concentrates on the impact of these subjects on individuals or smaller business groupings at the local level. The last item, the educational or motivational part, remains the same as originally designed, *i.e.*, business success stories and marketing and management features.

It has become obvious to us during our initial period of running the programme that the regional approach, rather than a country-by-country approach, is very valuable. Broadcasters in some of the islands first told us that they would be interested in carrying only those items that talked about their own situations directly. Now, however, they are telling us that it is often easier to look at some problems objectively by watching what other islands in the region are saying about the same issues, rather than considering only what is going on in "their own backyard." This had led them to accept the weekly, thematic approach as valuable and has stimulated us to make sure that the majority of our items have a regional application at some level or other.

One of our concerns when beginning the programme, knowing that we wanted the programme to be re-broadcast locally, was the degree to which discussions of political events or government policy as it affected business should be included in the programmes. In all of the islands we have found a realistic acceptance of items that draw clear parallels between political events, processes and policies on the one hand, and business activities, on the other. We do not, however, treat polities on its own, separate from trade.

In all respects, therefore, we have found that the programme has developed into one of both high credibility and established editorial independence.

DISTRIBUTION

Distribution has remained a serious problem. We have found that not enough of our target audience (that is, small and medium-size business people, government officials and opinion makers) have access to shortwave radio. That has confirmed our original opinion that, for the programme to be successful, it has to be broadcast on local radio stations. It has also been proven that one of the key success factors of the programme is its ability to provide up-to-date relevant information. Almost none of the managers of the radio station we have spoken to is willing to accept the far-from-perfect reproduction of an off-air recording from Radio Australia, and they have the problem of insufficient staff resources to record the programme at the times we broadcast it on Radio Australia. We are not willing to sacrifice the currency of the programme by sending the programme in tape-recorded form through the mail into the region—this would involve at least a two-week delay.

There is some hope that point-to-multi-point satellite delivery may become possible in some of our target countries in the not-too-distant future. In the meantime, we have attempted to solve the problem partially be re-scheduling the programme so that it immediately follows the "South Pacific News" and "Current Affairs" bulletins, which these stations are already recording and re-broadcasting daily. This will not, of course, solve the quality problems, but if may solve the rostering problems. We have agreed, however, to send the tape recording of the programme by post to two islands that we believe will receive the material within two or three days. We are yet to assess the success of this change. Certainly all of the local stations we have spoken to are keen to broadcast the programme as a service to their business communities.

FEEDBACK

Feedback on a programme such as this is not easy to obtain and assess. Nonetheless, after nine months of broadcasting we decided that there was sufficient awareness of the programme to spend some time in five key islands of the region to both assess its impact and further market "Pacific Sunrise." We found broad enthusiasm for the programme, not only among the business communities but alsokey opinion makers in the government and elsewhere.

In general terms, the business community has applauded the programme as a rare opportunity for business issues to be given a good platform for debate, on a par with other current issues and problems. Both the radio stations and the business communities have been impressed by the editorial stance of the programme and its quality, both in terms of the information and packaging.

The value of the programme appears to be its obvious ability to network ideas and information quickly and effectively around the region. The programme results not so much in the creation of new business as in making people aware of business opportunities and how to realize them. It allows for a better informed debate among isolated business communities on regional issues that affect them directly, and for some listeners it has helped them recognize that they face problems in common with others throughout the region.

Perhaps the most talked about section of the programme during our visits was that on training. This is recognized as potentially the most useful part of the programme. Of all the material used for that portion, the success stories of local business people have been most appreciated. These provide examples that can be followed, as well as solid business training information. In these islands, where business activity is new, if a success story can include several initial failures in the process that were used as learning experiences to achieve success, this can encourage young business people to continue their efforts. Also appreciated on this part of the programme is the better understanding of the kind and variety of support services provided by the SPTC.

None of this, of course, is quantifiable feedback—but it does come after speaking with the leaders and members of all the business communities of those islands, and with officials of government agencies and trade-related institutions.

We have also had feedback in terms of inquiries about individual products, ideas or scientific developments mentioned on the programme. It will take some time, however, to assess whether they have matured into new business ventures.

We know that relevant, cost-effective and accessible information is very hard to come by for the business communities of these islands, and we believe that the positive response to "Pacific Sunrise" has been recognition that we have come up with something new that, to an extent, fills that information vacuum.

SPIN-OFFS

The programme has given rise to a number of actual and potential spin-offs. The most obvious is the newsletter that we publish monthly with selected material from the programme, as well as additional material. This further allows us to disseminate what we believe to be important ideas and opportunities and to raise the public profile of the STPC. We have distributed the newsletter to all of the chambers of commerce and manufacturers, selected business leaders and key government sectors in the region. There was initially a problem of circulating the newsletter within the receiving organizations, as it was often kept in the office to which it was sent rather than handed around, but we have now taken steps to ensure a more universal distribution. The newsletter is now incorporated as a permanent feature in the monthly *Islands Business* magazine, which has a circulation of 6,000 and is expanding rapidly.

Other spin-offs of the radio programme are currently being discussed. In addition, a number of business organizations in the region have expressed strong interest in using "Pacific Sunrise" as a model to network their own information. Also, business groups are very keen to have the training component of the programme significantly extended and are willing to support the idea in concrete ways.

FUTURE DEVELOPMENTS

Our key problem for the moment is to provide fast, universal, high-quality distribution of the programme to the local stations. This, we have every reason to believe, should be effected within the next several months. All of the local stations we contacted are keen to take the programme (and, incidentally, any companion programmes we may wish to produce). After that, I believe our main challenge will be the same as many maturing programmes—to keep it fresh and relevant. It is doubtful that the programme itself will be changed substantially, but we are considering companion proposals to extend the more valuable elements of the programme in other ways.

SUGGESTIONS FOR OTHERS

For those wishing to begin a similar project, we would make the following recommendations:

1. Target the audience very clearly and specifically.

2. Consider not only the information needs of that audience, but also the way in which that audience most

easily assimilates information. This is not simply a question of packaging but of culture, language and history—perhaps even the medium used.

3. Maintain the credibility of the programme by leaving it free of vested interests. We believe that the obvious editorial independence of our programme has won it greater across-the-board acceptance than any other approach we might have taken.

4. Make certain that both the contractual and less formal relationship between the funding organization and the producer it clear and unambiguous. It has been possible for Radio Australia and the SPTC to negotiate the difficult area of editorial policy only because of such a clear relationship from the beginning.

5. It is absolutely essential that the individuals responsible for a programme of this type have not only a strong information background but also a sensitive understanding and respect for the people to whom they are broadcasting. A programme such as ours is not a traditional current affairs programme.

CONCLUSION

In conclusion, this radio programme has been an attempt to treat both the successes and the failures of business and trade activities in the region and to learn, for the benefit of the audience, something from each. Its underlying feature has been to use the somewhat "hard-nosed" approach to information of a radio's current affairs department to better enable those listening to further their own ends—in this case to assist business development in the Forum Island countries and territories of the South Pacific.

13

A Management Overview of Public Relations

R.P. BILLIMORIA

The function of management is to formulate policies and gear the organisation to achieve the aims and objectives of the enterprise. Thus the Public Relations Department (PRD) as a department should contribute in each of its activities towards the objective of the corporate body namely, to produce goods and services at a profit for the benefit of the community and those who work in the organisation. Any activity which does not contribute towards this end is redundant. This is not only to describe the public relations (PR) speciality but to lay down a system by which top management and the PRD could ensure that the public relations function which contributes towards the objective of the enterprise and to monitor its functioning towards this end.

PR, AXIOMS AND INTERESTS

How does management view public relations? It looks upon it as that function of management which ensures good will and acceptance for the organisation and its products or services, with identifiable groups of people effecting its present and future existence, and growth.

There are some axioms which public relations experts, advertisers and businessmen often fail to accept:

PR effort has marginal or negative value in case of all sub-standard products or a product whose price is non-competitive.

PR effort has significant effect in the case of a quality product vis-a-vis its competitors.

Broadly, the following may be considered as interests which are to be catered to by the Public Relations Department.

INTERNAL

Employees

Workers

Share-holders

EXTERNAL

Customers or potential customers
Suppliers
Distributors
State Governments and Central Government at all levels
Trading/Educational Institutions; and
Media.

It is understood that under 'External', the international markets and their Governments and other bodies concerned, have also to be kept in mind.

SYSTEMS APPROACH

A systems approach to management, consisting of input, activity and output, would bear application to functions like public relations and personnel as well.

In giant enterprises in the private sector and public sector as well, there is crying need for an integrated systems view emphasising the direct relationship between sub-systems like public relations and the total business objective of the organisation. We have to start thinking of PR not as a cosmetic appendage of management but as a major supporting sub-system of the total management system. One has to complement and support the other by being logically and sequentially related. This will be of importance to top management in that the systems view will enable the evaluation of PR activities by the degree to which they are determined by and contribute directly to the accomplishment of business objectives.

Let us, therefore, try and propose a systems concept not in a strait-jacket but as a tentative approach to be modified and adapted from time to time. This will help in planning, designing, implementing and assessing the value of PR programmes. In this concept, management would be able to answer the questions: Does the design of each PR programme or activity contribute to or, does it have no relevance or bears no discernible relationship to overall objectives?

WHAT EXISTS

You will notice that the traditional PR activities such as internal PR, and external PR are functioning separately under a titular chief of public relations. There is hardly any formalised communication and feedback among these sub-functions which may be working as separate empires pursuing their own individual objectives. This would result in few ties among the sub-functions, no logical flow of plan and action and no formal use of feedback form performance in order to modify plans for the future. May it be emphasised that the ritual of a monthly or ad hoc meeting does not serve the purpose.

We have spoken of company objectives. Some may argue that these are not enunciated in many organisations. But virtually all of them have objectives whether in writing or implied. There is no clear or direct relationship between such objective and in any direct functions of PR. The PR programmes do not flow out of the objectives and the sub-functions of PR. The PR programmes do not flow out of the objective in any definable manner. And hence the programmes and processes do not depend upon the objectives. For example, the PRD may plan or conduct training programmes or seminars merely because it has been done in the past or because some boss has spoken vaguely about the need for such training which is given by another prestigeous company as well. In quite a few cases you do not find any direct relationship between the programme and the requirements of the organisation as specified.

In some, the tendency is for each function and each sub-function to view itself as independent and to aim at the optimisation of its own speciality. Each tries to measure its own performance by the yard-stick of its own internal standards. This in turn leads to a 'subject optimisation' because the separate parties are not logically fitting together and balanced as an integrated system pursuing a unified set of goals directed towards achieving the objectives of the enterprise.

CLOSED-LOOP FEED BACK SYSTEM

Now let us study a Closed-Loop Feed Back System integrated with the total management system of the organisation. This system is geared to PR making the maximum contribution to the objectives of the organisation. The inputs, it will be noticed, are from the larger total management system consisting of items such as government policy forecast financial forecast and marketing forecast. The system is aimed to produce outputs for the individual employee as well as for the organisation.

The PR system has within it, systems for employment and placement of killed personnel, that training and development and external and internal PR. It indicates one full cycle of PR planning performance and feed back process. As may be obvious, this process of feed back does not take place in separate or clearly definable cycles. Each of the sub-systems is actually in various continuing stages of planning, performing and receiving feed back all at the same time.

At the beginning of every planning cycle, various forecasts (inputs) on Government policy, market, finance and others as also what the company is capable of doing in terms of material and human resources are considered while formulating the objectives of the organisation. This statement of company objectives now becomes the single input into the PR system. This leads in turn, to PR organisation plans consisting of statements of various steps which need be taken in order to meet the objectives of the company. Such action is largely of three types: staffing of the organisaton; working on external and internal PR activities; and evaluation.

Manpower requirements are tied up with the inventory of manpower resources from the Personnel Department or elsewhere, in order to produce staffing and placement plants. To make this inventory of value, PR requirements of manpower are enunciated in terms of skill, training, performance and other requirements. This is followed by appropriate training and development which provides a direct feed back to the manpower inventory and to the inputs of personnel an d industrial-relations (IR) and internal capability forecasts.

The organisation plans lead to plans for external and internal PR, both of which are determined in order to ensure that they are consistent and complementary and do not over-lap or confict. Furthermore, their needs must contribute to what is required of them so as to meet the company's objectives. For example, PR should not embark on programmes to improve its style of performance or because somebody else is doing it. According to the systems approach no activity or change in activity is appropriate unless it can be demonstrably be related to and be functional for achieving company objectives.

EVALUATION

It is with this background that the PR performance of individuals and the organisation is evaluated and analysed by matching results against objectives, enumerating various factors effecting results, analysing strengths and weaknesses and chalking out action plans which are fed back to the column of inputs.

Evaluation of PR activity is mostly difficult. It is easy for product publicity. For example, if a press get-together with a goad press kit announcing a new product leads to many enquiries and higher sales, evaluation is easy. But many results are less tangible. Take for instance, the company journal. It is difficult to prove that if the house journal had not existed for three years, there would have been a strike! Nor is it easy to attribute the upward or downward movement of share value to a particular PR programme.

Public opinion research in an added tool for evaluation and analysis. Reliable organisations in this field of speciality are unfortunately few in this country. But it has been proved that such projects can often indicate the source of discontent among employees or reveal previously unknown reasons of lagging sales. All this information can be used by the PRD to re-orient various action plans and initiate new ones.

RESULTS

The function of top management is certainly not to understand all the technicalities of PR but a closed loop feed back system would indicate, at any point of time, periodically or whenever there is a review, whether the department as a whole or any individual action plan is contributing towards the total corporate objectives. It will prevent PRD executive and other individuals from looking upon themselves as specialists of separate functions. They will start looking at their sub-system as a part of the total management system. The Director of PR will not ask: Is our programme conforming to the latest thinking in public relation? Can we make it more extensive? He will, instead ask: Do PR activities mesh with the activities and programmes in other sub-systems in order to make the total system more effective? This will be the first major management step towards a total re-orientation and gearing of the whole organisation to make it effective in fast changing items.

14

Audit of Information and Reporting Systems

P. CHATTOPADHYAY

Audit signifies regular and systematic review and apppraisal of specific activities from the point of view of knowing and judging the direction of efforts in practice and the ways in which such efforts could be brought back on the rail whenever centrifugal tendencies were noticed. This paper purports to bring these aspects in bolder relief so that management remained aware and conscious of the facts and the expectations as well as the deviations noticed in practice. The paper underlines that data and information are often misconstrued in practice. While data are facts as they are, information is the result of action-oriented analysis so that management is fed with the right impulses for moving forward. There appears to be a sort of inverse correlation between the availability of organized data in a processed form and their use for managerial purposes of looking into the future. While the usefulness of information based on hindsight is indeed useful, it is so only for a limited purpose such as to apply diagnostic tools, to know the causal relationships of factors to be reckone with and the reasons why targets could not be fulfilled so that they could be sorted out either by way of removal of snags or by that of revision of targets of attainment. The process of audit of information and reporting systems in the organizational context is a composite of multi-disciplinary approaches. The audit activities as such would require a composite team of experts so that each problem in the field of information and reporting systems was examined on its merit with reference to each of the facets involved. Economics of information systems, cost-benefits of analysis of such information and aspects of information explosion are matters with which management would be increasingly concerned with the see-change in information technology, on the one hand, and the process of management itself, on the other. Audit in its comprehensive sense underlines regular and systematic review and appraisal of systems and procedures concerning various factors and forces contributing to the realization of organization goals Review implies looking backward, going into the relationship of different factors accounting for performance and contributing to improvement in the state of affairs with respect to both stock and flow aspects. Appraisal relates to linking up past with the present for projecting into the future. The subtle distinction between review and appraisal is not always appreciated and used interchangeably in many cases. Recognition of this distinction, however, opens up vistas that otherwise remain closed.

On the other hand, 'regular' means that with reference to both time intervals and continuity of assessment. 'Systematic,' from our point of view, focuses attention of objectivity in the assessments made, application of tools and techniques of analysis for making such assessment and shifting various factors that account for better or worse performance in relation to the present. Thus regular and systematic review and appraisal imply much bigger and deeper dimensions that what merely financial audit indicates. The comprehensive span envisaged in audit as understood in this way has the sole objective of keeping track of factors of production in their static and dynamic ramification in practice and in their potential and kinetic characteristics. We have attempted to show all these elements in a summarized form in the Charts I and II.

Information and reporting systems in organizations are designed to help management in their decision making processes. Naturally such information and reporting are concerned with both back and forth thrusts of information so that management remains wiser on the basis of studied interrelationships of different variables and projecting into the future with the required degree of confidence. This is important especially when one considers what Peter Drucker mentioned of decision making as 'making the future today.' Since today's decision would manifest itself in actions tomorrow, it is absolutely essential that management is fed with the required information and analysis to know and judge the impacts anticipated of different alternative courses of action from which selection of one is to be made.

Here one may mention the aspects concerned primarily with hindsight, those connected with present activities and those that in the main relate to foreseeing what is going to happen tomorrow, day after and later. Time horizon is, therefore, an important aspect of planning into the future. There are different questions that remain innate in information reporting systems that should be considered for the purpose not only of designing such systems but also of making them more sensitive to the requirements for different levels of management. We say different levels purposely. The dimension of information needs, the character of information to be supplied and the nature of action to be taken thereon differ according to hierarchical positions in organizational set up, apart from the functional typicalities and requirements in different operational areas.

The first question that concerns one is related to different terms that are current in the context of information and reporting systems. One, it is essential to know the difference of meaning and significance of such terms as datum, data and information. While datum is a single bit event, data are many such bits, data being the plural of datum. When data are put into analytical processes, what comes out is information. Thus, processed, analyzed and sensitized data may finally result in giving information which, in their raw form, data are simply incapable of doing. Moreover, the same set of data may provide different type of information for different executives relating to both hierarchical levels and functional areas. Two, it is curious indeed that there occurs an inverse correlation between the immediately available data and their usability for decision making purposes of different levels of management.

Complete knowledge exists only with reference to the past. Since decision making implies projecting into the future, experience is hardly a complete and final guide to what would be happening tomorrow and day after. Trends may be dysfunctional due to various reasons. In fact, and most significant, most crucial decisions of management, infested as they are with risks and uncertainties, are commonly based essentially on grossly inadequate information figuring as no better than faint signs and symptoms, either showing broadly the direction or showing very vaguely the magnitude of possibility or the character of impacts that particular actions may trigger off. Last but not the least, one carries the feeling that a computer is a be-all and end-all of information systems, not quite appreciative of the fact that inadequate information. analysed in whatsoever dextrous and sophisticated manner, may not inform in the desired manner.

The tone of our reference to hindsight may suggest as if we do not appreciate the value of experience; far from it. We underline that past experience is only as good as lt shows how things could have happened if certain factors could be taken better care of, what relationships exist between individual factors and among factors of some significance so that the relationship itself can be taken as a knowledge for future projection. Curiously indeed, accounting information, though most detailed and most organized most of the time, is not immediately helpful to management for projecting into the future, unless the future is itself taken as an extension of what happened in the past. Extrapolation is indeed one of the tools of analysis of the 'decisioning phenomena', a term used by Gore and Dyson, but extrapolated extensions may not help management except very vaguely.

The information needs of management, manner in which data are collected and processed into information, the methods by which such information is conveyed to different decision and action centres are matters of immediate interest to not only the top management but also various levels of functional management. The manner in which data are collected from different sources, both from within and outside the organization, and the communication process, come in for emphasis for different reasons in the present context. Management, as it ramifies in practice, both in the context of general management and functional management, involves certain essential skills and activities like planning, organizing, decision making, measuring and controlling, or shall we say planning, coordinating, motivating and controlling.

Planning involves setting objectives for the area of activity of a particular manager; perception of opportunities, problems and alternatives surrounding the achievement of the objective diagnosis of opportunities, analysis of objectives and selection of a course of action; design of a programme of action to achieve objectives; and assessment and integration of sectional objectives into overall objectives, either with reference to the area of activity of an invidual executive or to the span of operations of the whole enterprise. Coordination, on the other hand, involves fixation of responsibility for actions, communication of the objectives, policies and goals top downward and bottom upward in a process of give and take; coordination implies striking balance among different factors put into action; and lastly, it also means the paoportionalities of different factors for achieving this balance for maximum efficiency.

Motivation means ensuring teamwork in action. This may sound nebulous to many. However, the alternative courses of action available to the managers for achieving the required levels of motivation both among executives and among other employees; that state and status of morale among different classes of executive and non-executive employees known from different sources—mainly opinionated, the preparation of organizational profiles, shall we any motivational profiles, in the hight of what Professor Rensis Likert underlined on the basis of his organizational surveys in the United States. The assumptions, inadequacies of impressionistic, opinionated data and indicators available may differ so widely that would tend to render common conclusions totally unrealistic.

Controlling implies knowing performance, judging performance, measuring and analysing variances and initiating corrective action; corrective action implies removal of snags or revision of targets, goals and objectives in a scheme of what is known as management by exception or responsibility accounting or responsibility budgeting or responsibility reporting—implying finding the grain from the chaff, sifting the relevant details from the mass and initiating action thereupon. Knowing and judging performance would require introduction of the budget or standard or norm, finding actuals and measuring and analysing variances for helping managerial action. Messrs Gore and Dyson give detaiia of the information content of the decisioning phenomena, covering predecion analysis, decisions taken and impacts generated. On the other hand, with the specifics of investment proposals and decisions, Professor B.R. Williams presented an inner story of the decisioning phenomena in his book entitled *Investment Proposals and Decisions*. The information needs, organization for making such information available and communication of all such information thus provide the crux of the matter.

Collection, compilation, collation, computation and tabulation of data, their analysis in different ways and their interpretation involve cost. Cost of information incurred has got to have some direct relationship with the benefit derived from such information. The information cost has also got several classificatory details like all other costs. Economics of information system thus occupies the prime of place in the overall context of managerial functions. In many cases, however, information gets collected and stored almost in its own independent momentum. Purposiveness of such information is hardly ever assessed. While the decision makers grope in the dark for relevant information and analysis; huge piles of data remain totally unanalysed; in their raw form, such data do not help anybody. On the contrary, considerable confusion results. Thus, data collection and transformation of data into information have two basic points to be established. One, the uses to which information will be put. Two, the character of information and actions taken on the basis of such information. As such, both assessment of use-value and study of impacts have a key role to play.

Analytical sophistication, on the other hand, has in many cases doubtful practical value especially because the decision makers are not specifically orienred to understand. interpret and apply the pointers raised by such analysis. Such sophistication in analysis and even application of different complicated management techniques figure in many a case as no better than ornaments. As if all this was not enough, the diseconomies of information system most of the time remain unstudied so that their use value in fact slides down. The tremendous potential created by MIS yet remains grossly underutilized in public sector enterprises in India. In a way, even private sector enterprises are no better, as regards the uses to which various threads of information are put to enhance the degree of confidence among the decision-makers.

After the collection phase of information, there is the reporting phase. While both in accounting and in management—general and functional, management by exception, responsibility accounting, responsibility budgeting and responsibility reporting have already developed a fairly rich core of knowledge based on fairly wide, international experience of industrial and commercial organizations. In practical terms, especially in this country, what happens is that everybody in the organization is dumped with every kind of information so that the decision-maker does not know what to do with so much of detail. Moreover, it appears that many public sector organizations have deliberately created gaps between the information-giver and the information-user.

There are several reports which are prepared on a daily basis. For instance, the daily return of cash and bank balance; daily statement of production and despatches; daily report of money receipts from sales effected; daily report of finished goods produced and despatched under different modes of transport; reports of daily purchases of key materials, payment commitments and actual payments to creditors for supplies, government statutory liabilities and others! and efficiency reporting on a daily basis with particular reference to capacity utilization and factors responsible for utilization below expected levels. When an organization has both on going projects and projects under construction, reports naturally are divided for establishing relevance of data and communicating information under both the heads.

The reports in such cases, particularly for projects under construction may relate to monthly return of cash position in the projects monthly statement of anticipated payments for drawal of funds, monthly expenditure statement, monthly statement of progress of expenditure and commitments, monthly estimated cost and production statements, detailed monthly cost sheet, monthly summary of production and sales from different plants with specific regard to products in a multi-product setup, monthly summary of production despatches under various modes of transport such as by road, by rail by sea or by air, contributory provident fund statement, monthly intimation of CPF contributions, trial balance head office reconciliation statement in the context of a plan, head office linkage, monthly profit and loss accounts, monthly progress report, monthly statement of specific depatches including export and money receipt therefrom, statement of dues from customers, bottlenecks in transport under different modes, demurrage, etc., payable and paid, statement of realizations, statement of closing stock at the end of each month, statement of overtime, travelling allowances, entertainment allowance showing both budget targets and actuals for the year to the end the of month and financial-cum-performance report.

Among the quarterly reports, mention may be made of quarterly financial report, quarterly statement of physical stock after due verification, surplus equipment stock and other statements of immediate relevance for quarterly check up. Half-yearly reports include the foreign exchange budget, revised estimates and budget estimates, report on despatch details particularly documentation, foreign exchange, incentives, duty drawback, refund, rebate, etc. Annual BPE return, annual accounts and summary assessment report on performance are presented on an annual basis. Data in the daily reports are added up for other reports in most cases, a process that can be avoided in large part.

Our studies of different government companies under the control of the Central Government have revealed the existence of about fifty reports tossing between end of an organization and another, between plants and head office, particularly when they are at distance, between head office and government departments and between head office and other public agencies. Of these, there are several reports, especially those on a quarterly, half-yearly and annual basis which are but additions and aggregations of figures presented on a daily, fortnightly, monthly and bi-monthly basis. In many cases, in spite of the fact that there are elaborate reporting systems in vogue and either plant, production shop, branch or depot is expected to furnish data within specified dates every month, even though too many reports move back and forth, the gaps in data caused by non-submission of reports by any of these points create difficuities in assessment.

Regular and systematic review and appraisal of reporting systems underlines pecifically the following aspects. One,e very report is required to be assessed both jointly and severally with reference to the actions taken. Two, the contents of each report should necessarily provide a fundamental span of focus. Three, the manner of compilation and computation of figure to be included in such reports are to be closely studied with reference to original documents for establishing veracity of such reports' Four unnecessary details, repetitive details, inadequately explained details and details without interpretation are to be sorted out, so that the cost-effectiveness of such reports remains favourable. Five, assessment of costs of the reporting system in vogue vis-a-vis the benefits derived from the system, tells management of the particular directions in which action should be initiated. Six, the report needs of management are like optimum points; too many reports cause confusion; too little reports cause ignorance. Management will have to be fed with that information which is immediately usable, information being supplied both in response to demand and in anticipation of demand. Seven, information and reporting systems are based not only on the data available from within the organization but also from outside, either through different agencies appointed for the purpose or through gleaning through various reports and studies brought out by sueh agencies, both within the country and abroad. The Economist's Intelligence Reports published on a weekly, monthly and quarterly basis from London have been used by many organizations in this country seeking to establish foreign markets, to plan and design marketing thrusts in particular areas and to launch new product campaigns. In India also, there are different agencies that bring out such Economic Intelligence Reports on the basis of which action programmes are designed by management in many an organization belonging to both sectors of the economy.

Information and reporting systems can naturally be divided into technical information systems, accounting information systems, cost and productivity information systems, marketing information systems and personnel information systems. Each of these sub-systems may have different degrees of significance depending on the thrust given by management and priorities attached. Audit helps management to proceed on reasonable lines in this respect and to develop practices and procedures that would make collection, computation and reporting of information responsive to requirements. For records keeping purposes, many organizations are now taking recourse to microfilming for reduction of bulk. Different capacities of computers coupled with appropriate programming look after both data storage and data retrieving in an expeditious manner. Selectivity, in fact acquires a particular significance in such situations because the computer can be utilized for those processes of analysis which are considered most relevant from the point of view of particular managerial levels and particular operations. Models and several other quantitative management techniques in general are both a cause and an effect of computerized programming approaches. The audit programme in the context of such a set up has to be sensitive enough to accommodate all these developments. However, the problem of beginning at the beginning remains. Over time, the audit function has to figure as a comprehensive screening process, analytical process and reporting process by itself.

Audit reports concerned with management information and reporting systems are not those that one is accustomed to seeing in the context of financial audit, both statutory and internal. The audit function has to be not only deep-probing but also constructive enough, looking at the ineffectiveness of existing systems for initiating improvements. Punitive approaches are, therefore, ruled out. The auditors also do not end up with submitting high sounding recommendations but are expected to see to the implementation of the suggestions. This puts on them an extra responsibility in so far as the improvements suggested would have to bear the feasibility constraints, apart from resource constraints and time constraints. Teamwork is immediately underlined in the context of audit of management information and reporting systems in so far as many matters connected with such review and appraisal may be beyond the capacity and comprehension of any one individual. The formation of audit team, to function under the umbrella of the top management, may figure as a more effective way of approach to the problem than imposition of any individual, from inspite or outside, figuring as an omnipotent personality. Resistance is a big roadblock to the effectiveness of such audit. The audit team has got to devise ways to overcome this resistance. As long as the audit function compensates all the costs that is incurred thereon, it justifies its work.

A TENTATIVE AUDIT PROGRAMME

A. Information

1. Scrutiny of the management information and reporting systems in vogue as a whole and in various segments and sub systems under both information and reporting.
2. The staff position for data processing and the level of expertise available for this purpose.
3. Examination of the various types of data figuring in the information system.
4. Assessing the information content of individual reports underlining the existence of either various alternatives from such selections are to be made or impacts created from earlier decisions.
5. The character of information conveyed—in anticipation of demand from various levels of management or in response to demand expressed by managers in charge of different functions, operations and various levels of hierarchy.
6. The shifting of data for processing into information, different types of information conveyed from the same sets of data or data stored earlier for different types of analysis resulting in specific conclusions to be used as information by managers.
7. Cost of data processing and information.

B. Reporting

1. Study of the reporting system in operation with particular reference to the organising points and destinations of such reports.

2. Accounting for similar types of data figuring in different reports and number of copies made of individual reports and same or similar reports sent to different managers belonging to different levels of the hierarchy.

3. Frequency and periodicity of reports—daily, weekly, fortnigthtly, monthly, quarterly, six monthly and annually.

4. Are the reports too short or too long? The kind of details that figure in individual reports.

5. Are the reports intended to carry a message? Examination of formats, contents and frequency of individual reports, charting out the criss-cross movements of these reports.

6. The gap between processing of information and reporting, on the one hand, and reports and specific actions, on the other—scrutiny of details, may be on a case study basis.

7. Are there deadwood among the reports in use? Consideration of feasibility of elimination of such reports.

8. How far individual types of data originating from particular quarters are integrated for developing messages for conveying them to managers—such integration may be on the basis of techno-economic, techno-financial and techno-managerial considerations.

9. If there is a budgetary control system in operation, do managers follow the concept of management by exception? What is its actual content? Are variances analysed and significant ones reported to concerned managers for appropriate action? If so, case study of actions taken on the basis of information received.

C. General

1. The cost effectiveness of management information and reporting systems, assessment underlining both the cost part and the effectiveness part and their relationships.
2. Do managers use external information. Are data collected from outside? If so, what are the sources? Are they first hand or secondhand?
3. Are there systems of survey of marketing, markets, customers of assessing acceptability of products? If so, how are the data used? How frequently are such data collected, especially for analysis of perspectives?
4. Are they gross perceptions regarding information needed and information supplied? Do managers believe that forewarned is forearmed?
5. It is possible to assess the degree of confidence of managers for purposes of decision making, particularly when it relates to foreseeing the future.

CHART—I

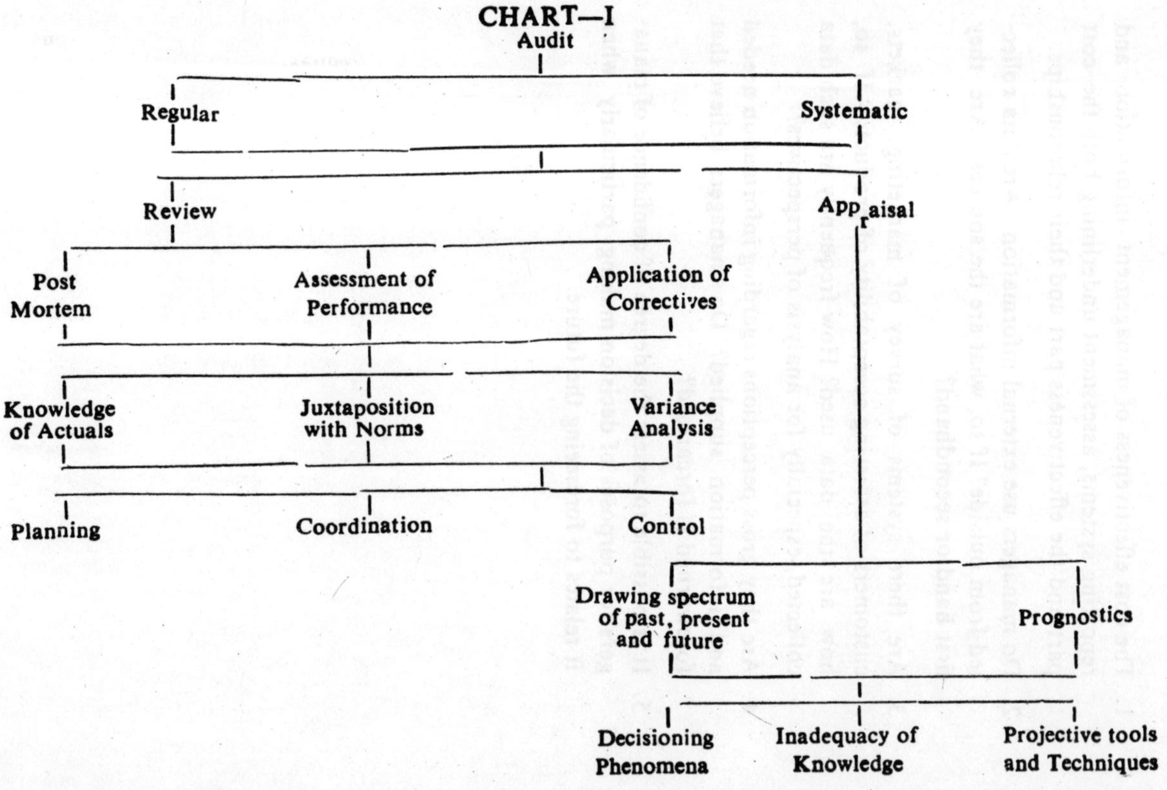
Audit
Regular
Systematic
Review
Appraisal
Post Mortem
Assessment of Performance
Application of Correctives
Knowledge of Actuals
Juxtaposition with Norms
Variance Analysis
Planning
Coordination
Control
Drawing spectrum of past, present and future
Prognostics
Decisioning Phenomena
Inadequacy of Knowledge
Projective tools and Techniques

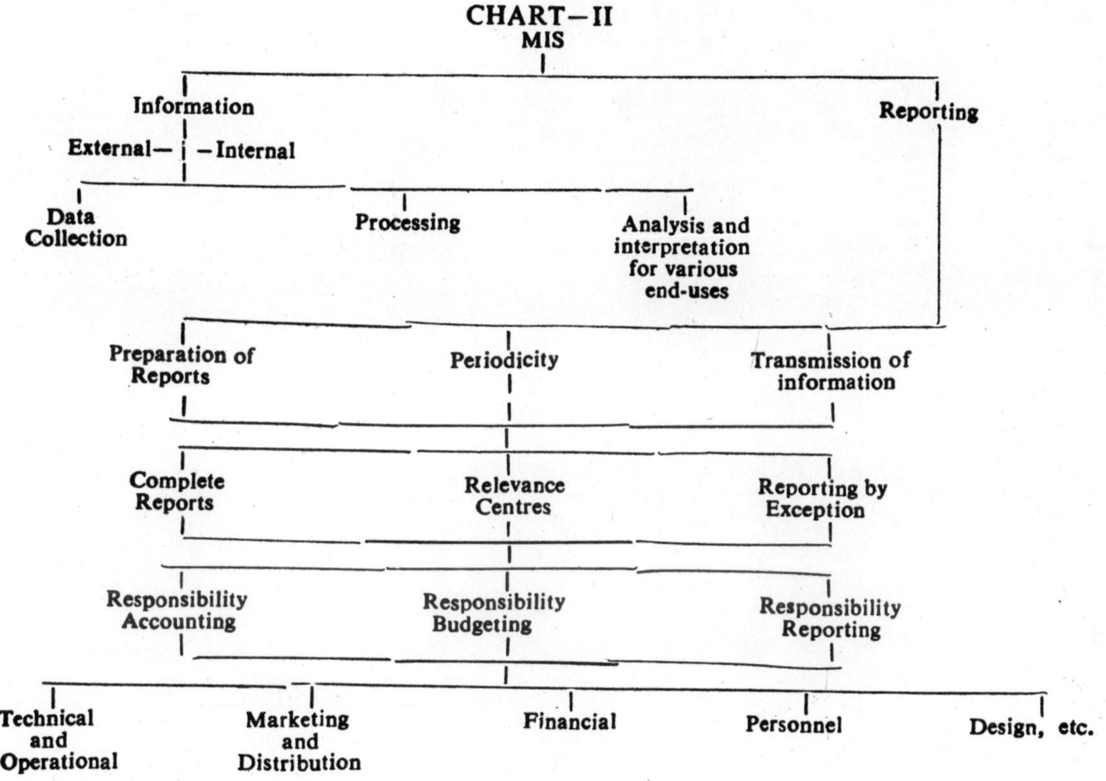
CHART—II
MIS
Information
Reporting
External—
—Internal
Data Collection
Processing
Analysis and interpretation for various end-uses
Preparation of Reports
Periodicity
Transmission of information
Complete Reports
Relevance Centres
Reporting by Exception
Responsibility Accounting
Responsibility Budgeting
Responsibility Reporting
Technical and Operational
Marketing and Distribution
Financial
Personnel
Design, etc.